Growing Fanaticism, Terrorism and Terrorist Outfits

About the Book

Terrorism is, in the broadest sense, the use of intentionally indiscriminate violence as a means to create terror among masses of people; or fear to achieve a religious or political aim. Terrorism involves the use or threat of violence and seeks to create fear, not just within the direct victims but among a wide audience. The book covers a lot of topics and on each topic it gives very comprehensive and in-depth review. The aim of the book is to generate an understanding of the growing fanaticism, terrorism and terrorist outfits. The purpose of this study is to focus attention on the types of individuals and groups that are prone to terrorism.

About the Author

Albert Robert presently Associate Professor in University of Pennsylvania, United States of America. He is a research fellow at AEI and the research manager for AEI's Critical Threats Project. As AEI's senior analyst studying terrorist groups, he focuses on the global Al-Qaeda network and covers the Salafi-Jihadi movement and related trends in the Middle East and Africa. He also specializes in Al-Qaeda in the Arabian Peninsula and Yemen, Al- Shabaab in Somalia, and Al-Qaeda in the Sahel.He has testified before Congress about the threats to US national security interests emanating from Al-Qaeda and its network. He has also briefed members of Congress, their staff, and US military, diplomatic, and intelligence community personnel. His analyses have been widely published, including in Foreign Affairs, Hill, Huffington Post, Wall Street Journal, and Washington Post.

Growing Fanaticism, Terrorism and Terrorist Outfits

Albert Robert

AMIGA PRESS INC.
Delhi: - 110051 (India)

AMIGA PRESS INC.
H.O:- 28-A, Indra Park, St.No-9
Chander Nagar, Krishna Nagar
Delhi: - 110051 (India)
Tel: - 011-22504028, +91-98736-57000
Email: - amigapress@gmail.com
info@amigapress.co.in
amigaeditorial@gmail.com
amigapub@gmail.com

Website: - www.amigapress.co.in

This edition is published by Amiga Press Inc.

ISBN: 978-93-84533-74-8

First Published 2020

Printed and bound in India by Replika Press Pvt. Ltd.

Preface

This edition of the Growing Fanaticism, Terrorism and Terrorist Outfits which provides a comprehensive summary of the key global trends and patterns in terrorism over the last 16 years, covering the period from the beginning of 2000 to the end of 2015. Produced by the Institute for Economics and Peace, the GTI is based on data from the Global Terrorism Database which is collected and collated by the National Consortium for the Study of Terrorism and Responses to Terrorism (START), a Department of Homeland Security Centre of Excellence led by the University of Maryland. The Global Terrorism Database is considered to be the most comprehensive dataset on terrorist activity globally and has now codified over 150,000 terrorist incidents.

The research presented in this report highlights a complex and rapidly changing set of dynamics in global terrorism. While on the one hand the top-line statistics highlight an improvement in the levels of global terrorism, the continued intensification of terrorism in some countries is a cause for serious concern, and highlights the fluid nature of modern terrorist activity. The complexity of this year's GTI is underscored by the fact that although 76 countries improved their GTI scores compared to 53 countries that worsened, the overall global GTI score deteriorated by six per cent since last year as many moderately affected countries experienced record levels of terrorism.

–Author

Contents

1

Concepts of Terror and Terrorism

Introduction

Terrorism is, in the broadest sense, the use of intentionally indiscriminate violence as a means to create terror among masses of people; or fear to achieve a religious or political aim. It is used in this regard primarily to refer to violence during peacetime or in context of war against non-combatants (mostly civilians and neutral military personnel). The terms "terrorist" and "terrorism" originated during the French Revolution of the late 18th century but gained mainstream popularity in the 1970s in news reports and books covering the conflicts in Northern Ireland, the Basque Country and Palestine. The increased use of suicide attacks from the 1980s onwards was typified by the September 11 attacks in New York City and Washington, D.C. in 2001.

There are different definitions of terrorism. Terrorism is a charged term. It is often used with the connotation of something that is "morally wrong". Governments and non-state groups use the term to abuse or denounce opposing groups. Varied political organizations have been accused of using terrorism to achieve their objectives. These organizations include right-wing and left-wing political organizations, nationalist groups, religious groups, revolutionaries and ruling governments. Legislation declaring terrorism a crime has been adopted in many states. When terrorism is perpetrated by nation-states it is not considered terrorism by the state conducting it, making legality a largely grey-area issue. There is no consensus as to whether or not terrorism should be regarded as a war crime.

The Global Terrorism Database, maintained by the University of Maryland, College Park, has recorded more than 61,000 incidents of non-state terrorism, resulting in at least 140,000 deaths between 2000 and 2014.

The Committee of Public Safety agents that enforced the policies of "The Terror" were referred to as "Terrorists". The word "terrorism" was first recorded in English-language dictionaries in 1798 as meaning "systematic use of terror as a policy".

Although the Reign of Terror was imposed by the French government, in modern times "terrorism" usually refers to the killing of people by non-governmental political activists for political reasons, often as a public statement. This meaning originated with Russian radicals in the 1870s. Sergey Nechayev, who founded the People's Reprisal in 1869, described himself as a «terrorist». German radicalist writer Johann Most helped popularize the modern sense of the word by dispensing "advice for terrorists" in the 1880s.

According to Myra Williamson: "The meaning of "terrorism" has undergone a transformation. During the reign of terror a regime or system of terrorism was used as an instrument of governance, wielded by a recently established revolutionary state against the enemies of the people. Now the term "terrorism" is commonly used to describe terrorist acts committed by non-state or subnational entities against a state."

There is no universal agreement on the definition of terrorism. Various legal systems and government agencies use different definitions. Moreover, governments have been reluctant to formulate an agreed-upon and legally binding definition. Difficulties arise from the fact that the term has become politically and emotionally charged. In the United States of America, terrorism is defined in Title 22 Chapter 38 U.S. Code § 2656f as "premeditated, politically motivated violence perpetrated against noncombatant targets by subnational groups or clandestine agents". In general, terrorism is classified as:

the use of violence or of the threat of violence in the pursuit of political, religious, ideological or social objectives

acts committed by non-state actors (or by undercover personnel serving on the behalf of their respective governments)

acts reaching more than the immediate target victims and also directed at targets consisting of a larger spectrum of society

both mala prohibita (i.e., crime that is made illegal by legislation) and mala in se (i.e., crime that is inherently immoral or wrong)

The following criteria of violence or threat of violence fall outside of the definition of terrorism:

wartime (including a declared war) or peacetime acts of violence committed by a nation state against another nation state regardless of legality or illegality that are carried out by properly uniformed forces or legal combatants of such nation states

reasonable acts of self-defense, such as the use of force to kill, apprehend, or punish criminals who pose a threat to the lives of humans or property

legitimate targets in war, such as enemy combatants and strategic infrastructure that form an integral part of the enemy's war effort

collateral damage, including the infliction of incidental damage to non-combatant targets during an attack on or attempting to attack legitimate targets in war

There are many reasons for the failure to achieve universal consensus regarding the definition of terrorism. In a briefing paper for the Australian Parliament, Angus Martyn stated that "[t]he international community has never succeeded in developing an accepted comprehensive definition of terrorism. During the 1970s and 1980s, the United Nations attempts to define the term foundered mainly due to differences of opinion between various members about the use of violence in the context of conflicts over national liberation and self-determination." These divergences have made it impossible to conclude a Comprehensive Convention on International Terrorism that incorporates a single, all-encompassing, legally binding, criminal-law definition of terrorism.

In international law

The need to define terrorism in international criminal law

Ben Saul has noted that a "A combination of pragmatic and principled arguments supports the case for defining terrorism in international law", including the need to condemn violations to human rights, to protect the state and deliberative politics, to differentiate public and private violence, and to ensure international peace and security.

Carlos Diaz-Paniagua, who coordinated the negotiations of the proposed United Nations Comprehensive Convention on International Terrorism, noted, on his part, the need to provide a precise definition of terrorist activities in international law: "Criminal law has three purposes: to declare that a conduct is forbidden, to prevent it, and to express society's condemnation for the wrongful acts. The symbolic, normative role of criminalization is of particular importance in the case of terrorism. The criminalization of terrorist acts expresses society's repugnance at them, invokes social censure and shame, and stigmatizes those who commit them. Moreover, by creating and reaffirming values, criminalization may serve, in the long run, as a deterrent to terrorism, as those values are internalized." Thus, international criminal law treaties that seek to prevent, condemn and punish terrorist activities, require precise definitions:

The definition of the offence in criminal law treaty plays several roles. First and foremost, it has the symbolic, normative role of expressing society's condemnation of the forbidden acts. Second, it facilitates agreement. Since states tend to be reluctant to undertake stringent obligations in matters related to the exercise of their domestic jurisdiction, a precise definition of the crime, which restricts the scope of those obligations, makes agreement less costly. Third, it provides an inter-subjective basis for the homogeneous application of the treaty's obligations on judicial and police cooperation. This function is of particular importance in extradition treaties because, to grant an extradition, most legal systems require that the crime be punishable both in the requesting state and the requested state. Fourth, it helps states to enact domestic legislation to criminalize and punish the wrongful acts defined in the treaty in conformity with their human rights' obligations. The principle of nullum crimen sine lege requires, in particular, that states define precisely which acts are prohibited before anyone can be prosecuted or punished for committing those same acts.

Saul noted in this sense that, missing a generally agreed, all-encompassing, definition of the term:

'Terrorism' currently lacks the precision, objectivity and certainty demanded by legal discourse. Criminal law strives to avoid emotive terms to prevent prejudice to an accused, and shuns ambiguous or subjective terms as incompatible with the principle of non-retroactivity. If the law is to admit the term, advance definition is essential on grounds of fairness, and it is not sufficient to leave definition to the unilateral interpretations of States. Legal definition could plausibly retrieve terrorism from the ideological quagmire, by severing an agreed legal meaning from the remainder of the elastic, political concept. Ultimately it must do so without criminalizing legitimate violent resistance to oppressive regimes – and becoming complicit in that oppression.

Obstacles to a comprehensive definition

Diaz-Paniagua has noted that, to "...create an effective legal regime against terrorism, it would be necessary to formulate a comprehensive definition of that crime that, on the one hand, provides the strongest moral condemnation to terrorist activities while, on the other hand, has enough precision to permit the prosecution of criminal activities without condemning acts that should be deemed to be legitimate. Nonetheless, due to major divergences at the international level on the question of the legitimacy of the use of violence for political purposes, either by states or by self-determination and revolutionary groups, this has not yet been possible." In this sense, M. Cherif Bassiouni notes:

to define 'terrorism' in a way that is both all-inclusive and unambiguous is very difficult, if not impossible. One of the principle difficulties lies in the fundamental values at stake in the acceptance or rejection of terror-inspiring violence as means of accomplishing a given goal. The obvious and well known range of views on these issues are what makes an internationally accepted specific definition of what is loosely called 'terrorism,' a largely impossible undertaking. That is why the search for and internationally agreed upon definition may well be a futile and unnecessary effort.

Sami Zeidan, a diplomat and scholar, explained the political reasons underlying the current difficulties to define terrorism as follows:

There is no general consensus on the definition of terrorism. The difficulty of defining terrorism lies in the risk it entails of taking positions. The political value of the term currently prevails over its legal one. Left to its political meaning, terrorism easily falls prey to change that suits the interests of particular states at particular times. The Taliban and Osama bin Laden were once called freedom fighters (mujahideen) and backed by the CIA when they were resisting the Soviet occupation of Afghanistan. Now they are on top of the international terrorist lists. Today, the United Nations views Palestinians as freedom fighters, struggling against the unlawful occupation of their land by Israel, and engaged in a long-established legitimate resistance, yet Israel regards them as terrorists [...] The repercussion of the current preponderance of the political over the legal value of terrorism is costly, leaving the war against terrorism selective, incomplete and ineffective.

In the same vein, Jason Burke, a British reporter who writes about radical Islamist activity, said:

There are multiple ways of defining terrorism, and all are subjective. Most define terrorism as "the use or threat of serious violence" to advance some kind of "cause". Some state clearly the kinds of group ("sub-national", "non-state") or cause (political, ideological, religious) to which they refer. Others merely rely on the instinct of most people when confronted with innocent civilians being killed or maimed by men armed with explosives, firearms or other weapons. None is satisfactory, and grave problems with the use of the term persist. Terrorism is after all, a tactic. The term "war on terrorism" is thus effectively nonsensical. As there is no space here to explore this involved and difficult debate, my preference is, on the whole, for the less loaded term "Militancy". This is not an attempt to condone such actions, merely to analyse them in a clearer way.

The political and emotional connotation of the term "terrorism" makes difficult its use in legal discourse. In this sense, Saul notes that:

Despite the shifting and contested meaning of "terrorism" over time, the peculiar semantic power of the term, beyond its literal signification, is its capacity to stigmatize, delegitimize, denigrate, and dehumanize those at whom it is directed, including political opponents. The term is ideologically and politically loaded; pejorative; implies moral, social, and value judgment; and is "slippery and much-abused." In the absence of a definition of terrorism, the struggle over the representation of a violent act is a struggle over its legitimacy. The more confused a concept, the more it lends itself to opportunistic appropriation.

Historically, the dispute on the meaning of terrorism arose since the laws of war were first codified in 1899. The Martens Clause was introduced as a compromise wording for the dispute between the Great Powers who considered francs-tireurs to be unlawful combatants subject to execution on capture, and smaller states who maintained that they should be considered lawful combatants.

More recently the 1977 Protocol Additional to the Geneva Conventions of 12 August 1949, and relating to the Protection of Victims of International Armed Conflicts, which applies in situations Article 1. Paragraph 4 "... in which peoples are fighting against colonial domination and alien occupation and against racist regimes...", contains many ambiguities that cloud the issue of who is or is not a legitimate combatant. These difficulties have led Pamala Griset to conclude that: "the meaning of terrorism is embedded in a person's or nation's philosophy. Thus, the determination of the 'right' definition of terrorism is subjective."

The sectoral approach

To elaborate an effective legal regime to prevent and punish international terrorism—rather than only working on a single, all-encompassing, comprehensive definition of terrorism—the international community has also adopted a "...'sectoral' approach aimed at identifying offences seen as belonging to the activities of terrorists and working out treaties in order to deal with specific categories thereof". The treaties that follow this approach focus on the wrongful nature of terrorist activities rather than on their intent:

On the whole, therefore, the 'sectoral' conventions confirm the assumption that some offences can be considered in themselves as offences of international concern, irrespective of any 'terrorist' intent or purpose. Indeed, the principal merit of the 'sectoral approach' is that it avoids the need to define 'terrorism' of 'terrorist acts' ... So long as the 'sectoral' approach is followed, there is no need to define terrorism; a definition would only be necessary if the punishment of the relevant offences were made conditional on the existence of a specific 'terrorist' intent; but this would be counter-productive, inasmuch as it would result in unduly restricting their suppression.

Following this approach, the international community has adopted the following sectoral counter-terrorism conventions, open to the ratification of all states:

The 1963 Convention on Offences and Certain Other Acts Committed On Board Aircraft

The 1970 Convention for the Suppression of Unlawful Seizure of Aircraft

The 1971 Convention for the Suppression of Unlawful Acts against the Safety of Civil Aviation

The 1979 Convention on the Physical Protection of Nuclear Material

The 1988 Protocol for the Suppression of Unlawful Acts of Violence at Airports Serving International Civil Aviation

The 1988 Convention for the Suppression of Unlawful Acts against the Safety of Maritime Navigation

The 1988 Protocol for the Suppression of Unlawful Acts against the Safety of Fixed Platforms Located on the Continental Shelf

The 1991 Convention on the Marking of Plastic Explosives for the Purpose of Identification

The 1997 International Convention for the Suppression of Terrorist Bombings.

The 1999 International Convention for the Suppression of the Financing of Terrorism

The 2005 International Convention for the Suppression of Acts of Nuclear Terrorism

Analyzing these treaties, Andrew Byrnes observed that:

These conventions – all of which are described by the United Nations as part of its panoply of anti-terrorist measures – share three principal characteristics:

(a) they all adopted an "operational definition" of a specific type of terrorist act that was defined without reference to the underlying political or ideological purpose or motivation of the perpetrator of the act – this reflected a consensus that there were some acts that were such a serious threat to the interests of all that they could not be justified by reference to such motives;

(b) they all focused on actions by non-state actors (individuals and organisations) and the State was seen as an active ally in the struggle against terrorism – the question of the State itself as terrorist actor was left largely to one side; and

(c) they all adopted a criminal law enforcement model to address the problem, under which States would cooperate in the apprehension and prosecution of those alleged to have committed these crimes.

Byrnes notes that "this act-specific approach to addressing problems of terrorism in binding international treaties has continued up until relatively recently. Although political denunciation of terrorism in all its forms had continued apace, there had been no successful attempt to define 'terrorism' as such in a broad sense that was satisfactory for legal purposes. There was also some scepticism as to the necessity, desirability and feasibility of producing an agreed and workable general definition." Nonetheless, since 2000, the United Nations General Assembly has been working on a proposed Comprehensive Convention on International Terrorism.

Comprehensive conventions

The international community has worked on two comprehensive counter-terrorism treaties, the League of Nations' 1937 Convention for the Prevention and Punishment of Terrorism, which never entered into force, and the United Nations' proposed Comprehensive Convention on International Terrorism, which hasn't been finalized yet.

League of Nations

In the late 1930s, the international community made a first attempt at defining terrorism. Article 1.1 of the League of Nations' 1937 Convention for the prevention and punishment of Terrorism, which never entered into force, defined "acts of terrorism" as "criminal acts directed against a State and intended or calculated to create a state of terror in the minds of particular persons or a group of persons or the general public". Article 2 included as terrorist acts, if they were directed against another state and if they constituted acts of terrorism within the meaning of the definition contained in article 1, the following:

1. Any willful act causing death or grievous bodily harm or loss of liberty to:

a) Heads of State, persons exercising the prerogatives of the head of the State, their hereditary or designated successors;

b) The wives or husbands or the above-mentioned persons;

c) Persons charged with public functions or holding public positions when the act is directed against them in their public capacity.

2. Willful destruction of, or damage to, public property or property devoted to a public purpose belonging to or subject to the authority of another High Contracting Party.

3. Any willful act calculated to endanger the lives of members of the public.

4. Any attempt to commit an offence falling within the foregoing provisions of the present article.

5. The manufacture, obtaining, possession, or supplying of arms, ammunition, explosives or harmful substances with the view to the commission in any country whatsoever of an offence falling within the present article.

Networked Infrastructure

Electrical grids, the banking system, water distribution, traffic management, communication systems, air traffic control, mass transit, military systems, etc. all tend to be operate in some sort of a networked fashion. Connectivity in this case does not imply that these systems are openly connected to the Internet and may use private networks (physical or virtual). The problems occur when you consider that security is often compromised for the sake of convenience and corners are cut. If you want to manage the electrical grid or the traffic management system in a city remotely, you need connectivity. Does it make sense to build a completely private network (dedicated cables) for each of these infrastructure systems? In some cases yes, but many implementations tend to piggyback off of existing shared infrastructure believing that it can be secured fully. Hackers and cyber terrorists are able to find these vulnerabilities and exploit them to access core systems which can be destructive to this networked infrastructure. Therefore security this infrastructure is much harder than expected and leads to vulnerabilities that can only be countered by constant vigilance and expert personnel - a cost that is often overlooked.

How to protect against Cyber Terrorism

Most of targets of cyber terrorism are large organizations; governments, utilities, infrastructure, businesses, financial institutions, etc.; but there are things that individuals can do to ensure they can protect themselves or minimize the impact of cyberterrorism.

- Use strong passwords (long in length and combination of alphabets, numbers and special characters)
- Use different passwords for different websites and if needed, consider using a password manager
- Update your systems when patches are released or vulnerabilities discovered (update your operating system, browsers, anti-virus/security programs, firmware, etc.)
- Use more secure operating systems (like Linux) where possible
- Use virtual machines (with software like Virtualbox) when installing unkown software or visiting sketchy web sites or if you require some anonymity.

- Secure your personal networks (Wi-Fi passwords with encryption and firewalls)
- Do not install random, untrusted software on your computers/devices - especially on smartphones and tablets
- Test your personal network for vulnerabilities
- Secure your data by using strong encryption where possible

Criminal elements

Cybercrime and cyberterrorism do often intersect in that one can be used to fund the other (either in its virtual or physical form). Organized crime is deeply involved in sophisticated cybercrime activities that one would see with spam, identity theft, bank fraud, shady prescription medication sales, drugs, pornography, human trafficking, prostitution, virtual heists - including stealing bitcoin and other cryptocurrency fraud, credit card fraud, money laundering, peddling fake or stolen merchandise, phone fraud, malware/spyware/ransomeware and other nefarious activities. The funds and expertise they gain from their cybercrime sprees allow them to expand their virtual and "brick and mortar" operations, often making them cyber mercenaries available to the highest bidder - be they terrorist groups, countries or other criminals.

Terrorist Propaganda

The Internet has also proven to be a great venue for terrorist groups to spread their propaganda. Websites extolling terrorist views started cropping up almost as soon as the Internet started on its ascent as a revolutionary medium for communication. This is problematic but those that try to use this as an excuse to censor online content and discussions do miss the point that this is also a great eye opener to the majority of the people that do not subscribe to such views. It exposes terrorists to law enforcement agencies (as part of their investigations and by attracting terrorists to disclose their agendas through "honey pots"), the media and the public. As we mentioned in the above section, networked infrastructure and websites, though they may be "secured" by passwords, encryption or other more sophisticated tactics will always be vulnerable - in this case to those helping expose terrorist agendas.

Terrorist Behavior

There is clearly a wide choice of definitions for terrorism. Despite this, there are elements in common among the majority of useful definitions. Common threads of the various definitions identify terrorism as:

- Coercive
- Dynamic
- Deliberate

Political

A terrorist act is a political act or is committed with the intention to cause a political effect. Clausewitz' statement that "war is a continuation of policy by other means" is taken as a truism by terrorists. They merely eliminate the intermediate step of armies and warfare, and apply violence directly to the political contest.

Psychological

The intended results of terrorist acts cause a psychological effect ("terror"). They are aimed at a target audience other than the actual victims of the act. The intended target audience of the terrorist act may be the population as a whole, some specific portion of a society (an ethnic minority, for example), or decision-making elites in the society's political, social, or military populace.

Coercive

Violence and destruction are used in the commission of the act to produce the desired effect. Even if casualties or destruction are not the result of a terrorist operation, the threat or potential of violence is what produces the intended effect. For example, a successful hostage taking operation may result in all hostages being freed unharmed after negotiations and bargaining. Regardless of the outcome, the terrorist bargaining chips were nothing less than the raw threat of applying violence to maim or kill some or all of the hostages. When the threat of violence is not credible, or the terrorists are unable to implement violence effectively, terrorism fails.

Dynamic

Terrorist groups demand change, revolution, or political movement. The radical worldview that justifies terrorism mandates drastic action to destroy or alter the status quo. Even if the goals of a movement are reactionary in nature, they require action to "turn back the clock" or restore some cherished value system that is extinct. Nobody commits violent attacks on strangers or innocents to keep things "just the way they are."

Deliberate

Terrorism is an activity planned and intended to achieve particular goals. It is a rationally employed, specifically selected tactic, and is not a random act. Since the victims of terrorist violence are often of little import, with one being as good for the terrorists' purposes as another, victim or target selection can appear random or unprovoked. But the target will contain symbolic value or be capable of eliciting emotional response according to the terrorists' goals. Remember that the actual target of terrorism is not the victim of the violence, but the psychological balance.

Media Exploitation

Terrorism's effects are not necessarily aimed at the victims of terrorist violence. Victims are usually objects to be exploited by the terrorists for their effect on a third party. In order to produce this effect, information of the attack must reach the target audience. So any terrorist organization plans for exploitation of available media to get the message to the right audiences. Victims are simply the first medium that transmits the psychological impact to the larger target audience. The next step in transmission will depend on what media is available, but it will be planned, and it will frequently be the responsibility of a specific organization within the terrorist group to do nothing else but exploit and control the news cycle.

Some organizations can rely on friendly or sympathetic news outlets, but this is not necessary. News media can be manipulated by planning around the demands of the "news cycle", and the advantage that control of the initiative gives the terrorist. Pressures to report quickly, to "scoop" competitors, allow terrorists to present claims or make statements that might be refuted or critically commented on if time were available. Terrorists often provide names and details of individual victims to control the news media through its desire to humanize or personalize a story. For the victims of a terrorist attack, it is a certainty that the impact on the survivors (if there are any) is of minimal importance to the terrorists. What is important is the intended psychological impact that the news of their death or suffering will cause in a wider audience.

Historical background

The term terroriste, meaning "terrorist", is first used in 1794 by the French philosopher François-Noël Babeuf, who denounces Maximilien Robespierre's Jacobin regime as a dictatorship. In the years leading up to the Reign of Terror, the Brunswick Manifesto threatened Paris with an "exemplary, never to be forgotten vengeance: the city would be subjected to military punishment and total destruction" if the royal family was harmed, but this only increased the Revolution's will to abolish the monarchy. Some writers attitudes about French Revolution grew less favorable after the French monarchy was abolished in 1792. During the Reign of Terror, which began in July 1793 and lasted thirteen months, Paris was governed by the Committee of Public safety who oversaw a regime of mass executions and public purges.

Prior to the French Revolution, ancient philosophers wrote about tyrannicide, as tyranny was seen as the greatest political threat to Greco-Roman civilization. Medieval philosophers were similarly occupied with the concept of tyranny, though the analysis of some theologians like Thomas Aquinas drew a distinction between usurpers, who could be killed by anyone, and legitimate rulers who abused their power – the latter, in Aquinas' view, could only be punished by a public authority. John of Salisbury was the first medieval Christian scholar to defend tyrannicide.

Most scholars today trace the origins of the modern tactic of terrorism to the Jewish Sicarii Zealots who attacked Romans and Jews in 1st century Palestine. They follow its development from the Persian Order of Assassins through to 19th-century anarchists. The "Reign of Terror" is usually regarded as an issue of etymology. The term terrorism has generally been used to describe violence by non-state actors rather than government violence since the 19th-century Anarchist Movement.

In December 1795, Edmund Burke used the word "Terrorists" in a description of the new French government called 'Directory':

At length, after a terrible struggle, the [Directory] Troops prevailed over the Citizens (…) To secure them further, they have a strong corps of irregulars, ready armed. Thousands of those Hell-hounds called Terrorists, whom they had shut up in Prison on their last Revolution, as the Satellites of Tyranny, are let loose on the people.(emphasis added)

The terms "terrorism" and "terrorist" gained renewed currency in the 1970s as a result of the Israeli–Palestinian conflict, the Northern Ireland conflict, the Basque conflict, and the operations of groups such as the Red Army Faction. Leila Khaled was described as a terrorist in a 1970 number of Life magazine. A number of books on terrorism were published in the 1970s. The topic came further to the fore after the 1983 Beirut barracks bombings and again after the 2001 September 11 attacks and the 2002 Bali bombings.

Modern definitions terrorism

There are over 109 different definitions of terrorism. American political philosopher Michael Walzer in 2002 wrote: "Terrorism is the deliberate killing of innocent people, at random, to spread fear through a whole population and force the hand of its political leaders". Bruce Hoffman, an American scholar, has noted that

It is not only individual agencies within the same governmental apparatus that cannot agree on a single definition of terrorism. Experts and other long-established scholars in the field are equally incapable of reaching a consensus. C.A.J. Coady has written that the question of how to define terrorism is "irresolvable" because "its natural home is in polemical, ideological and propagandist contexts".

French historian Sophie Wahnich distinguishes between the revolutionary terror of the French Revolution and the terrorists of the September 11 attacks:

Revolutionary terror is not terrorism. To make a moral equivalence between the Revolution's year II and September 2001 is historical and philosophical nonsense ... The violence exercised on 11 September 2001 aimed neither at equality nor liberty. Nor did the preventive war announced by the president of the United States.

Experts disagree about "whether terrorism is wrong by definition or just wrong as a matter of fact; they disagree about whether terrorism should be defined in terms of its aims, or its methods, or both, or neither; they disagree about whether or not states can perpetrate terrorism; they even disagree about the importance or otherwise of terror for a definition of terrorism."

State terrorism

Alternatively, responding to developments in modern warfare, Paul James and Jonathan Friedman distinguish between state terrorism against non-combatants and state terrorism against combatants, including 'Shock and Awe' tactics:

Shock and Awe" as a subcategory of "rapid dominance" is the name given to massive intervention designed to strike terror into the minds of the enemy. It is a form of state-terrorism. The concept was however developed long before the Second Gulf War by Harlan Ullman as chair of a forum of retired military personnel.

United Nations

In November 2004, a Secretary-General of the United Nations report described terrorism as any act "intended to cause death or serious bodily harm to civilians or non-combatants with the purpose of intimidating a population or compelling a government or an international organization to do or abstain from doing any act". The international community has been slow to formulate a universally agreed, legally binding definition of this crime. These difficulties arise from the fact that the term "terrorism" is politically and emotionally charged. In this regard, Angus Martyn, briefing the Australian parliament, stated,

The international community has never succeeded in developing an accepted comprehensive definition of terrorism. During the 1970s and 1980s, the United Nations attempts to define the term floundered mainly due to differences of opinion between various members about the use of violence in the context of conflicts over national liberation and self-determination.

These divergences have made it impossible for the United Nations to conclude a Comprehensive Convention on International Terrorism that incorporates a single, all-encompassing, legally binding, criminal law definition of terrorism. The international community has adopted a series of sectoral conventions that define and criminalize various types of terrorist activities.

Since 1994, the United Nations General Assembly has repeatedly condemned terrorist acts using the following political description of terrorism:

Criminal acts intended or calculated to provoke a state of terror in the public, a group of persons or particular persons for political purposes are in any circumstance unjustifiable, whatever the considerations of a political, philosophical, ideological, racial, ethnic, religious or any other nature that may be invoked to justify them.

U.S. law

Various legal systems and government agencies use different definitions of terrorism in their national legislation.

U.S. Code Title 22 Chapter 38, Section 2656f(d) defines terrorism as: "Premeditated, politically motivated violence perpetrated against noncombatant targets by subnational groups or clandestine agents, usually intended to influence an audience".

18 U.S.C. § 2331 defines "international terrorism" and "domestic terrorism" for purposes of Chapter 113B of the Code, entitled "Terrorism":

"International terrorism" means activities with the following three characteristics:

Involve violent acts or acts dangerous to human life that violate federal or state law; Appear to be intended (i) to intimidate or coerce a civilian population; (ii) to influence the policy of a government by intimidation or coercion; or (iii) to affect the conduct of a government by mass destruction, assassination, or kidnapping; and occur primarily outside the territorial jurisdiction of the U.S., or transcend national boundaries in terms of the means by which they are accomplished, the persons they appear intended to intimidate or coerce, or the locale in which their perpetrators operate or seek asylum.

Media spectacle

A definition proposed by Carsten Bockstette at the George C. Marshall European Center for Security Studies, underlines the psychological and tactical aspects of terrorism:

Terrorism is defined as political violence in an asymmetrical conflict that is designed to induce terror and psychic fear (sometimes indiscriminate) through the violent victimization and destruction of noncombatant targets (sometimes iconic symbols). Such acts are meant to send a message from an illicit clandestine organization. The purpose of terrorism is to exploit the media in order to achieve maximum attainable publicity as an amplifying force multiplier in order to influence the targeted audience(s) in order to reach short- and midterm political goals and/or desired long-term end states.

Terrorists attack national symbols, which may negatively affect a government, while increasing the prestige of the given terrorist group or its ideology.

Political violence

Terrorist acts frequently have a political purpose. Some official, governmental definitions of terrorism use the criterion of the illegitimacy or unlawfulness of the act. to distinguish between actions authorized by a government (and thus "lawful") and those of other actors, including individuals and small groups. For example, carrying out a strategic bombing on an enemy city, which is designed to affect civilian support for a cause, would not be considered terrorism if it were authorized by a government. This criterion is inherently problematic and is not universally accepted, because: it denies the existence of state terrorism. An associated term is violent non-state actor.

According to Ali Khan, the distinction lies ultimately in a political judgment.

Pejorative use

Having the moral charge in our vocabulary of 'something morally wrong', the term 'terrorism' is often used to abuse or denounce opposite parties, either governments or non-state-groups.

Those labeled "terrorists" by their opponents rarely identify themselves as such, and typically use other terms or terms specific to their situation, such as separatist, freedom fighter, liberator, revolutionary, vigilante, militant, paramilitary, guerrilla, rebel, patriot, or any similar-meaning word in other languages and cultures. Jihadi, mujaheddin, and fedayeen are similar Arabic words that have entered the English lexicon. It is common for both parties in a conflict to describe each other as terrorists.

On whether particular terrorist acts, such as killing non-combatants, can be justified as the lesser evil in a particular circumstance, philosophers have expressed different views: while, according to David Rodin, utilitarian philosophers can (in theory) conceive of cases in which the evil of terrorism is outweighed by the good that could not be achieved in a less morally costly way, in practice the "harmful effects of undermining the convention of non-combatant immunity is thought to outweigh the goods that may be achieved by particular acts of terrorism". Among the non-utilitarian philosophers, Michael Walzer argued that terrorism can be morally justified in only one specific case: when "a nation or community faces the extreme threat of complete destruction and the only way it can preserve itself is by intentionally targeting non-combatants, then it is morally entitled to do so".

In his book Inside Terrorism Bruce Hoffman offered an explanation of why the term terrorism becomes distorted:

On one point, at least, everyone agrees: terrorism is a pejorative term. It is a word with intrinsically negative connotations that is generally applied to one's enemies and opponents, or to those with whom one disagrees and would otherwise prefer to ignore. 'What is called terrorism,' Brian Jenkins has written, 'thus seems to depend on one's point of view. Use of the term implies a moral judgment; and if one party can successfully attach the label terrorist to its opponent, then it has indirectly persuaded others to adopt its moral viewpoint.' Hence the decision to call someone or label some organization terrorist becomes almost unavoidably subjective, depending largely on whether one sympathizes with or opposes the person/group/cause concerned. If one identifies with the victim of the violence, for example, then the act is terrorism. If, however, one identifies with the perpetrator, the violent act is regarded in a more sympathetic, if not positive (or, at the worst, an ambivalent) light; and it is not terrorism.

The pejorative connotations of the word can be summed up in the aphorism, "One man's terrorist is another man's freedom fighter". This is exemplified when a group using irregular military methods is an ally of a state against a mutual enemy, but later falls out with the state and starts to use those methods against its former ally. During World War II, the Malayan People's Anti-Japanese Army was allied with the British, but during the Malayan Emergency, members of its successor (the Malayan Races Liberation Army), were branded "terrorists" by the British. More recently, Ronald Reagan and others in the American administration frequently called the mujaheddin "freedom fighters" during the Soviet–Afghan War yet twenty years later, when a new generation of Afghan men were fighting against what they perceive to be a regime installed by foreign powers, their attacks were labelled "terrorism" by George W. Bush. Groups accused of terrorism understandably prefer terms reflecting legitimate military or ideological action. Leading terrorism researcher Professor Martin Rudner, director of the Canadian Centre of Intelligence and Security Studies at Ottawa's Carleton University, defines "terrorist acts" as unlawful attacks for political or other ideological goals, and said:

There is the famous statement: 'One man's terrorist is another man's freedom fighter.' But that is grossly misleading. It assesses the validity of the cause when terrorism is an act. One can have a perfectly beautiful cause and yet if one commits terrorist acts, it is terrorism regardless.

Some groups, when involved in a "liberation" struggle, have been called "terrorists" by the Western governments or media. Later, these same persons, as leaders of the liberated nations, are called "statesmen" by similar organizations. Two examples of this phenomenon are the Nobel Peace Prize laureates Menachem Begin and Nelson Mandela. WikiLeaks editor Julian Assange has been called a "terrorist" by Sarah Palin and Joe Biden.

Sometimes, states that are close allies, for reasons of history, culture and politics, can disagree over whether or not members of a certain organization are terrorists. For instance, for many years, some branches of the United States government refused to label members of the Provisional Irish Republican Army (IRA) as terrorists while the IRA was using methods against one of the United States' closest allies (the United Kingdom) that the UK branded as terrorism. This was highlighted by the Quinn v. Robinson case.

Media outlets who wish to convey impartiality may limit their usage of "terrorist" and "terrorism" because they are loosely defined, potentially controversial in nature, and subjective terms.

History of terrorism

Depending on how broadly the term is defined, the roots and practice of terrorism can be traced at least to the 1st-century AD. Sicarii Zealots, though some dispute whether the group, a radical offshoot of the Zealots which was active in Judaea Province at the beginning of the 1st century AD, was in fact terrorist. According to the contemporary Jewish-Roman historian Josephus, after the Zealotry rebellion against Roman rule in Judea, when some prominent Jewish collaborators with Roman rule were killed, Judas of Galilee formed a small and more extreme offshoot of the Zealots, the Sicarii, in 6 AD. Their terror was directed against Jewish "collaborators", including temple priests, Sadducees, Herodians, and other wealthy elites.

The term "terrorism" itself was originally used to describe the actions of the Jacobin Club during the "Reign of Terror" in the French Revolution. "Terror is nothing other than justice, prompt, severe, inflexible", said Jacobin leader Maximilien Robespierre. In 1795, Edmund Burke denounced the Jacobins for letting "thousands of those hell-hounds called Terrorists ... loose on the people" of France.

In January 1858, Italian patriot Felice Orsini threw three bombs in an attempt to assassinate French Emperor Napoleon III. Eight bystanders were killed and 142 injured. The incident played a crucial role as an inspiration for the development of the early terrorist groups.

Arguably the first organization to utilize modern terrorist techniques was the Irish Republican Brotherhood, founded in 1858 as a revolutionary Irish nationalist group that carried out attacks in England. The group initiated the Fenian dynamite campaign in 1881, one of the first modern terror campaigns. Instead of earlier forms of terrorism based on political assassination, this campaign used modern, timed explosives with the express aim of sowing fear in the very heart of metropolitan Britain, in order to achieve political gains.

Another early terrorist group was Narodnaya Volya, founded in Russia in 1878 as a revolutionary anarchist group inspired by Sergei Nechayev and "propaganda by the deed" theorist Carlo Pisacane. The group developed ideas – such as targeted killing of the 'leaders of oppression' – that were to become the hallmark of subsequent violence by small non-state groups, and they were convinced that the developing technologies of the age – such as the invention of dynamite, which they were the first anarchist group to make widespread use of – enabled them to strike directly and with discrimination.

Scholars of terrorism refer to four major waves of global terrorism: "the Anarchist, the Anti-Colonial, the New Left, and the Religious. The first three have been completed and lasted around 40 years; the fourth is now in its third decade."

Types of terrorism

Depending on the country, the political system, and the time in history, the types of terrorism are varying. In early 1975, the Law Enforcement Assistant Administration in the United States formed the National Advisory Committee on Criminal Justice Standards and Goals. One of the five volumes that the committee wrote was titled Disorders and Terrorism, produced by the Task Force on Disorders and Terrorism under the direction of H. H. A. Cooper, Director of the Task Force staff.

The Task Force defines terrorism as "a tactic or technique by means of which a violent act or the threat thereof is used for the prime purpose of creating overwhelming fear for coercive purposes". It classified disorders and terrorism into six categories:

Civil disorder – A form of collective violence interfering with the peace, security, and normal functioning of the community.

Political terrorism – Violent criminal behaviour designed primarily to generate fear in the community, or substantial segment of it, for political purposes.

Non-Political terrorism – Terrorism that is not aimed at political purposes but which exhibits "conscious design to create and maintain a high degree of fear for coercive purposes, but the end is individual or collective gain rather than the achievement of a political objective".

Quasi-terrorism – The activities incidental to the commission of crimes of violence that are similar in form and method to genuine terrorism but which nevertheless lack its essential ingredient. It is not the main purpose of the quasi-terrorists to induce terror in the immediate victim as in the case of genuine terrorism, but the quasi-terrorist uses the modalities and techniques of the genuine terrorist and produces similar consequences and reaction. For example, the fleeing felon who takes hostages is a quasi-terrorist, whose methods are similar to those of the genuine terrorist but whose purposes are quite different.

Limited political terrorism – Genuine political terrorism is characterized by a revolutionary approach; limited political terrorism refers to "acts of terrorism which are committed for ideological or political motives but which are not part of a concerted campaign to capture control of the state".

Official or state terrorism – "referring to nations whose rule is based upon fear and oppression that reach similar to terrorism or such proportions". It may be referred to as Structural Terrorism defined broadly as terrorist acts carried out by governments in pursuit of political objectives, often as part of their foreign policy.

Other sources have defined the typology of terrorism in different ways, for example, broadly classifying it into domestic terrorism and international terrorism, or using categories such as vigilante terrorism or insurgent terrorism. One way the typology of terrorism may be defined:

- Political terrorism
- Sub-state terrorism
- Social revolutionary terrorism
- Nationalist-separatist terrorism
- Religious extremist terrorism
- Religious fundamentalist Terrorism
- New religions terrorism
- Right-wing terrorism
- Left-wing terrorism
- Communist terrorism
- State-sponsored terrorism
- Regime or state terrorism
- Criminal terrorism
- Pathological terrorism
- Growing Fanaticism

Fanatics are gaining power and legitimacy. Some countries are already dominated by fanaticism — think North Korea, Syria and Myanmar. Some are flirting with it — think Hungary, Poland and the United States. Some countries are repeated victims of fanatic terrorists — think England, France and Spain. The United States has always had its share of fanatical groups, but never before Trump have they felt so emboldened or been given such legitimization from the White House.

We will be helpless to deal with rising fanaticism if we fail to understand its political, economic, religious and psychological roots. I have invited Andre Haynal, a world's expert on fanaticism, to help explain it to us.

Professor Haynal has been a close observer of fanaticism for 80 years. He vividly remembers Hitler's terrifying speech exulting in Germany's takeover of Austria and lived under three different fanatic regimes in Hungary (the Nazis, the Communists, the Hungarian Fascists). He has studied with concern the Trump phenomena in the U.S. and the growth of fanatic nationalism in many European countries.

Professor Haynal is the former Chair of the Department of Psychiatry at the University of Geneva; former President of the Swiss Psychoanalytic Association; and the author of "Encounters with The Irrational". He is assisted by his wife Veronique Haynal, a psychotherapist in Geneva, who shares fully in all his work.

In Gulliver's Travels, Jonathan Swift describes the bitter and bloody war between fanatic Lilliputians and equally fanatic Blefuscudians- over the proper way to crack open a soft-boiled egg. Eleven thousand people chose death over the dishonor of cracking open the egg in the middle or on the narrow end.

Many factors are promoting fanaticism:

Rapid societal change- in technology, economic opportunity, living arrangements, traditions, ideals, values, expectations

Leaving people feeling disconnected from the past, frightened in the present, not in control of the future

Fierce job competition from computers and multinational outsourcing

Feeling that others (especially minorities and immigrants) are stealing status and resources

Comfort in belonging to a closed community of like-minded believers

Socio-economic deprivation and inequality

A charismatic leader who confidently comes forth with grand promises offering prosperity, security, and stability

Why is fanaticism on the rise now?

Crushing overpopulation – the world census, 1 billion in 1800, is now 7.6 billion and growing at the astounding rate 1 billion people every 12 years

- War, famine, and drought- resulting in massive migrations
- Political turmoil and societal instability
- Weakening of previous consensus cultural norms
- Dissolution of family ties
- Increasing concentration of wealth
- Religious tensions

Humans are less necessary as producers and consumers in a world increasingly dominated by computers

What are the characteristics of fanatic leaders?

They may differ widely in intelligence, personality and goals - but all use similar methods to turn followers into fanatics.

They convey a simple message with powerful conviction and constant propaganda.

They deny truth, manipulate objective reality, distort facts, and create fake news.

- They are intolerant of contradiction and destroy opposition.
- They delegitimize and censor alternative views.
- They divide issues and people sharply into good and bad.
- They create scapegoats and targets of anger.

Fanatical followers need:

- A simple answer, black or white
- To be protected against imagined 'evil'
- A sense of community
- To feel important
- To feel better than the 'others'
- To secure special rights and resources, in this life or in the next
- Redemption

What can reduce fanaticism?

Empowering the people; giving them a sense of responsibility for the community; educating them to distinguish real facts from surreptitious falsities; encouraging them to see through propaganda on talk radio, social media and the Rupert Murdoch fake news outlets.

Fanaticism thrives where there is deprivation and inequality. If we hope to reduce it, we must make the world a better place — reducing inequality, controlling population, and ensuring a life worth living."

Although individual fanaticism is probably as old as human psychology, institutionalized fanaticism is a creature of the agricultural revolution. The clear delineation of a powerful, rich, ruling class from their chattel subjects depended upon the religious doctrines that promoted fanatic devotion to defined leaders. Religious movements have ever since been the cause of, or excuse for, much of the world's wars and prejudice. In the last few centuries, fanatic nationalist and political ideologies have added to fanatic religion as a cause of war and terrorism.

The seeming victory of rational thought over religious doctrine during the 18th century Enlightenment promised a possible reduction in the power of fanaticism. But the Reign of Terror ending the French Revolution proved that secular fanaticism could be quite as deadly as religious.

The Internet has been a great disappointment. Hailed as a promoter of knowledge and democracy, it has instead become more a propagator of propaganda.

Trump, a creature of fanaticism and its egregious exploiter, has raised social networking into an art form of prejudice and hate. Fanaticism breeds fanaticism in a self-reinforcing, vicious cycle.

Trump will never be cured, nor will his very most bigoted followers. But many of Trump's supporters are much more reasonable people, temporarily deceived now, but likely eventually to return to rationality and moderation once the US returns to normal leadership.

We must elect anti-Trumps- leaders who will bring us together as one people, rather than encourage fanatical and self-destructive divisions.

During our long history as a nation, we have almost always been much better as a people than we are today. I have faith we will again become much better as a people when the Trump blight is overcome.

There will always be bigots- racists, misogynists, anti-gays, anti-migrants, and anti-Semites. But they must be contained- never again encouraged and exploited by the president of the United States.

Fanaticism: A brief history of the concept

Since the spectacular arrival of the threat of terrorism put an end to our complacent post-communist interregnum, the Other of parliamentary democracies has been presented – in the media but also by ubiquitous psychological "experts" – as a "fanatic". Prominent figures have identified fanaticism as a cultural syndrome, or even a deep psychopathology that could enable us to explain the supposed increase in supranational violence. While Savater's text boasts an anti-clerical irreverence of a libertarian sort that spares no one, Finkielkraut, as shown in several of his recent works, shows an obsession for confrontation with "Islamic" intolerance, with "their" illiberal fanaticism. This seems again to reiterate, in French Republican guise, Huntington's noxious theses on the clash of civilizations. In both cases, the spectacle of fanaticism, in its rapid circulation through the global media, is the object of observation and opinion, rather than the causes of fanaticism or the realities from which it originates (realities like that of the concrete intolerance towards Muslim immigrants in Denmark).

The introduction of the concept of fanaticism into the debate on today's ideological conflicts indeed seems to lean more towards cultural and psychological causes than political, strategic, and material ones. Fanaticism often appears as an invariable that transcends historical events, or even, in an Orientalist and racist vein, a characteristic of fantastical entities such as "the Arab mind". The anti-historicity of the concept in part allows for its often arbitrary and hypocritical use. Fanaticism, as we cannot help but notice with painful frequency, is often projected onto an enemy with which, by definition, one cannot negotiate. As Amos Oz writes in How to Cure a Fanatic, "it is enough to read the newspaper, or watch the news on television, to explain the ease with which people become fanatically anti-fanatic, anti-fundamentalist, with which they undertake an anti-Jihad crusade". Words that ironically gain weight when one notes that the very same Oz, who advocates "imagining" the Other, was initially spurred by the recent war in Lebanon to abandon his own reasoning, proposing an apologia for Israel and a demonization of Hezbollah that fails any test, empirical or moral. Alone the Orwellian title of one of his recent opinion pieces gives us a sense of the dangers of partisan anti-fanaticism: "Why Israeli missiles strike for peace".

The growing use of the term "fanaticism" to identify the dangers of the present, particularly the exacerbation of religious politics and the terrorist phenomenon, is rarely accompanied by a reflection on the genealogy of the term and the variety of its applications. A look at its philosophical history allows us instead to view its many facets and to initiate a critique of its rhetorical and analytical functions. In this essay, I would simply like to assess a few moments in the history of this exquisitely polemical concept, moments that allow us to recognize the persistence of certain leitmotifs in the discourse on fanaticism, including the psychologization of politics, the problem of the universal, and the image of Islam.

Luther: Fanatical anti-fanaticism

The discourse on fanaticism emerged from the crucible of ideological, theological, and political battles that accompanied the Reformation. Born, more precisely, of Luther and Melanchthon's ferocious polemics against the various urban and peasants' movements against the German lords. They tried, by defending the peasants' modus vivendi from the first manifestations of that which Marx would call primitive accumulation, to avert the expropriation of the products of their labour. As we will see, the term SchwÃrme, used by the founder of Protestantism to condemn the rebels, ended up playing an important role in Kant's critiques. But what did this concept refer to in the midst of the violent battles of 1524-25? Following Augustinian terminology, the ideologues of the Reformation saw in this social movement an attempt to eliminate the key distinction between the earthly city and the City of God, or rather to push madly – through a politicized and plebeian millennialism – for the realization of the kingdom of heaven on earth. According to Melanchthon, who refers here to the translations of Aristotle's Politics, this meant eliminating the role of "civil society". For Luther, the attempt to overthrow the secular authorities was a sign of disastrous pride, a religious catastrophe.

The conflict between Luther and the peasant rebels demonstrates extremely well the plurisecular mechanism that turns the condemnation of "fanaticism" into the justification for exceedingly cruel (and fanatical) political and military repression. Mixing theological arguments and characteristically political calculations (such as allowing the Reformation to survive in the midst of the crisis caused by the peasants' wars), in May 1525 Luther, who had earlier criticized the German principles very harshly, wrote the text Against the robbing and murdering mobs of peasants. In it, he exhorts with great enthusiasm the armies of the princes to exterminate the rebels "like dogs", and claims, quoting St Paul, that whoever (on the princes' side) dies in such battles couldn't have "a more blessed death". Luther saw in the "fanaticism" of the peasants, above all in the case of the fanatic par excellence, the preacher MÃ¼ntzer, an assault against social order as such. It is here, at the dawn of the discourse on fanaticism, that the oppositional and biased character of the term shows itself most clearly. Firstly, as one will see later with the sans-culottes of the French Revolution – for example in Edmund Burke's remarks on "epidemical fanaticism" – the "fanatic" is always the rebellious plebeian; fanaticism is often identified as the "mad" request for social equality. As many have noted, the etymology of the German term shares this theme of "fear of the masses", to quote Etienne Balibar, inasmuch as the fanatics are a swarm (Schwarm), the plebs, a multitude in revolt. As demonstrated by recent historical research, that which presented itself largely as an articulated movement – with specific institutional and constitutional demands (the maintenance of the peasant assemblies, the alleviation of levies and taxes) – and which used the religious discourse (the Gospel) in minimalist and pragmatic terms, is depicted by its detractors (in order to better justify an unsparing repression) as a theological aberration, a disease of the spirit.5

It is instead in the austerity of Kant's Enlightenment that the theme of fanaticism detaches itself clearly from a culturalist discourse. For Kant it is in the very structure of subjectivity, in the relationship between knowledge and practice, that the fanatic bacillus is to be found. In his Critique of Practical Reason, Kant distinguishes between "religious fanaticism", which pertains to the supposed knowledge of God, and the much more dangerous "moral fanaticism", which, instead of making its actions right through a simple duty, tries to base morals on sentiments, noble beliefs, and sublime faith. The moral fanatic is a subject who, in refusing to submit himself to the universality of duty, can easily turn into a well-meaning murderer. For Kant, fanaticism is always a transgression of the limits of human reason, a metaphysical delirium. In the Critique of Judgement, fanaticism – which for Luther was caused by an excess of iconoclasm (the anti-representational fury of the radical Reform) – is described "aesthetically" as a desire to "see something beyond all bounds of sensibility". This is almost a kind of metaphysical idolatry (in fact, Kant praises Jewish iconoclasm here). Finally, in his essay "What Does it Mean to Orient Oneself in Thinking?", fanaticism – projected onto Spinoza (who others regard, justifiably, as a sworn enemy of fanatical subjectivity) – is identified with an ontological dogmatism that claims dangerously to have access to the supersensible.

What is the political core of the Kantian discourse on fanaticism? Firstly, for Kant fanaticism is linked to an obsession which, although it believes itself to be universal, reveals itself to be particularist. This is the case in nationalistic fanaticism, which Kant sets against cosmopolitanism. In Kant, the defence of authority that we encountered in Luther reemerges: denial of any right to rebellion and the requirement in politics for a respect of authority, laws, and representative institutions. This is explained not only by Kant's cautious disposition, but by one of his possible definitions of fanaticism, as the confusion of a regulatory idea (the republic, for example) with a constituent plan that may be affirmed materially and subjectively. This tendency to neutralize a "constituent fanaticism" can be seen clearly in Kant's complex reaction to the French Revolution, well analyzed by Hannah Arendt in her lectures on Kant and judgement. While the rebel sans-culotte is implicitly seen as a fanatical and pathological figure, the revolutionary movement is saved and universalized through its effect on the spectator, who judges it in terms of human history and the sign of universality that it conveys. In this way, Kant's Conflict of the Faculties, paradoxically without justifying the actors of the revolution, sees the revolution as a test of the moral inclination of our species, and (repeating a dichotomy presented in the Critique of Judgement, the Anthropology [1798], and various other texts) distinguishes between fanaticism and enthusiasm, with the latter understood as a passion for the ideal that does not flow over into the "fanatical" effort to achieve it hic et nunc.

Hegel and the excess of Islamic universality

The concept of fanaticism (for which the German philosopher uses both SchwÃ¤rmerei and Fanatismus) plays an extremely interesting role in the works of Hegel. While in Kant we are dealing with a cognitive and affective disposition, a spurious result of our inevitable metaphysical impulse, in Hegel fanaticism is depicted as a necessary passage in the progressive universalization of Spirit. As rightly noted by Domenico Losurdo, German thought from Kant to Hegel can be characterized as a philosophical response to the historical trauma and prospect of emancipation represented by the French Revolution. In the conceptual transcription of the revolution, fanaticism appears as a short circuit between the abstract universal and its concrete realization, a manifestation of subjective freedom in its pure negativity, in its active refusal of any determination. As is well-known, in the Phenomenology of Spirit Hegel recognizes in this negating movement of abstract, subjective freedom the spiritual force behind the Reign of Terror and its ruthless logic of suspicion – an idea that Alain Badiou has recently brought back in The Century in order to summarize the essence of the twentieth century.

In the Philosophy of Right (1821), Hegel returns to this subject, speaking of a "fanaticism of destruction" that is exemplified in the elimination of suspected individuals, in the rejection of the stabilization of the revolution in any determined institutional order. In the field of politics, if the fanatic strives for the realization of an ideal, he at any rate ends up fatally undermining any particular organization, inasmuch as his "negative freedom" manifests itself only in the destruction of the particular. In an addition to the Philosophy of Right, Hegel associates this "nihilistic" rage with the injection of religious subjectivity into the objectivity of the State. Insofar as religion is characterized by a strict impetus towards totality, and the State instead depends on the differentiation of its "organs", the introduction of religion into politics is destructive. "The wish to have the whole in every particular", writes Hegel, "could be fulfilled only by the destruction of the particular, and fanaticism is just the refusal to give scope to particular differences." When devotion enters into the State, it reveals itself as pure, explosive intolerance. This could give the impression of a simple refutation, liberal or conservative, of a radical politics of principle. Transferring our attention to Hegel's more specifically historical reflections, we can instead note that this fanaticism of destruction, this terror of the abstract, can represent an inevitable passage, and not simply, like Kant, an inclination against which we may be immunized by a healthy dose of Enlightenment. At this point it is useful to note that Hegel's use of the concept of fanaticism, even if it plays an extremely specific role in the development of Spirit, shares a notable plasticity with its more recent usages. One can even say that the specificity of the concept of "fanaticism of destruction" goes hand in hand with its extension to apparently disconnected cases – the rituals of the tribes of Dahomey, Hinduism, Islam. Or better, in the Hegelian discourse on fanaticism there is a strange short circuit between an exquisitely immanent moment of the European spirit and the appearance of its non-European and ahistorical other. Leaving aside the stereotypical images of a savage and frenetic Africa, and of an India that drowns in the tepid waters of the Absolute, the discourse on "fanatical" Islam, which seems to retrace the worst of eighteenth-century Orientalism, contains interesting and at times surprising ideas.

Firstly, it is worth noting that in Hegel Islam appears as a spiritual and political phenomenon. In a symptomatic phrase, Hegel defines it as the "Revolution in the East". Far from the fashion for "Oriental despotism", he sees in Islam a movement of universalization, although one that, dominated by the "Oriental principle", is centred around abstract unity (monotheism without trinity), thereby leading to the abandonment or forcible dissolution of particularity, differences, and multiplicity. In the Philosophy of History, Islam appears as a triumph over Jewish particularism, the birth of a true and proper universal character. Therefore it is not in a pathological obsession for the particular – as in the case of nationalistic fanaticism condemned by Kant's cosmopolitan thinking – but in the excess of universality that Hegel recognizes the spiritual and political limits of Islam, whose subject is without predicates, without qualities. It is therefore on the basis of his theory of fanaticism as abstract and negative subjectivity that Hegel ends up revitalizing Orientalist discourse: Islam is "expansionist", because it cannot stabilize itself in a differentiated manifold; Islam decays into "sensuality" (another element of the Orientalist discourse, present in the fantasies of an Orient made of harems and opium), because social cohesion is granted only by the One, by Allah, and not by institutions of the State. So, though recognizing the universalizing force of Islam (also embodied, according to him, by the dignity and courage of its warriors), for Hegel its spirituality necessarily issues into a "desolate destruction".

Setting aside the utter neglect of Islamic political, legal, and scientific thought, which conditions such verdicts, and remaining within the bounds of Hegel's discourse, is it possible to treat Islamic "fanaticism" as a mere dead end of Spirit? Inasmuch as it portrays it as a movement of radical universalization, I do not believe that Hegel's thought permits a simple expulsion of Islamic "fanaticism". In his Lectures on the Philosophy of Religion (1821-31), the "pure formalism" of Islam is explicitly flanked with the French Revolution and its "terrorist" dissolution of the pre-revolutionary ties. Insofar as the Hegelian State aims to integrate subjectivity and freedom into an organic and differentiated system of institutional determinations, Hegel's historical thought cannot ignore the inevitable, and in a certain sense "progressive", nature of the "fanatical" moment. We are reminded of this political power of abstraction, for example, in the experience of the African-American leader Malcolm X, for whom conversion to Islam functioned as a break in the particularism of black nationalism. As he wrote in a letter from Jeddah in 1964 (during the hajj dramatized in the famous film by Spike Lee), for him Islam represented "the one religion that erases the race problem from its society".

Remaining closer to Hegel, the inevitability and the local necessity of "fanaticism" (as a movement of radical universalization) were noted by the young Hegelian Arnold Ruge in a text entitled "Hegel's Philosophy of Right and the Politics of Our Times", published in the Deutsche JahrbÃ¼cher in 1842. In which sense does "fanaticism" appear necessary to Ruge? Reflecting on the key problem of his time, the relationship between Church and State, Ruge declares that religion manifests itself as desire (Lust) for liberation, and that fanaticism represents an "intensified religion", or rather a passion (Wollust) for liberation that is born from a prior failure, from a blockage of the routes to emancipation. Again the example of France returns, with its "insane" but comprehensible repeated attempt to destroy the obstacles to social equality. It is in his phenomenology of the "practical pathos" of the fanatic that Ruge shows himself to be one of our contemporaries. Indeed, he writes: "When there is something to explode, one goes up in smoke with it, so that ultimately, while not sparing oneself, one also sacrifices others horribly to one's purposes". But while many of our intellectuals might read this pathos (or this pathology) in an abstract sense, for Ruge it was a consequence of the failure to incorporate the passion for liberation into the mechanisms of the State. That is why he declares that "as long as there are batteries to man and positions to defend with one's life, we will have no history without fanaticism".

Conclusion: Beyond liberalism and fanaticism

Today it is good to keep Ruge's considerations in mind. During the Cold War, the discourse on "totalitarianism" operated for a long time with an extremely impoverished version of the concept of fanaticism that had already been articulated in German philosophy. This is especially evident in this discourse's desire simply to nullify the egalitarian force of the French Revolution, often read (by authors like Talmon and even Arendt) as the remote, but fundamental source of all the ills of our time. State socialism too was often read in a psychological and religious key, leaving aside serious historical and sociological analyses. Sensationalist texts on the psychopathology of Stalin, for example, have obscured the institutional mechanisms of terror and their material and economic context, ignoring for example the eminently pragmatic and opportunistic character of the decisions that led to the gulags, as well as the Machiavellian role of ideological "moderation" in Stalin's political trajectory.

The anti-communist thought of the twentieth century, which has often regarded "fanaticism" as the cause rather than the effect of social evils (see for example the reflections of Emil Cioran and Raymond Aron), has given rise to the purely ideological dichotomy between a liberalism of scepticism and compromise, on one hand, and fanaticism, on the other. According to such thinkers, "fanaticism" is not simply an erroneous but inevitable tendency of human reason (Kant) or a necessary phase of extremism in the development of humanity (Hegel). It is a pathology to be eradicated. Such a vision of fanaticism not only forgets that sceptics and liberals are perfectly capable of causing enormous harm, or indeed evil (especially when legitimated by a "just war", which wars against "fanatics" are by definition), and that not all reactionaries can be classified as "fanatics", but it also ignores the lesson of Ruge: a "history without fanaticism" can only be the result of a politics of real emancipation and not of an abstract battle of ideas. Does this perhaps signify that the term "fanaticism" should simply be abandoned? That the fanatic is an illusion, a chimera?

Not necessarily, but, following the traces of the great thinkers who wrestled with it, it is up to us contemporaries to rethink fanaticism as a precise historical, political, and psychological concept for the present and not simply as a talisman for exorcising or eliminating absolute enemies. Perhaps a first step would be to treat fanaticism as predicate of certain actions and political discourses, refraining from defining political subjects as "fanatics" sans phrase. For, as the case of Luther and the rebel peasants shows, the designation of one's enemies as "fanatics" is often the sinister prelude to treating them "like dogs", or like "unlawful combatants".

2

Religious Fanaticism and Communalism

Religious fanaticism is uncritical zeal or with an obsessive enthusiasm related to one's own, or one's group's, devotion to a religion – a form of human fanaticism which could otherwise be expressed in one's other involvements and participation, including employment, role, and partisan affinities.

Terrorist acts throughout history have been performed on religious grounds with the goal to either spread or enforce a system of belief, viewpoint or opinion. The validity and scope of religious terrorism is limited to an individual's view or a group's view or interpretation of that belief system's teachings.

Religious terrorism is terrorism carried out based on motivations and goals that may have a predominantly religious character or influence.

In the modern age, after the decline of ideas such as the divine right of kings and with the rise of nationalism, terrorism has more often been based on anarchism, and revolutionary politics. Since 1980, however, there has been an increase in terrorist activity motivated by religion.

Former United States Secretary of State Warren Christopher has said that terrorist acts in the name of religion and ethnic identity have become "one of the most important security challenges we face in the wake of the Cold War." However, the political scientists Robert Pape and Terry Nardin, the social psychologists M. Brooke Rogers and colleagues, and the sociologist and religious studies scholar Mark Juergensmeyer have all argued that religion should only be considered one incidental factor and that such terrorism is primarily geopolitical.

According to Juergensmeyer, religion and violence have had a symbiotic relationship since before the Crusades and even since before the Bible. He defines religious terrorism as consisting of acts that terrify, the definition of which is provided by the witnesses – the ones terrified – and not by the party committing the act; accompanied by either a religious motivation, justification, organization, or world view. Religion is sometimes used in combination with other factors, and sometimes as the primary motivation. Religious terrorism is intimately connected to current forces of geopolitics.

Bruce Hoffman has characterized modern religious terrorism as having three traits:

The perpetrators must use religious scriptures to justify or explain their violent acts or to gain recruits.

Clerical figures must be involved in leadership roles.

Perpetrators use apocalyptic images of destruction to justify the acts.

Martyrdom and suicide terrorism

Important symbolic acts such as the blood sacrifice link acts of violence to religion and terrorism. Suicide terrorism, self-sacrifice, or martyrdom has throughout history been organized and perpetrated by groups with both political and religious motivations. The Christian tradition has a long history of heterodoxical and heretical groups which stressed self-immolative acts and scholarship has to some degree linked this to modern political groups such as the Irish Republican Army. Suicide terrorism or martyrdom is efficient, inexpensive, easily organized, and extremely difficult to counter, delivering maximum damage for little cost. The shocking nature of a suicide attack also attracts public attention. Glorifying the culture of martyrdom benefits the terrorist organization and inspires more people to join the group. According to one commentator, retaliation against suicide attacks increases the group's sense of victimization and commitment to adhere to doctrine and policy. This process serves to encourage martyrdom, and so suicide terrorism, self-sacrifice, or martyrdom represent "value for money". Robert Pape, a political scientist who specializes in suicide terrorism, has made a case for secular motivations and reasons as being the foundations of most suicide attacks, which are often labelled as "religious".

Financing

Terrorism activities worldwide are supported through not only the organized systems that teach holy war as the highest calling, but also through the legal, illegal, and often indirect methods financing these systems; these sometimes use organizations, including charities, as fronts to mobilize or channel sources and funds. Charities can involve the provision of aid to those in need, and oblations or charitable offerings are fundamental to nearly all religious systems, with sacrifice as a furtherance of the custom.

Criticism of the concept

Robert Pape compiled the first complete database of every documented suicide bombing from 1980–2003. He argues that the news reports about suicide attacks are profoundly misleading – "There is little connection between suicide terrorism and Islamic fundamentalism, or any one of the world's religions". After studying 315 suicide attacks carried out over the last two decades, he concludes that suicide bombers' actions stem from political conflict, not religion.

Michael A. Sheehan stated in 2000, "A number of terrorist groups have portrayed their causes in religious and cultural terms. This is often a transparent tactic designed to conceal political goals, generate popular support and silence opposition."

Terry Nardin wrote,

"A basic problem is whether religious terrorism really differs, in its character and causes, from political terrorism... defenders of religious terrorism typically reason by applying commonly acknowledged moral principles... But the use (or misuse) of moral arguments does not in fact distinguish religious from nonreligious terrorists, for the latter also rely upon such arguments to justify their acts... political terrorism can also be symbolic... alienation and dispossession... are important in other kinds of violence as well. In short, one wonders whether the expression 'religious terrorism' is more than a journalistic convenience".<

Professor Mark Juergensmeyer wrote,

"...religion is not innocent. But it does not ordinarily lead to violence. That happens only with the coalescence of a peculiar set of circumstances – political, social, and ideological – when religion becomes fused with violent expressions of social aspirations, personal pride, and movements for political change." and "Whether or not one uses 'terrorist' to describe violent acts depends on whether one thinks that the acts are warranted. To a large extent the use of the term depends on one's world view: if the world is perceived as peaceful, violent acts appear to be terrorism. If the world is thought to be at war, violent acts may be regarded as legitimate. They may be seen as preemptive strikes, as defensive tactics in an ongoing battles, or as symbols indicating to the world that it is indeed in a state of grave and ultimate conflict."

David Kupelian wrote, "Genocidal madness can't be blamed on a particular philosophy or religion."

Riaz Hassan wrote, "It is politics more than religious fanaticism that has led terrorists to blow themselves up."

On July 2, 2013 in Lahore, 50 Muslim scholars of the Sunni Ittehad Council (SIC) issued a collective fatwa against suicide bombings, the killing of innocent people, bomb attacks, and targeted killings declaring them as Haraam or forbidden.

According to the Global Terrorism Index by the University of Maryland, College Park, religious extremism has overtaken national separatism and become the main driver of terrorist attacks around the world. Since 9/11 there has been a five-fold increase in deaths from terrorist attacks. The majority of incidents over the past several years can be tied to groups with a religious agenda. Before 2000, it was nationalist separatist terrorist organizations such as the IRA and Chechen rebels who were behind the most attacks. The number of incidents from nationalist separatist groups has remained relatively stable in the years since while religious extremism has grown. The prevalence of Islamist groups in Iraq, Afghanistan, Pakistan, Nigeria and Syria is the main driver behind these trends.

Four of the terrorist groups that have been most active since 2001 are Boko Haram, Al Qaeda, the Taliban and ISIL. These groups have been most active in Iraq, Afghanistan, Pakistan, Nigeria and Syria. 80 percent of all deaths from terrorism occurred in one of these five countries.

Terrorism in Pakistan has become a great problem. From the summer of 2007 until late 2009, more than 1,500 people were killed in suicide and other attacks on civilians for reasons attributed to a number of causes – sectarian violence between Sunni and Shia Muslims; easy availability of guns and explosives; the existence of a "Kalashnikov culture"; an influx of ideologically driven Muslims based in or near Pakistan, who originated from various nations around the world and the subsequent war against the pro-Soviet Afghans in the 1980s which blew back into Pakistan; the presence of Islamist insurgent groups and forces such as the Taliban and Lashkar-e-Taiba. On July 2, 2013 in Lahore, 50 Muslim scholars of the Sunni Ittehad Council (SIC) issued a collective fatwa against suicide bombings, the killing of innocent people, bomb attacks, and targeted killings declaring them as Haraam or forbidden.

In 2015, the Southern Poverty Law Center released a report on terrorism in the United States. The report (titled The Age of the Wolf) found that during that period, "more people have been killed in America by non-Islamic domestic terrorists than jihadists." The "virulent racist and anti-semitic" ideology of the ultra-right wing Christian Identity movement is usually accompanied by anti-government sentiments. Adherents of Christian Identity believe that whites of European descent can be traced back to the "Lost Tribes of Israel" and many consider Jews to be the Satanic offspring of Eve and the Serpent. This group has committed hate crimes, bombings and other acts of terrorism. Its influence ranges from the Ku Klux Klan and neo-Nazi groups to the anti-government militia and sovereign citizen movements. Christian Identity's origins can be traced back to Anglo-Israelism, which held the view that British people were descendants of ancient Israelites. By the 1930s, the movement had been infected with anti-Semitism, and eventually Christian Identity theology diverged from traditional Anglo-Israelism, and developed what is known as the "two seed" theory. According to the two-seed theory, the Jewish people are descended from Cain and the serpent (not from Shem). The white European seedline is descended from the "lost tribes" of Israel. They hold themselves to "God's laws", not to "man's laws", and they do not feel bound to a government that they consider run by Jews and the New World Order.

Israel has had problems with Jewish religious terrorism. Yigal Amir assassinated Israeli Prime Minister Yitzhak Rabin in 1995. For Amir, killing Rabin was an exemplary act that symbolized the fight against an illegitimate government that was prepared to cede Jewish Holy Land to the Palestinians.

Features of Religious Fanaticism

Steffen gives several features associated with religious fanaticism or extremism:

"Spiritual needs"... human beings have a spiritual longing for understanding and meaning, and given the mystery of existence, that spiritual quest can only be fulfilled through some kind of relationship with ultimacy, whether or not that takes the form as a "transcendent other." Religion has power to meet this need for meaning and transcendent relationship.

"Attractiveness"... it presents itself in such a way that those who find their way into it come to express themselves in ways consistent with the particular vision of ultimacy at the heart of this religious form.

A "live option"... it is present to the moral consciousness as a live option that addresses spiritual need and satisfies human longing for meaning, power, and belonging.

Examples of religious fanaticism

Christianity

Ever since Christianity was established, some of those in authority have sought to expand and control the church, often through the fanatical use of force. Grant Shafer says, "Jesus of Nazareth is best known as a preacher of nonviolence" , although in Matthew 10:34 he says, "Think not that I am come to send peace on earth; I came not to send peace, but a sword." The start of Christian fanatic rule came with the Roman Emperor Constantine I. Ellens says, "When Christianity came to power in the empire of Constantine, it proceeded almost to viciously repress all non-Christians and all Christians who did not line up with official Orthodox ideology, policy, and practice". An example of Christians who didn't line up with Orthodox ideology is the Donatists, who "refused to accept repentant clergy who had formerly given way to apostasy when persecuted". Fanatic Christian activity, continued into the Middle Ages with the Crusades. These wars were attempts by the Catholics, sanctioned by the Pope, to reclaim the Holy Land from the Muslims. However many Catholics see the crusades as a just war in self-defense. Charles Selengut, in his book Sacred Fury: Understanding Religious Violence, said:

The Crusades were very much holy wars waged to maintain Christianity's theological and social control. On their way to conquering the Holy Land from the Muslims by force of arms, the crusaders destroyed dozens of Jewish communities and killed thousands because the Jews would not accept the Christian faith. Jews had to be killed in the religious campaign because their very existence challenged the sole truth espoused by the Christian Church.

Shafer adds that, "When the crusaders captured Jerusalem in 1099, they killed Muslims, Jews, and native Christians indiscriminately". Another prominent form of fanaticism according to some came a few centuries later with the Spanish Inquisition. The Inquisition was the monarchy's way of making sure their people stayed within Catholic Christianity. Selengut said,

"The inquisitions were attempts at self-protection and targeted primarily "internal enemies" of the church". The driving force of the Inquisition was the Inquisitors, who were responsible for spreading the truth of Christianity. Selengut continues, saying:

The inquisitors generally saw themselves as educators helping people maintain correct beliefs by pointing out errors in knowledge and judgment... Punishment and death came only to those who refused to admit their errors ... during the Spanish Inquisitions of the fifteenth century, the clear distinction between confession and innocence and remaining in error became muddled.... The investigators had to invent all sorts of techniques, including torture, to ascertain whether ... new converts' beliefs were genuine.

During the reformation Christian fanaticism increased between Catholics and the recently formed protestants, many Christians were killed for having rival view point. The reformation set of a chain of sectarian wars between the Catholics and the sectarian protestant culminating in the wars of religions.

Islam

Extremism within Islam goes back to the 7th century to the Kharijites. From their essentially political position, they developed extreme doctrines that set them apart from both mainstream Sunni and Shi□a Muslims. The Kharijites were particularly noted for adopting a radical approach to Takfir, whereby they declared other Muslims to be unbelievers and therefore deemed them worthy of death.

Sayyid Qutb, a figurehead of the Muslim Brotherhood in Egypt, was influential in promoting a Pan-Islamist ideology in the 1960s. When Qutb was executed by the Egyptian government, Ayman al-Zawahiri formed the organization Egyptian Islamic Jihad to replace the government with an Islamic state that would reflect Qutb's ideas for Islamic revival. The Qutbist ideology has been influential in jihadist movements that seek to overthrow secular governments, and Qutb's books have been frequently been cited by Osama bin Laden and Anwar al-Awlaki.

Since Osama bin Laden's fatwa in 1998, radical jihad has increasingly become an internationally recognized term. Bin Laden's concept, though, is very different from the actual meaning of the term. In the religious context, jihad most nearly means "working urgently for a certain godly objective, generally an imperialist one". The word jihad in Arabic means 'struggle'. The struggle can be a struggle of implementing the Islamic values in daily activities, a struggle with others to counter arguments against Islam, or self-defense when physically attacked because of belief in Islam. According to Steffen, there are portions of the Qur'an where military jihad is used. As Steffen says, though, "Jihad in these uses is always defensive. Not only does 'jihad' not endorse acts of military aggression, but 'jihad' is invoked in Qur'anic passages to indicate how uses of force are always subject to restraint and qualification". This kind of jihad differs greatly from the kind most commonly discussed today.

Thomas Farr, in an essay titled "Islam's Way to Freedom", says that, "Even though most Muslims reject violence, the extremists' use of sacred texts lends their actions authenticity and recruiting power". (Freedom 24) He goes on to say, "The radicals insist that their central claim – God's desire for Islam's triumph – requires no interpretation. According to them, true Muslims will pursue it by any means necessary, including dissimulation, civil coercion, and the killing of innocents". (Freedom 24)

According to certain observers this disregard for others and rampant use of violence is markedly different from the peaceful message that jihad is meant to employ. Although fanatic jihadists have committed many terroristic acts throughout the world, perhaps the best known is the September 11 attacks. According to Ellens, the al-Qaeda members who took part in the terrorist attacks did so out of their belief that, by doing it, they would "enact a devastating blow against the evil of secularized and non-Muslim America. They were cleansing this world, God's temple".

Religious war

A religious war or holy war (Latin: bellum sacrum) is a war primarily caused or justified by differences in religion. In the modern period, debates are common over the extent to which religious, economic, or ethnic aspects of a conflict predominate in a given war. According to the Encyclopedia of Wars, out of all 1,763 known/recorded historical conflicts, 123, or 6.98%, had religion as their primary cause. Matthew White's The Great Big Book of Horrible Things gives religion as the cause of 13 of the world's 100 deadliest atrocities. In several conflicts including the Israeli–Palestinian conflict, the Syrian civil war, and the wars in Afghanistan and Iraq, religious elements are overtly present but variously described as fundamentalism or religious extremism—depending upon the observer's sympathies. However, studies on these cases often conclude that ethnic animosities drive much of the conflicts.

Some historians argue that what is termed "religious wars" is a largely "Western dichotomy" and a modern invention from the past few centuries, arguing that all wars that are classed as "religious" have secular (economic or political) ramifications. Similar opinions were expressed as early as the 1760s, during the Seven Years' War, widely recognized to be "religious" in motivation, noting that the warring factions were not necessarily split along confessional lines as much as along secular interests.

According to Jeffrey Burton Russell, numerous cases of supposed acts of religious wars such as the Thirty Years' War, the French Wars of Religion, the Sri Lankan Civil War, 9/11 and other terrorist attacks, the Bosnian War, and the Rwandan Civil War were all primarily motivated by social, political, and economic issues rather than religion. For example, in the Thirty Years' War the dominant participant on the "Protestant" side for much of the conflict was France, led by Cardinal Richelieu.

History of the concept of religion

The modern word religion comes from the Latin word religio. In the ancient and medieval world, the etymological Latin root religio was understood as an individual virtue of worship, never as doctrine, practice, or actual source of knowledge. The modern concept of "religion" as an abstraction which entails distinct sets of beliefs or doctrines is a recent invention in the English language since such usage began with texts from the 17th century due to the splitting of Christendom during the Protestant Reformation and more prevalent colonization or globalization in the age of exploration which involved contact with numerous foreign and indigenous cultures with non-European languages. It was in the 17th century that the concept of "religion" received its modern shape despite the fact that the Bible, the Quran, and other ancient sacred texts did not have a concept of religion in the original languages and neither did the people or the cultures in which these sacred texts were written. For example, the Greek word threskeia, which was used by Greek writers such as Herodotus and Josephus and is found in texts like the New Testament, is sometimes translated as "religion" today, however, the term was understood as "worship" well into the medieval period.

In the Quran, the Arabic word din is often translated as "religion" in modern translations, but up to the mid-1600s translators expressed din as "law". Even in the 1st century AD, Josephus had used the Greek term ioudaismos, which some translate as "Judaism" today, even though he used it as an ethnic term, not one linked to modern abstract concepts of religion as a set of beliefs. It was in the 19th century that the terms "Buddhism", "Hinduism", "Taoism", and "Confucianism" first emerged. Throughout its long history, Japan had no concept of "religion" since there was no corresponding Japanese word, nor anything close to its meaning, but when American warships appeared off the coast of Japan in 1853 and forced the Japanese government to sign treaties demanding, among other things, freedom of religion, the country had to contend with this Western idea.

According to the philologist Max Müller in the 19th century, the root of the English word "religion", the Latin religio, was originally used to mean only "reverence for God or the gods, careful pondering of divine things, piety" (which Cicero further derived to mean "diligence"). Max Müller characterized many other cultures around the world, including Egypt, Persia, and India, as having a similar power structure at this point in history. What is called ancient religion today, they would have only called "law".

Some languages have words that can be translated as "religion", but they may use them in a very different way, and some have no word for religion at all. For example, the Sanskrit word dharma, sometimes translated as "religion", also means law. Throughout classical South Asia, the study of law consisted of concepts such as penance through piety and ceremonial as well as practical traditions. Medieval Japan at first had a similar union between "imperial law" and universal or "Buddha law", but these later became independent sources of power.

There is no precise equivalent of "religion" in Hebrew, and Judaism does not distinguish clearly between religious, national, racial, or ethnic identities. One of its central concepts is "halakha", meaning the "walk" or "path" sometimes translated as "law", which guides religious practice and belief and many aspects of daily life.

Criteria for classification

The Crusades against Muslim expansion in the 11th century was recognized as a "holy war" or bellum sacrum by later writers in the 17th century. The early modern wars against the Ottoman Empire were seen as a seamless continuation of this conflict by contemporaries. The term "religious war" was used to describe, controversially at the time, what are now known as the European wars of religion, and especially the then-ongoing Seven Years' War, from at least the mid 18th century.

In their Encyclopedia of Wars, authors Charles Phillips and Alan Axelrod document 1763 notable wars in world history out of which 121 wars are in the "religious wars" category in the index. They note that before the 17th century, much of the "reasons" for conflicts were explained through the lens of religion and that after that time wars were explained through the lens of wars as a way to further sovereign interests. Some commentators have concluded that only 123 wars (7%) out of these 1763 wars were fundamentally originated by religious motivations.

The Encyclopedia of War, edited by Gordon Martel, using the criteria that the armed conflict must involve some overt religious action, concludes that 6% of the wars listed in their encyclopedia can be labelled religious wars.

William T. Cavanaugh in his Myth of Religious Violence (2009) argues that what is termed "religious wars" is a largely "Western dichotomy" and a modern invention, arguing that all wars that are classed as "religious" have secular (economic or political) ramifications. Similar opinions were expressed as early as the 1760s, during the Seven Years' War, widely recognized to be "religious" in motivation, noting that the warring factions were not necessarily split along confessional lines as much as along secular interests.

It is evident that religion as one aspect of a people's cultural heritage may serve as a cultural marker or ideological rationalisation for a conflict that has deeper ethnic and cultural differences. This has been specifically argued for the case of The Troubles in Northern Ireland, often portrayed as a religious conflict of a Catholic vs. a Protestant faction, while the more fundamental cause of the conflict was in fact ethnic or nationalistic rather than religious in nature. Since the native Irish were mostly Catholic and the later British-sponsored immigrants were mainly Protestant, the terms become shorthand for the two cultures, but it is inaccurate to describe the conflict as a religious one.

According to Irfan Omar and Michael Duffey's review of violence and peacemaking in world religions, they note that studies of supposed cases of religious violence often conclude that violence is strongly driven by ethnic animosities.

The concept of "Holy War" in individual religious traditions

While early empires could be described as henotheistic, i.e. dominated by a single god of the ruling elite (as Marduk in the Babylonian empire, Assur in the Assyrian empire, etc.), or more directly by deifing the ruler in an imperial cult, the concept of "Holy War" enters a new phase with the development of monotheism.

Ancient warfare and polytheism

Classical Antiquity had a pantheon with particular attributes and interest areas. Ares personified war. While he received occasional sacrifice from armies going to war, there was only a very limited "cult of Ares". In Sparta, however, each company of youths sacrificed to Enyalios before engaging in ritual fighting at the Phoebaeum.

Islam

The Muslim conquests were a military expansion on an unprecedented scale, beginning in the lifetime of Muhammad and spanning the centuries, down to the Ottoman wars in Europe. Until the 13th century, the Muslim conquests were those of a more or less coherent empire, the Caliphate, but after the Mongol invasions, expansion continued on all fronts (other than Iberia which was lost in the Reconquista) for another half millennium until the final collapse of the Mughal Empire in the east and the Ottoman Empire in the west with the onset of the modern period.

There were also a number of periods of infighting among Muslims; these are known by the term Fitna and mostly concern the early period of Islam, from the 7th to 11th centuries, i.e. before the collapse of the Caliphate and the emergence of the various later Islamic empires.

While technically, the millennium of Muslim conquests could be classified as "religious war", the applicability of the term has been questioned. The reason is that the very notion of a "religious war" as opposed to a "secular war" is the result of the Western concept of the separation of Church and State. No such division has ever existed in the Islamic world, and consequently there cannot be a real division between wars that are "religious" from such that are "non-religious". Islam does not have any normative tradition of pacifism, and warfare has been integral part of Islamic history both for the defense and the spread of the faith since the time of Muhammad. This was formalised in the juristic definition of war in Islam, which continues to hold normative power in contemporary Islam, inextricably linking political and religious justification of war. This normative concept is known as Jihad, an Arabic word with the meaning "to strive; to struggle" (viz. "in the way of God"), which includes the aspect of struggle "by the sword".

The first forms of military Jihad occurred after the migration (hijra) of Muhammad and his small group of followers to Medina from Mecca and the conversion of several inhabitants of the city to Islam. The first revelation concerning the struggle against the Meccans was surah 22, verses 39-40:

To those against whom war is made, permission is given (to fight), because they are wronged;- and verily, Allah is most powerful for their aid. (They are) those who have been expelled from their homes in defiance of right,- (for no cause) except that they say, "our Lord is Allah". Did not Allah check one set of people by means of another, there would surely have been pulled down monasteries, churches, synagogues, and mosques, in which the name of Allah is commemorated in abundant measure. Allah will certainly aid those who aid his (cause);- for verily Allah is full of Strength, Exalted in Might, (able to enforce His Will).

This happened many times throughout history, beginning with Muhammad's battles against the polytheist Arabs including the Battle of Badr (624), and battles in Uhud (625), Khandaq (627), Mecca (630) and Hunayn (630).

Christianity

In early Christianity, St. Augustine's concept of just war (bellum iustum) was widely accepted, but warfare was not regarded as a virtuous activity and expressions of concern for the salvation of those who killed enemies in battle, regardless of the cause for which they fought, was common. According to historian Edward Peters, before the 11th century Christians had not developed a concept of "Holy War" (bellum sacrum), whereby fighting itself might be considered a penitential and spiritually meritorious act. During the 9th and 10th centuries, multiple invasions occurred which lead some regions to make their own armies to defend themselves and this slowly lead to the emergence of the Crusades, the concept of "holy war", and terminology such as "enemies of God" in the 11th century.

During the time of the Crusades, some of those who fought in the name of God were recognized as the Milites Christi, soldiers or knights of Christ. The Crusades were a series of military campaigns that took place during the 11th through 13th centuries against the Muslim Conquests. Originally, the goal was to recapture Jerusalem and the Holy Land from the Muslims, and support the besieged Christian Byzantine Empire against the Muslim Seljuq expansion into Asia Minor and Europe proper. Later, Crusades were launched against other targets, either for religious reasons, such as the Albigensian Crusade, the Northern Crusades, or because of political conflict, such as the Aragonese Crusade. In 1095, at the Council of Clermont, Pope Urban II raised the level of war from bellum iustum ("just war"), to bellum sacrum ("holy war"). In 16th-century France there was a succession of wars between Roman Catholics and Protestants (Hugenots primarily), known as the French Wars of Religion. In the first half of the 17th century, the German states, Scandinavia (Sweden, primarily) and Poland were beset by religious warfare in the Thirty Years War. Roman Catholicism and Protestantism figured in the opposing sides of this conflict, though Catholic France did take the side of the Protestants but purely for political reasons.

The Battle of Las Navas de Tolosa, known in Arab history as the Battle of Al-Uqab, took place on 16 July 1212 and was an important turning point in the

Reconquista and in the medieval history of Spain. The forces of King Alfonso VIII of Castile were joined by the armies of his Christian rivals, Sancho VII of Navarre, Pedro II of Aragon and Afonso II of Portugal in battle against the Berber Muslim Almohad conquerors of the southern half of the Iberian Peninsula.

Judaism

In the Jewish religion, the expression Milkhemet Mitzvah (Hebrew: "commandment war") refers to a war that is obligatory for all Jews (men and women). Such wars were limited to territory within the borders of the land of Israel. The geographical limits of Israel and conflicts with surrounding nations are detailed in the Tanakh, the Hebrew Bible, especially in Numbers 34:1-15 and Ezekiel 47:13-20. The concept of a religious war was absent in Jewish thought for approximately 2000 years, though it reemerged in some factions of the Zionist movement, particularly Revisionist Zionism. "From the earliest days of Israel's existence as a people, holy war was a sacred institution, undertaken as a cultic act of a religious community.

According to Reuven Firestone, ""Holy War" is a Western concept referring to war that is fought for religion, against adherents of other religions, often in order to promote religion through conversion, and with no specific geographic limitation. This concept does not occur in the Hebrew Bible, whose wars are not fought for religion or in order to promote it but, rather, in order to preserve religion and a religiously unique people in relation to a specific and limited geography."

Religious conflict in the modern period

Israeli–Palestinian conflict

The Israeli–Palestinian conflict can be viewed primarily as an ethnic conflict between two parties where one party is most often portrayed as a singular ethno-religious group consisting only of the Jewish majority and ignores non-Jewish minority Israeli citizens who at varying levels support a Zionist state, especially the Druze and Circassians who for example volunteer in higher numbers for IDF combat service and are represented in the Israeli parliament in greater percentages than Israeli Jews are as well as Israeli Arabs, Samaritans, various other Christians, and Negev Bedouin; the other party is sometimes presented as an ethnic group which is multi-religious (although most numerously consisting of Muslims, then Christians, then other religious groups up to and including Samaritans and even Jews). Yet despite the multi-religious composition of both of the parties in the conflict, elements on both sides often view it as a religious war between Jews and Muslims. In 1929, religious tensions between Muslim and Jewish Palestinians over Jews praying at the Wailing Wall led to the 1929 Palestine riots including the Hebron and Safed ethnic cleansings of Jews.

In 1947, the UN decided on partitioning the Mandate of Palestine, led to the creation of the state of Israel and Jordan annexing the West Bank portion of the mandate, since then the region has been plagued with conflict. The 1948 Palestinian exodus also known as the Nakba (Arabic:), occurred when approximately 711,000 to 726,000 Palestinian Arabs fled or were expelled from their homes, during the 1948 Arab–Israeli War and the Civil War that preceded it. The exact number of refugees is a matter of dispute, though the number of Palestine refugees and their unsettled descendants registered with UNRWA is more than 4.3 million. The causes remain the subject of fundamental disagreement between Palestinians and Israelis. Jews make a religious and historical claim to the land, and Palestinians make historic, religious and ethnic claims to the land.

Pakistan and India

The All India Muslim League (AIML) was formed in Dhaka in 1906 by Muslims who were suspicious of the Hindu-majority Indian National Congress. They complained that Muslim members did not have the same rights as Hindu members. A number of different scenarios were proposed at various times.This was fuelled by the British policy of "Divide and Rule", which they tried to bring upon every political situation. Among the first to make the demand for a separate state was the writer/philosopher Allama Iqbal, who, in his presidential address to the 1930 convention of the Muslim League said that a separate nation for Muslims was essential in an otherwise Hindu-dominated subcontinent.

After the dissolution of the British Raj in 1947, two new sovereign nations were formed—the Union of India and the Dominion of Pakistan. The subsequent partition of the former British India displaced up to 12.5 million people, with estimates of loss of life varying from several hundred thousand to a million. India emerged as a secular nation with a Hindu majority, while Pakistan was established as an Islamic republic with Muslim majority population.

Abyssinia – Somalia

The Abyssinian–Adal war was a military conflict between the Abyssinians and the Adal Sultanate from 1529 until 1559. The Imam Ahmad ibn Ibrahim al-Ghazi (nicknamed Gurey in Somali and Gragn in Amharic (Graññ), both meaning "the left-handed") came close to extinguishing the ancient realm of Abyssinia, and forcibly converting all of its surviving subjects to Islam; the intervention of the European Cristóvão da Gama, son of the famous navigator Vasco da Gama, attempted to help to prevent this outcome but was killed by al-Ghazi. However, both polities exhausted their resources and manpower in this conflict, allowing the northward migration of the Oromo into their present homelands to the north and west of Addis Ababa. Many historians trace the origins of hostility between Somalia and Ethiopia to this war. Some historians also argue that this conflict proved, through their use on both sides, the value of firearms such as the matchlock musket, cannons, and the arquebus over traditional weapons.

Nigerian conflict

Inter-ethnic conflict in Nigeria has generally had a religious element. Riots against Igbo in 1953 and in the 1960s in the north were said to have been sparked by religious conflict. The riots against Igbo in the north in 1966 were said to have been inspired by radio reports of mistreatment of Muslims in the south. A military coup d'état led by lower and middle-ranking officers, some of them Igbo, overthrew the NPC-NCNC dominated government. Prime Minister Balewa along with other northern and western government officials were assassinated during the coup. The coup was considered an Igbo plot to overthrow the northern dominated government. A counter-coup was launched by mostly northern troops. Between June and July there was a mass exodus of Ibo from the north and west. Over 1.3 million Ibo fled the neighboring regions in order to escape persecution as anti-Ibo riots increased. The aftermath of the anti-Ibo riots led many to believe that security could only be gained by separating from the North.

In the 1980s, serious outbreaks between Christians and Muslims occurred in Kafanchan in southern Kaduna State in a border area between the two religions.

The 2010 Jos riots saw clashes between Muslim herders against Christian farmers near the volatile city of Jos, resulting in hundreds of casualties. Officials estimated that 500 people were massacred in night-time raids by rampaging Muslim gangs.

Buddhist uprising

During the rule of the Catholic Ngo Dinh Diem in South Vietnam, the discrimination against the majority Buddhist population generated the growth of Buddhist institutions as they sought to participate in national politics and gain better treatment. The Buddhist Uprising of 1966 was a period of civil and military unrest in South Vietnam, largely focused in the I Corps area in the north of the country in central Vietnam.

In a country where the Buddhist majority was estimated to be between 70 and 90 percent, Diem ruled with a strong religious bias. As a member of the Catholic Vietnamese minority, he pursued pro-Catholic policies that antagonized many Buddhists.

Chinese conflict

The Dungan revolt (1862–1877) and Panthay Rebellion (1856–1873) by the Hui were also set off by racial antagonism and class warfare, rather than the mistaken assumption that it was all due to Islam that the rebellions broke out. During the Dungan revolt fighting broke out between Uyghurs and Hui.

In 1936, after Sheng Shicai expelled 20,000 Kazakhs from Xinjiang to Qinghai, the Hui led by General Ma Bufang massacred their fellow Muslims, the Kazakhs, until there were only 135 of them left.

Tensions with Uyghurs and Hui arose because Qing and Republican Chinese authorities used Hui troops and officials to dominate the Uyghurs and crush Uyghur revolts. Xinjiang's Hui population increased by over 520 percent between 1940 and 1982, an average annual growth rate of 4.4 percent, while the Uyghur population only grew by 1.7 percent. This dramatic increase in the Hui population led inevitably to significant tensions between the Hui and Uyghur Muslim populations. Some old Uyghurs in Kashgar remember that the Hui army at the Battle of Kashgar (1934) massacred 2,000 to 8,000 Uyghurs, which caused tension as more Hui moved into Kashgar from other parts of China. Some Hui criticize Uyghur separatism, and generally do not want to get involved in conflicts in other countries over Islam for fear of being perceived as radical. Hui and Uyghur live apart from each other, praying separately and attending different mosques.

Lebanese Civil War

There is no consensus among scholars on what triggered the Lebanese Civil War. However, the militarization of the Palestinian refugee population, with the arrival of the PLO guerrilla forces did spark an arms race amongst the different Lebanese political factions. However the conflict played out along three religious lines, Sunni Muslim, Christian Lebanese and Shiite Muslim, Druze are considered among Shiite Muslims.

It has been argued that the antecedents of the war can be traced back to the conflicts and political compromises reached after the end of Lebanon's administration by the Ottoman Empire. The Cold War had a powerful disintegrative effect on Lebanon, which was closely linked to the polarization that preceded the 1958 political crisis. During the 1948 Arab–Israeli War an exodus of Palestinian refugees who fled the fighting or were expelled from their homes, arrived in Lebanon. Palestinians came to play a very important role in future Lebanese civil conflicts, whilst the establishment of Israel radically changed the local environment in which Lebanon found itself.

Lebanon was promised independence and on 22 November 1943 it was achieved. Free French troops, who had invaded Lebanon in 1941 to rid Beirut of the Vichy French forces, left the country in 1946. The Christians assumed power over the country and economy. A confessional parliament was created, where Muslims and Christians were given quotas of seats in parliament. As well, the President was to be a Christian, the Prime Minister a Sunni Muslim and the Speaker of Parliament a Shia Muslim.

In March 1991, parliament passed an amnesty law that pardoned all political crimes prior to its enactment. The amnesty was not extended to crimes perpetrated against foreign diplomats or certain crimes referred by the cabinet to the Higher Judicial Council. In May 1991, the militias (with the important exception of Hezbollah) were dissolved, and the Lebanese Armed Forces began to slowly rebuild themselves as Lebanon's only major non-sectarian institution.

Some violence still occurred. In late December 1991 a car bomb (estimated to carry 220 pounds of TNT) exploded in the Muslim neighborhood of Basta. At least thirty people were killed, and 120 wounded, including former Prime Minister Shafik Wazzan, who was riding in a bulletproof car.

Yugoslav Wars

The Croatian War (1991–95) and Bosnian War (1992–95), have been viewed of as religious wars between the Orthodox, Catholic and Muslim populations of former Yugoslavia, that is, Serbs, Croats and Bosniaks. Traditional religious symbols were used during the wars. Notably, foreign Muslim volunteers came to Bosnia to wage jihad ("jihad" doesn't mean "holy war", it means "struggle"), and were thus known as "Bosnian mujahideen".

Sudanese Civil War

The Second Sudanese Civil War from 1983 to 2005 have describe the conflict as an ethnoreligious one where the Muslim central government's pursuits to impose sharia law on non-Muslim southerners led to violence, and eventually to the civil war. The war resulted in the independence of South Sudan six years after the war ended. Sudan is Muslim and South Sudan is Christian.

Religion and Secularism in India

The Constitution of India declares the nation as a secular entity but unlike the concept of secularism followed in countries like France and Turkey, Indian secularism believes in the tolerance of all religions. The term secularism implies the absence of any divine element or aspect. But for a nation that has Mahatma Gandhi as its ideologue, religion cannot be divorced from politics and the society. It is not just that Gandhi prayed a lot, his principles of non-violence and truth had seeds in religious philosophy. However, for Gandhi there were two forms of religion. The first form consisted of a set of principles and a code of ethics that all major religions propagated. For instance, theft, murder etc are wrong and punishable by all religions. The other form of religion is the approach and rituals which varies from group to group. Many secular countries, especially those of Europe treat the universal code of ethic as secular progressive thought but Gandhi and his contemporary leaders of India redefined secularism not as a godless concept but as a concept that gives space to all religions. Religion in India was to play a unifying role as well as help individuals evolve spiritually unlike the role it was to play in Pakistan.

Religious Fundamentalism and Fanaticism

Religious fundamentalism and fanaticism are again terms that need to be astutely defined. If fundamentalism means adhering to the fundamentals of a religious doctrine then even Gandhi was a fundamentalist as he was a strict vegetarian and performed ritualistic worship every day. In that sense fundamentalism is rather desirable since the fundamentals of all major religions require adherents to conform to the principles of peaceful co-existence and perform acts for spiritual evolution.

Fanaticism on the other hand is dedication to fundamentals with such devotion and so devoid of reason that the followers end up overdoing or even doing the opposite of what the fundamentals required. Muslims in India imitating Arabic culture (even those unrelated to Islam) is an example of harmless fanaticism. More serious fanaticism is manifested in instances where scientific facts are discarded in preference to superstitions and myths or where religious decrees (usually in matters of personal laws) are passed which are found to be contradictory to the law of the land as well as to religious laws (it is found in both Muslim and Hindu communities).

Communalism

Communalism is a concept which has least to do with religion although it almost always uses religion to manifest itself. Broadly defining, communalism is identifying one's own aspirations and fear (especially socio-political-economic) with the aspirations and fears of one's own community rather than society as a whole. However, in the context of the Indian subcontinent the term communalism denotes an organization/mobilization of like-minded but aggressive, intolerant and nearly violent group of individuals against other sections of society. Communalism plays a major role in the subcontinent as it is home to numerous religious, linguistic and ethnic groups, jostling for place in political mainstream, often with antagonism for those belonging to the "other community" which is held responsible for past violations as well as nefarious designs for the future. A very disturbing aspect of communalism is the fact that primary loyalty is shown towards the group that has the highest degree of commonality not on the basis of conscious and deliberate actions, belief and other elements of social contract but accidental factors like membership of religious, linguistic or ethnic community. Religious fanaticism is often result of convoluted logic but there is no logic in communalism because reasoning and rationalism are concepts alien to it.

It took mankind thousands of years to evolve into civil society based on rationalism, reason and even faith but it takes one moment of hatred to takes us back to the prehistoric times when our ancestors battled for survival. In fact, underneath our sophisticated and civilized demeanor many of us remain the same primitive hunters, fighters, warring for survival in a hostile world. Apart from other wild animals and furious nature herself we also have to fight against fellow humans from the "other clan/tribe" who are constantly conspiring to attack us and steal our food, women and our children. To protect our own possessions and interests we would have to attack first and incapaciate the enemy or, at the least, be prepared for retaliation in case of an attack on us. It is this primitive "herd mentality" of distrust and hatred that drives the force of communalism in the civil society.

As opposed to prehistory, this trend in modern society has always been driven by a few individuals who exploit it to acquire leadership of their respective communities. From blatantly provocative orations and sloganeering to indoctrination at the grass root level, all efforts to create an atmosphere of fear, distrust, mass hysteria and self-righteous rage are often found to be politically motivated and hollow. India has had the misfortune of being turned into a laboratory of such violent and divisive political experiments more than once. The first one led to the partition of the nation and a bloodbath that left an indelible scar in the national psyche of all three nations. The Muslim League's experiment was later emulated by Hindu communalists even if faith based antagonism was incompatible with the Hindu ethos. Hindu communalism actually predates its Muslim counterpart but it could never command the same level of popularity as the latter did. Hindu communalism reached its climax in the late 80's and early 90's riding on the wave of Hindutva ideology centered around Babri Masjid/Ram Janmabhoomi issue. The Sangh Parivar led by the lesser radical BJP waged an all out war on the existing political arrangement , evoking sub-nationalist emotion of a people already dismayed by years of congress misrule. Communalists always view civilization as a perpetual war between communities and rewrite history portraying their own community of being historically wronged. It painted the Muslim rule of India as one of intolerance, subjugation and systematic persecution of the majority community although historical evidences reveal a completely different picture (will talk on that in some other post). In post-independence politics, it portrayed the Muslims as the "pariah" group with whose support the corrupt and inefficient Congress remained in power and the group that was in one way or the other responsible for all ills of the Indian society. It accused the Congress of appeasing Muslims for vote-bank politics and it accused Muslims of keeping a corrupt and inefficient Congress in power for selfish ends.

It never explained how a community constituting less than 15% of the population could be held responsible for hijacking the government's agenda. Equally intriguing was the charge of appeasement when Sachar Commission reported that post-independence, while other under-privileged sections had seen some upliftment the Muslims had in fact become poorer and more backward. Shouldn't the pampered minority constitute the creamy layer of the society like the Jews of Al-Andulas or to cite a contemporary analogy, the Jews of the US?

But more than indoctrination or misinformation campaigns it is the remnants of the tribal mentality in us that fans communalism. For a long time I used to call this gorilla mentality but lately i have been wondering if it would be judicious to attribute a human vice to beasts! That very Sunday i came across another news item of a baby elephant having fallen into a pit 2 kms from a village in the Simlipal region of Orissa. The adult elephants did not allow forest guards to get close enough to attempt rescue operation. Instead the elephants summoned their comrades from the jungle and formed a large chain to pull out the baby.

Secularism as Stretegic Prevention

A recent study provides a fresh and illuminating perspective on the surge in religion's political influence across the globe. And despite recent claims that religion is exclusively irrational and violent, its political influence is in fact diverse, sometimes promoting civil war and terrorism but at other times fostering democracy, reconciliation, and peace. In our diverse and sort of 'mixed' world today, the forces of secularism are at work in our age of reason and science despite trends in fanaticism and inclinations of selected politicians attempting to use religion for political gains in several parts of the world. I contend that despite mixed messages on the subject, forces for secularism with its various components may play a sobering influence in keeping a handle on the forces of religious intolerance and extremism.

Terrorists and terrorist organizations, including governments in a few countries, have taken an increased interest during the past few decades in articulating religious reasoning to rationalize or justify violent means for achieving their political and economic goals.18However, no formal religion in the world actually may have condoned violence against innocent people. It seems that it is time we reverse the cycle and advocate its "right or proper" use in human relationships, i.e. for initiatives against violence. Contemporary societies need to develop and adopt an optimistic tone that seeks to find the future-oriented ways of preventing religion-based terrorism or any other related form of violence against the humanity and enhance the opportunities for the promotion of secularism and a global peace.

I take the position that secularism, as functioning process and practice in any society, needs to be acceptable to people just as much or even more than it is to their government. It is an ideology and a source of liberating human beings from dogma, superstitions, cultism, and any form of fanaticism. It emphasizes that people's attitudes toward other religions in their society need to become positive toward the freedom and equality in matters of conscience and freedom in exercising religion with a 'secular mind.' Secularism demands religious groups give flexibility to people in civil matters. Thus, religion may need to maintain some degree of neutrality in dealing with individuals' private lives.

Characteristics of Secularism

I have in the exploratory study reported here at least made a beginning toward identifying selected ideal characteristics of secularism, first through a relatively extensive review of literature relevant to the topic and then by consulting some 'experts' in trying to sort as well as rank those characteristics in as much meaningful way as could be possible in a limited effort addressing a complex topic inherently plagued by confusions, philosophical controversies, and a lack of research that could solidify logical and empirical dilemmas. The characteristics appear to be realistic, internally consistent, theoretically meaningful, and conceptually relevant to secularism. However, they should be repeatedly tested, through a systematic methodology, in empirical contexts for reliability and validity before becoming established in the literature. My identification of multiple characteristics organized under topics of multiple categories should be useful for continuous efforts needed in broadening the operational definition as well as the base of the concept of secularism. Indeed, matters of rationality and religion will require people to continue to engage in dialogs and open communication in order to deal with such sensitive issues as what we are dealing with in this chapter.

Separation of Religion and State

- Assure all people an equal liberty of conscience (or conviction/ faith) in society. Constitutional principles and civil laws relevant to a secularist perspective in the state should be explicitly stated and implemented.
- No oppression of any religion should be permitted. State shall promote or recognize formally any dominant religion. Political candidates should refrain from publically advocating any particular religion in democratic elections.
- Implement a completely free exercise of religion, along with a prohibition of economic and political controls, regulation, or interference from government in affairs of all religions.
- Assure an unconditional judicial monitoring and protection to all ethnic and religious minorities from domination by majorities.
- Fully implement through all branches of the government (executive, legislative and judiciary), the accommodation principle, the non-establishment principle, and separation of each religion in the country and state.
- Guarantee the state's neutrality by avoiding the establishment of any particular religion and in basing civil and criminal jurisprudence on logical and democratic processes than on any scripture of faith.
- Modernism and Religion
- Low degree of cultist and orthodox orientations in religions.
- Advocacy of moderate, tolerant, non-militant, open-minded, and humanist (rather than inflexible, rigid, fanatic, fundamentalist, authoritarian, heroworship-oriented, enthusiast, domineering; aggressive, expansionist, separatist, intrusive, or radical) outlook in every religion.
- There should be no public bashing of any religion.
- Separation of religion from educational programs (specifically, promote no schooling of children solely brainwashing them for any religious training) which must be based on academic freedom and scientific enquiry.
- Separation of religion from magical, fatalist, or superstitious approaches; every religion recognizing individualism, equality, and freedom for all people.
- Preventing all religious organizations from engaging in a business model or from soliciting monetary charges for 'divine favors or interventions' to help people overcoming life problems.
- Promote freedom to people to practice whatever level of religiosity they choose in terms of participation in religious rituals and organizations.
- Increased emphasis on spirituality as the primary goal of religion; and religious organizations recognizing needs and realities of change and rationality-oriented progress in society.

- Increased recognition for non-violence and humanitarian goals and outlooks in religion and spirituality.
- Secularism reinforces critical and diverse thinking; a process that promotes unity in diversity.

Communal tensions in British South Asian communities are on the rise. Conflict between Sikh and Muslim youths and Hindu and Muslim is becoming a more common occurrence in Asian areas. Religious fanaticism - of the kind that promotes hostility toward others - holds a grip on a small but increasing number. And the tensions on Britain's streets are increasingly tied to events abroad, not least the US-led 'war on terrorism'.

In the northern town of Bradford, early last year, violence flared up between Hindu and Muslim communities. And last October in Derby, a 15-year-old Hindu girl was hospitalised following an argument about the events of September 11. Tensions were already high in the town following the distribution of an anti-Sikh leaflet, credited to the non-existent group 'Real Khilafah'.

There are less violent signs too. In January, Sunrise Radio - Britain's 'leading Asian radio station' - took the bizarre step of banning the word 'Asian'. This was the culmination of a long campaign by groups such as the UK branch of the Vishwa Hindu Parishad that want to dissociate themselves from Muslims in the public mind by dropping the secular term 'Asian' (which has long been the standard description for those who have a heritage in India, Pakistan, Bangladesh and Sri Lanka). Although the term has always been problematic, this campaign is premised on the idea that racist whites could be persuaded to exclude Hindus and Sikhs from their hatred and instead focus just on Muslims.

The tendency took on a disturbing twist after September 11 when many South Asians in America became victims of revenge attacks. Some Sikhs - instead of marching with Muslims and calling for an end to any revenge attacks - marched separately with banners saying 'we are not Muslims', as if American Muslims were any more valid as targets for revenge than they were. And in January 2002, for the first time ever, the extreme-Right, racist British National Party (BNP) managed to convince a tiny faction of Asians - the Shere-e-Punjab grouping - to co-operate on anti-Muslim propaganda.

Later in the year, three British Muslims on holiday in India were killed in the state-sponsored anti-Muslim pogroms that swept through Gujarat in February and March. On one level these deaths are unrelated to developments in Britain. But, with the increase in ideologies and even funds flowing across continents, such distinctions become less tenable.

It would be tempting to try and blame just one side for the cycle of mutual demonisation. But, as Arundhati Roy has written in the context of the Gujarat carnage, for anybody to 'arbitrarily decree exactly where the cycle started is malevolent and irresponsible'; all sides increasingly resemble each other the more they try to call attention to their religious differences by castigating the other.

As a new generation of British Asians, born in this country in the 1960s and 1970s, occupies more positions of influence in our communities, it is the future orientation of British Asian life that is at stake. Will we be divided and separated by religion or will we be able to find a place in our lives for both our own faith and an understanding of others, within a secular framework?

Democracy and domestic terrorism

Terrorism is most common in nations with intermediate political freedom, and it is least common in the most democratic nations. one study suggests that suicide attacks may be an exception to this general rule. Evidence regarding this particular method of terrorism reveals that every modern suicide campaign has targeted a democracy–a state with a considerable degree of political freedom. The study suggests that concessions awarded to terrorists during the 1980s and 1990s for suicide attacks increased their frequency. There is a connection between the existence of civil liberties, democratic participation and terrorism. According to Young and Dugan, these things encourage terrorist groups to organize and generate terror.

Some examples of "terrorism" in non-democratic nations include ETA in Spain under Francisco Franco (although the group's terrorist activities increased sharply after Franco's death), the Organization of Ukrainian Nationalists in pre-war Poland, the Shining Path in Peru under Alberto Fujimori, the Kurdistan Workers Party when Turkey was ruled by military leaders and the ANC in South Africa. Democracies, such as Japan, the United Kingdom, the United States, Israel, Indonesia, India, Spain, Germany, Italy and the Philippines, have experienced domestic terrorism.

While a democratic nation espousing civil liberties may claim a sense of higher moral ground than other regimes, an act of terrorism within such a state may cause a dilemma: whether to maintain its civil liberties and thus risk being perceived as ineffective in dealing with the problem; or alternatively to restrict its civil liberties and thus risk delegitimizing its claim of supporting civil liberties. For this reason, homegrown terrorism has started to be seen as a greater threat, as stated by former CIA Director Michael Hayden. This dilemma, some social theorists would conclude, may very well play into the initial plans of the acting terrorist(s); namely, to delegitimize the state and cause a systematic shift towards anarchy via the accumulation of negative sentiments towards the state system.

Islam and the 'war on terrorism'

Many South Asians in Britain were shocked by Rajinder Singh's open support for the BNP. Yet anti-Islamic feeling is becoming increasingly acceptable across society, especially under the guise of the 'war on terrorism', and anti-Muslim elements in all communities have found renewed confidence in the wake of Bush's 'You are either with us or against us' rhetoric. Hindu nationalists, both in India and the UK, believe that their own Islamophobia has now been vindicated. Meanwhile Muslims are finding that somehow they are all being held responsible for the September 11 attack. Muslims are being told that their loyalty to Britain must come before their faith, even by liberal commentators such as the Guardian's Hugo Young.

Shabana Najib, a community worker in Derby, says that following September 11, many Muslim women stopped going out, especially into the town centre. Anyone wearing a headscarf would get nasty comments. 'Why should my mum or my sister have to hear racist remarks?' she asks. 'You can't go around attacking all Muslims when only a tiny number were to blame.' But as well as the verbal and physical abuse, there is the feeling of always having to explain yourself. As Shabana says, 'I don't condone what happened in America, I think it was horrendous. But I shouldn't have to say that. You feel like you have to, because, if you don't, people don't necessarily understand. We get associated with terrorists and extremists constantly - you can't move away from it. You say Islam and automatically somebody is thinking "extremist" or "terrorist".'

In a context in which their faith is constantly being questioned, in schools and workplaces, Muslims are finding that they have to develop their own personal strategies for handling situations in which they are expected to be ambassadors for an entire world religion that has suddenly been put under the spotlight. Some have dealt with this by deepening their awareness of Islam, perhaps reconnecting with a Muslim community they had left behind; many have become a lot more aware of events in places like Palestine, Chechnya and Afghanistan. Islamic identity has been strengthened.

In addition, many Hindus and Sikhs have shown little solidarity with Muslims during this period of heightened anti-Muslim feeling, quickly forgetting their own experiences of racism. As Shabana Najib points out, 'Anybody who has experienced discrimination should have empathy for others who are going through it, not to pity them or sympathise to a great extent, but just to understand the pain.' Instead, each community is asking itself 'what have they ever done for us?' This has led to much of the common ground between Muslims and Asians of other faiths being stripped away.

With these tensions in the air, it has become easier for organised groups or gangs that define themselves by religion to persuade youngsters to join them. For some, the fear of bullying leads to outside groups being 'called in' for protection, especially as rumours fly around of the attacks being planned by 'the other side'. A lot of youthful male pride is at stake when your faith is being attacked or, worse, when there is a perceived threat to 'your' women. For others, these groups provide simple answers to the difficult questions young Muslims in particular now face. In either case, it feeds the growth of organised groups prepared to use violence in the name of religion.

3

Violence and Terrorism: The Role of the Mass Media

Introduction

With the advent of the new millennium, the number of terrorism attacks increased worldwide. The attacks inspired a series of empirical terrorism studies, and I received a wave of invitations to review the burgeoning research on media and terrorism. Certainly I could feel the topic was critically important, but I felt a troubling sense that behind the invitations was an assumption that my Middle Eastern background qualified me to pronounce on terrorism. And yet, unknown to most of the people asking me for help, they had tapped a raw nerve. During my university days I was the survivor of a terrorist attack, the witness of a deadly bombing when religious extremists detonated a bomb near Cairo's busiest square in Egypt.

Those haunting memories, coupled with a sense of global responsibility and academic enthusiasm, pushed me to ask Dr. Fuyuan Shen, the editor-in-chief of Mass Communication and Society, to offer a special issue on this topic. I felt this issue could offer a forum for inspiring new conversations and advancing studies pertaining to terrorism within the mass communication field. The proposal was competitively selected by Dr. Shen and his editorial board, and the response to the call was unprecedented—almost 50 national and international submissions solid, from which eight were selected after several rounds of peer reviews.

Whereas the literature offers no single embracing definition of terrorism, scholars can agree that terrorism includes the use of violence against civilians, with the intention of creating fear or terror, and the intention to force specific belief systems upon others. With the advance of technology, the threat of terrorism has been of growing concern, especially because the Internet has helped terrorists recruit new members, plan their attacks, and amplify their messages.

As all technology continues to evolve, it is not difficult to imagine how the advanced information and technology of the new millennium could cause more terrifying realities in the world today. Cooper explained that the onward sweep of technology makes it possible to undertake newer and more efficient ways to create the fear that is at the heart of terrorism.

Without doubt, during this period of profound technological changes, researchers should study the relationships among media, society, and the new paradigm of terrorism. As Cummings and Frost wrote, academic studies are an influencing source that legitimizes ideas and research findings. The studies here, therefore, provide valuable knowledge and offer key directions for current and future terrorism research within our discipline.

Research on media and terrorism is crucial, especially amid the increase in terrorism activities. According to the U.S. Department of State, there has been a 35% increase in terrorist attacks across the world between 2013 and 2014, with the total number of people killed by terrorism increasing by more than 80%. Comparatively, however, investigating the role of media in communicating such trends has been a relatively new field of research. These special issue articles, which have all been selected for their unique contribution to the literature, display this fast-emerging research area.

The special issue begins with Dan Berkowitz's work that applies a semiotic lens to examine the role images of terrorism play in mediating healing and solidarity in both the local and the global media arena. Using a qualitative examination of news reports and blogs related to the 2016 Brussels terrorist attacks, he found that a combination of photographs, editorial cartoons, and anchoring texts has the potential to build global solidarity against terrorism. One of the insights of his work emphasizes the importance of the anchoring function. Berkowitz explains that this function is essential for audience decoding, specifically when photographs and cartoons are global, and therefore not readily accessible to the broader audience.

In the next article, Grizzard and colleagues take us a step further in examining the role of visuals with an empirical study that challenges common wisdom and assesses whether visuals containing graphic violence yield prosocial responses (e.g., greater moral sensitivity). The authors set the stage by conducting two experimental studies using news footage of a mass execution conducted by the Islamic State group. Noting that graphically violent visuals can have prosocial effects, they suggest that editorial policies governing the display of graphic violence should take a more balanced approach to the issue. It might be possible, they note, that only by confronting graphic visuals does one becomes motivated to put an end to the violence that caused it.

The Role of Violence in Terrorism

An examination of the elements of terror and symbolic violence highlighted the value of physical violence in the creation of terror. While not as effective in inducing terror, information warfare tactics allow tomorrow's terrorist to cause great disruption without physical harm to individuals. The violence of the cyberterrorist exists exclusively in the virtual world of cyberspace. While conventional terrorism will still involve physical destruction of property and human life, cyberterrorism will utilize cyberviolence and "virtual" destruction of data in cyberspace. While directly causing no casualties, this action will still fulfill the goals of advertising, morale building, disorientation, and response provocation. Some cyberterror actions, such as attacking safety or control systems (avionics, air traffic control, etc.) have the potential to create cascading failures that will lead to loss of life. Cyberterrorists will in many cases, have the option of including destruction along with disruption to create terror and a more permanent result. While we have yet to see the combination of political motivation and criminal activity in cyberspace, we cannot disregard the potential of this type of terrorism.

Violence and terror have long been major themes of mythology, drama, literature, and popular culture. Concern about their influence on public life, on children and young people and on crime, -and their implications for social control in general is more recent. Such concern was stirred by the mass production and easy availability of both the implements and images of violence and terror in the mass media and has raised issues of conflict, fear, and power that reach into the structure of societies on the broadest, deepest, and, at times even the highest levels.

Reliable observation and systematic analysis usually require limited and objective definitions. Most research studies have defined media violence as the depiction of overt physical action that hurts or kills or threatens to do so. A terroristic act is typically defined as involving violence by, among, or against states or other authorities in order to spread fear and to make a statement, usually political.

Media violence and terror are closely related. They depict social relationships and the use of force to control, dominate, provoke, or annihilate. By demonstrating who can get away with what against whom, factual and fictional representations of violence or terror can: intimidate people; provoke resistance, aggression, or repression; and cultivate a sense of relative strength and vulnerability as they portray the social "pecking order." The very use of terms such as "terrorist" can also serve the interests of those who have the power to apply them. They can strip those so labeled of a sense of identity, history, and rationality and thus justify violence and terror against them.

Sensitivity to violence and the volatile nature of terrorism make it necessary for most countries to consider policies for the media in dealing with them. The policies, and access to information about them, depend on the extent of political, commercial, and public responsibility for the media. Most of the research available has been conducted on the broadcasting media, in countries where public licensing or ownership make them more accessible than other media to policy-oriented inquiry.

The public role of the mass media in most Western industrialized societies is (in addition to making a profit) to inform and educate citizens in the ways of democracy. By contrast, the goal of organized terrorists groups is to upset these orderly processes and to achieve private, usually unpopular, political and informational goals. Along the way, these violent groups use and abuse the media and the state. They, in turn, are reciprocally used and abused in the process.

Both terrorism's and media's roles, techniques, and expectations are explained and the media terrorist interactive system described. A case study of the Italian Red Brigades' (Brigate Rosse or BR) 1978 kidnapping and murder of Aldo Mow is presented for illustrative purposes. Some conclusions and suggestions for changing the cycle of violence system through media, governmental, diplomatic, and rhetorical reforms are also offered for consideration in the context of future public/media policymaking and publicizing terrorism for informational, rather than exploitative, purposes.

Types of violence

The World Health Organization divides violence into three broad categories:

- self-directed violence
- interpersonal violence
- collective violence

This initial categorization differentiates between violence a person inflicts upon himself or herself, violence inflicted by another individual or by a small group of individuals, and violence inflicted by larger groups such as states, organized political groups, militia groups and terrorist organizations. These three broad categories are each divided further to reflect more specific types of violence:

- physical
- sexual
- psychological
- emotional

Alternatively, violence can primarily be classified as either instrumental or reactive / hostile.

Self-directed violence

Self-directed violence is subdivided into suicidal behaviour and self-abuse. The former includes suicidal thoughts, attempted suicides – also called para suicide or deliberate self-injury in some countries – and completed suicides. Self-abuse, in contrast, includes acts such as self-mutilation.

Collective violence

Collective violence is subdivided into structural violence and economic violence. Unlike the other two broad categories, the subcategories of collective violence suggest possible motives for violence committed by larger groups of individuals or by states. Collective violence that is committed to advance a particular social agenda includes, for example, crimes of hate committed by organized groups, terrorist acts and mob violence. Political violence includes war and related violent conflicts, state violence and similar acts carried out by larger groups. Economic violence includes attacks by larger groups motivated by economic gain – such as attacks carried out with the purpose of disrupting economic activity, denying access to essential services, or creating economic division and fragmentation. Clearly, acts committed by larger groups can have multiple motives.

This typology, while imperfect and far from being universally accepted, does provide a useful framework for understanding the complex patterns of violence taking place around the world, as well as violence in the everyday lives of individuals, families and communities. It also overcomes many of the limitations of other typologies by capturing the nature of violent acts, the relevance of the setting, the relationship between the perpetrator and the victim, and – in the case of collective violence – possible motivations for the violence. However, in both research and practice, the dividing lines between the different types of violence are not always so clear. State violence also involves upholding, forms of violence of a structural nature, such as poverty, through dismantling welfare, creating strict policies such as 'welfare to work', in order to cause further stimulation and disadvantage Poverty as a form of violence may involve oppressive policies that specifically target minority or low socio-economic groups. The 'war on drugs', for example, rather than increasing the health and well-being of at risk demographics, most often results in violence committed against these vulnerable demographics through incarceration, stigmatization and police brutality

Warfare

War is a state of prolonged violent large-scale conflict involving two or more groups of people, usually under the auspices of government. It is the most extreme form of collective violence. War is fought as a means of resolving territorial and other conflicts, as war of aggression to conquer territory or loot resources, in national self-defence or liberation, or to suppress attempts of part of the nation to secede from it. There are also ideological, religious and revolutionary wars.

Since the Industrial Revolution the lethality of modern warfare has grown. World War I casualties were over 40 million and World War II casualties were over 70 million.

Interpersonal violence

Interpersonal violence is divided into two subcategories: Family and intimate partner violence – that is, violence largely between family members and intimate partners, usually, though not exclusively, taking place in the home. Community violence – violence between individuals who are unrelated, and who may or may not know each other, generally taking place outside the home. The former group includes forms of violence such as child abuse, intimate partner violence and abuse of the elderly. The latter includes youth violence, random acts of violence, rape or sexual assault by strangers, and violence in institutional settings such as schools, workplaces, prisons and nursing homes. When interpersonal violence occurs in families, its psychological consequences can affect parents, children, and their relationship in the short- and long-terms.

Youth violence

Following the World Health Organization, youth are defined as people between the ages of 10 and 29 years. Youth violence refers to violence occurring between youths, and includes acts that range from bullying and physical fighting, through more severe sexual and physical assault to homicide.

Worldwide some 250,000 homicides occur among youth 10–29 years of age each year, which is 41% of the total number of homicides globally each year ("Global Burden of Disease", World Health Organization, 2008). For each young person killed, 20-40 more sustain injuries requiring hospital treatment. Youth violence has a serious, often lifelong, impact on a person's psychological and social functioning. Youth violence greatly increases the costs of health, welfare and criminal justice services; reduces productivity; decreases the value of property; and generally undermines the fabric of society.

Prevention programmes shown to be effective or to have promise in reducing youth violence include life skills and social development programmes designed to help children and adolescents manage anger, resolve conflict, and develop the necessary social skills to solve problems; schools-based anti-bullying prevention programmes; and programmes to reduce access to alcohol, illegal drugs and guns. Also, given significant neighbourhood effects on youth violence, interventions involving relocating families to less poor environments have shown promising results. Similarly, urban renewal projects such as business improvement districts have shown a reduction in youth violence.

Different types of youth on youth violence include witnessing or being involved in physical, emotional and sexual abuse (e.g. physical attacks, bullying, rape), and violent acts like gang shootings and robberies. According to researchers in 2018, "More than half of children and adolescents living in cities have experienced some form of community violence." The violence "can also all take place under one roof, or in a given community or neighborhood and can happen at the same time or at different stages of life." Youth violence has immediate and long term adverse impact whether the individual was the recipient of the violence or a witness to it.

Youth violence impacts individuals, their families, and society. Victims can have lifelong injuries which means ongoing doctor and hospital visits, the cost of which quickly add up. Since the victims of youth-on-youth violence may not be able to attend school or work because of their physical and/or mental injuries, it is often up to their family members to take care of them, including paying their daily living expenses and medical bills. Their caretakers may have to give up their jobs or work reduced hours to provide help to the victim of violence. This causes a further burden on society because the victim and maybe even their caretakers have to obtain government assistance to help pay their bills. Recent research has found that psychological trauma during childhood can change a child's brain. "Trauma is known to physically affect the brain and the body which causes anxiety, rage, and the ability to concentrate. They can also have problems remembering, trusting, and forming relationships." Since the brain becomes used to violence it may stay continually in an alert state (similar to being stuck in the fight or flight mode). "Researchers claim that the youth who are exposed to violence may have emotional, social, and cognitive problems. They may have trouble controlling emotions, paying attention in school, withdraw from friends, or show signs of post-traumatic stress disorder".

It is important for youth exposed to violence to understand how their bodies may react so they can take positive steps to counteract any possible short- and long-term negative effects (e.g., poor concentration, feelings of depression, heightened levels of anxiety). By taking immediate steps to mitigate the effects of the trauma they've experienced, negative repercussions can be reduced or eliminated. As an initial step, the youths need to understand why they may be feeling a certain way and to understand how the violence they have experienced may be causing negative feelings and making them behave differently. Pursuing a greater awareness of their feelings, perceptions, and negative emotions is the first step that should be taken as part of recovering from the trauma they have experienced. "Neuroscience research shows that the only way we can change the way we feel is by becoming aware of our inner experience and learning to befriend what is going on inside ourselves".

Some of the ways to combat the adverse effects of exposure to youth violence would be to try various mindfulness and movement activities, deep breathing exercises and other actions that enable youths to release their pent up emotions. Using these techniques will teach body awareness, reduce anxiety and nervousness, and reduce feelings of anger and annoyance. Over time these types of activities will help these younger victims of violence to have greater control over their feelings and behaviors and avoid unhealthy ways of coping. Another way to help trauma victims of youth violence is through the arts. This can be accomplished by giving them the opportunity to engage in drawing, painting, music, and singing which will give them an outlet to express themselves and their emotions in a positive way.

Youth who have experienced violence benefit from having a close relationship with one or more people. This is important because the trauma victims need to have people who are safe and trustworthy that they can relate and talk to about their horrible experiences. Some youth do not have adult figures at home or someone they can count on for guidance and comfort. Schools in bad neighborhoods where youth violence is prevalent should assign counselors to each student so that they receive regular guidance. In addition to counseling/therapy sessions and programs, it has been recommended that schools offer mentoring programs where students can interact with adults who can be a positive influence on them. Another way is to create more neighborhood programs to ensure that each child has a positive and stable place to go when school in not in session. Many children have benefited from formal organizations now which aim to help mentor and provide a safe environment for the youth especially those living in neighborhoods with higher rates of violence. This includes organizations such as Becoming a Man, CeaseFire Illinois, Chicago Area Project, Little Black Pearl, and Rainbow House". These programs are designed to help give the youth a safe place to go, stop the violence from occurring, offering counseling and mentoring to help stop the cycle of violence. If the youth do not have a safe place to go after school hours they will likely get into trouble, receive poor grades, drop out of school and use drugs and alcohol. The gangs look for youth who do not have positive influences in their life and need protection. This is why these programs are so important for the youth to have a safe environment rather than resorting to the streets. For example, Derek grew up amongst the violence in Chicago in the 1980's and was even a former gang leader. It took him thirty years in a gang and time in jail to realize he was on the wrong path. He created a boxing program called "Boxing Out Negativity" which provides youth in high crime areas a safe place to get out their anger and energy. It helps them in a positive way and keeps them off the street. With the help of programs to help victims of youth violence there is a greater opportunity for these youth to turn their lives around.

Intimate partner violence

Intimate partner violence refers to behaviour in an intimate relationship that causes physical, sexual or psychological harm, including physical aggression, sexual coercion, psychological abuse and controlling behaviours.

Population-level surveys based on reports from victims provide the most accurate estimates of the prevalence of intimate partner violence and sexual violence in non-conflict settings. A study conducted by WHO in 10 mainly developing countries found that, among women aged 15 to 49 years, between 15% (Japan) and 70% (Ethiopia and Peru) of women reported physical and/or sexual violence by an intimate partner.

Intimate partner and sexual violence have serious short- and long-term physical, mental, sexual and reproductive health problems for victims and for their children, and lead to high social and economic costs. These include both fatal and non-fatal injuries, depression and post-traumatic stress disorder, unintended pregnancies, sexually transmitted infections, including HIV.

Factors associated with the perpetration and experiencing of intimate partner violence are low levels of education, history of violence as a perpetrator, a victim or a witness of parental violence, harmful use of alcohol, attitudes that are accepting of violence as well as marital discord and dissatisfaction. Factors associated only with perpetration of intimate partner violence are having multiple partners, and antisocial personality disorder.

A recent theory named "The Criminal Spin" suggests a mutual flywheel effect between partners that is manifested by an escalation in the violence. A violent spin may occur in any other forms of violence, but in Intimate partner violence the added value is the mutual spin, based on the unique situation and characteristics of intimate relationship.

The primary prevention strategy with the best evidence for effectiveness for intimate partner violence is school-based programming for adolescents to prevent violence within dating relationships. Evidence is emerging for the effectiveness of several other primary prevention strategies – those that: combine microfinance with gender equality training; promote communication and relationship skills within communities; reduce access to, and the harmful use of alcohol; and change cultural gender norms.

Sexual violence

Sexual violence is any sexual act, attempt to obtain a sexual act, unwanted sexual comments or advances, or acts to traffic, or otherwise directed against a person's sexuality using coercion, by any person regardless of their relationship to the victim, in any setting. It includes rape, defined as the physically forced or otherwise coerced penetration of the vulva or anus with a penis, other body part or object.

Population-level surveys based on reports from victims estimate that between 0.3–11.5% of women reported experiencing sexual violence. Sexual violence has serious short- and long-term consequences on physical, mental, sexual and reproductive health for victims and for their children as described in the section on intimate partner violence. If perpetrated during childhood, sexual violence can lead to increased smoking, drug and alcohol misuse, and risky sexual behaviors in later life. It is also associated with perpetration of violence and being a victim of violence.

Many of the risk factors for sexual violence are the same as for domestic violence. Risk factors specific to sexual violence perpetration include beliefs in family honor and sexual purity, ideologies of male sexual entitlement and weak legal sanctions for sexual violence.

Few interventions to prevent sexual violence have been demonstrated to be effective. School-based programmes to prevent child sexual abuse by teaching children to recognize and avoid potentially sexually abusive situations are run in many parts of the world and appear promising, but require further research. To achieve lasting change, it is important to enact legislation and develop policies that protect women; address discrimination against women and promote gender equality; and help to move the culture away from violence.

Elder maltreatment

Elder maltreatment is a single or repeated act, or lack of appropriate action, occurring within any relationship where there is an expectation of trust which causes harm or distress to an older person. This type of violence constitutes a violation of human rights and includes physical, sexual, psychological, emotional; financial and material abuse; abandonment; neglect; and serious loss of dignity and respect.

While there is little information regarding the extent of maltreatment in elderly populations, especially in developing countries, it is estimated that 4–6% of elderly people in high-income countries have experienced some form of maltreatment at home However, older people are often afraid to report cases of maltreatment to family, friends, or to the authorities. Data on the extent of the problem in institutions such as hospitals, nursing homes and other long-term care facilities are scarce. Elder maltreatment can lead to serious physical injuries and long-term psychological consequences. Elder maltreatment is predicted to increase as many countries are experiencing rapidly ageing populations.

Many strategies have been implemented to prevent elder maltreatment and to take action against it and mitigate its consequences including public and professional awareness campaigns, screening (of potential victims and abusers), caregiver support interventions (e.g. stress management, respite care), adult protective services and self-help groups. Their effectiveness has, however, not so far been well-established.

Targeted violence

Several rare but painful episodes of assassination, attempted assassination and school shootings at elementary, middle, high schools, as well as colleges and universities in the United States, led to a considerable body of research on ascertainable behaviors of persons who have planned or carried out such attacks. These studies (1995–2002) investigated what the authors called "targeted violence," described the "path to violence" of those who planned or carried out attacks and laid out suggestions for law enforcement and educators. A major point from these research studies is that targeted violence does not just "come out of the blue".

Everyday violence

As an anthropological concept, "everyday violence" may refer to the incorporation of different forms of violence (mainly political violence) into daily practices.

Factors

Violence cannot be attributed to a single factor. Its causes are complex and occur at different levels. To represent this complexity, the ecological, or social ecological model is often used. The following four-level version of the ecological model is often used in the study of violence:

The first level identifies biological and personal factors that influence how individuals behave and increase their likelihood of becoming a victim or perpetrator of violence: demographic characteristics (age, education, income), genetics, brain lesions, personality disorders, substance abuse, and a history of experiencing, witnessing, or engaging in violent behaviour.

The second level focuses on close relationships, such as those with family and friends. In youth violence, for example, having friends who engage in or encourage violence can increase a young person's risk of being a victim or perpetrator of violence. For intimate partner violence, a consistent marker at this level of the model is marital conflict or discord in the relationship. In elder abuse, important factors are stress due to the nature of the past relationship between the abused person and the care giver.

The third level explores the community context—i.e., schools, workplaces, and neighbourhoods. Risk at this level may be affected by factors such as the existence of a local drug trade, the absence of social networks, and concentrated poverty. All these factors have been shown to be important in several types of violence.

Finally, the fourth level looks at the broad societal factors that help to create a climate in which violence is encouraged or inhibited: the responsiveness of the criminal justice system, social and cultural norms regarding gender roles or parent-child relationships, income inequality, the strength of the social welfare system, the social acceptability of violence, the availability of weapons, the exposure to violence in mass media, and political instability.

Child-rearing

Cross-cultural studies have shown that greater prevalence of corporal punishment of children tends to predict higher levels of violence in societies. For instance, a 2005 analysis of 186 pre-industrial societies found that corporal punishment was more prevalent in societies which also had higher rates of homicide, assault, and war. In the United States, domestic corporal punishment has been linked to later violent acts against family members and spouses. While studies showing associations between physical punishment of children and later aggression cannot prove that physical punishment causes an increase in aggression, a number of longitudinal studies suggest that the experience of physical punishment has a direct causal effect on later aggressive behaviors. The American family violence researcher Murray A. Straus believes that disciplinary spanking forms "the most prevalent and important form of violence in American families", whose effects contribute to several major societal problems, including later domestic violence and crime.

Psychology

The causes of violent behavior in people are often a topic of research in psychology. Neurobiologist Jan Vodka emphasizes that, for those purposes, "violent behavior is defined as overt and intentional physically aggressive behavior against another person."

Based on the idea of human nature, scientists do agree violence is inherent in humans. Among prehistoric humans, there is archaeological evidence for both contentions of violence and peacefulness as primary characteristics.

Since violence is a matter of perception as well as a measurable phenomenon, psychologists have found variability in whether people perceive certain physical acts as "violent". For example, in a state where execution is a legalized punishment we do not typically perceive the executioner as "violent", though we may talk, in a more metaphorical way, of the state acting violently. Likewise, understandings of violence are linked to a perceived aggressor-victim relationship: hence psychologists have shown that people may not recognise defensive use of force as violent, even in cases where the amount of force used is significantly greater than in the original aggression.

The "violent male ape" image is often brought up in discussions of human violence. Dale Peterson and Richard Wranghamin "Demonic Males: Apes and the Origins of Human Violence" write that violence is inherent in humans, though not inevitable. However, William L. Ury, editor of a book called "We Must Fight! From the Battlefield to the Schoolyard—A New Perspective on Violent Conflict and Its Prevention" criticizes the "killer ape" myth in his book which brings together discussions from two Harvard Law School symposiums. The conclusion is that "we also have lots of natural mechanisms for cooperation, to keep conflict in check, to channel aggression, and to overcome conflict. These are just as natural to us as the aggressive tendencies."

The psychiatrist James Gilligan argues that most violent behavior represents an effort to eliminate feelings of shame and humiliation, which he calls "the death of self". The use of violence often is a source of pride and a defence of honor, especially among males who believe violence defines manhood.

In an article entitled "The History of Violence" in The New Republic, Steven Pinker posits that, on average, the amount and cruelty of violence to humans and animals has decreased over the last few centuries.

Pinker's observation of the decline in interpersonal violence echoes the work of Norbert Elias, who attributes the decline to a "civilizing process", in which the state's monopolization of violence, the maintenance of socioeconomic interdependencies or "figurations", and the maintenance of behavioural codes in culture all contribute to the development of individual sensibilities, which increase the repugnance of individuals towards violent acts.

Some scholars disagree with the argument that all violence is decreasing arguing that not all types of violent behaviour are lower now than in the past. They suggest that research typically focuses on lethal violence, often looks at homicide rates of death due to warfare, but ignore the less obvious forms of violence. However, non-lethal violence, such as assaults or bullying appear to be declining as well. In his article "The Coming Anarchy", Robert D. Kaplan introduces the notion of liberating violence. According to Kaplan, we will observe more violent civil wars in the future, which will be fought due to economic inequalities around the world.

The concept of violence normalization, is known as socially sanctioned or structural violence, and is a topic of increasing interest to researchers trying to understand violent behavior. It has been discussed at length by researchers in sociology, medical anthropology, psychology, philosophy, and bioarchaeology.

Evolutionary psychology offers several explanations for human violence in various contexts, such as sexual jealousy in humans, child abuse, and homicide. Goetz (2010) argues that humans are similar to most mammal species and use violence in specific situations. He writes that "Buss and Shackelford (1997a) proposed seven adaptive problems our ancestors recurrently faced that might have been solved by aggression: co-opting the resources of others, defending against attack, inflicting costs on same-sex rivals, negotiating status and hierarchies, deterring rivals from future aggression, deterring mate from infidelity, and reducing resources expended on genetically unrelated children."

Goetz writes that most homicides seem to start from relatively trivial disputes between unrelated men who then escalate to violence and death. He argues that such conflicts occur when there is a status dispute between men of relatively similar status. If there is a great initial status difference, then the lower status individual usually offers no challenge and if challenged the higher status individual usually ignores the lower status individual. At the same an environment of great inequalities between people may cause those at the bottom to use more violence in attempts to gain status.

Media

Research into the media and violence examines whether links between consuming media violence and subsequent aggressive and violent behaviour exists. Although some scholars had claimed media violence may increase aggression, this view is coming increasingly in doubt both in the scholarly community and was rejected by the US Supreme Court in the Brown v EMA case, as well as in a review of video game violence by the Australian Government (2010) which concluded evidence for harmful effects were inconclusive at best and the rhetoric of some scholars was not matched by good data.

Prevention

The threat and enforcement of physical punishment has been a tried and tested method of preventing some violence since civilisation began. It is used in various degrees in most countries.

Interpersonal violence

A review of scientific literature by the World Health Organization on the effectiveness of strategies to prevent interpersonal violence identified the seven strategies below as being supported by either strong or emerging evidence for effectiveness. These strategies target risk factors at all four levels of the ecological model.

Life skills in youth

Evidence shows that the life skills acquired in social development programmes can reduce involvement in violence, improve social skills, boost educational achievement and improve job prospects. Life skills refer to social, emotional, and behavioural competencies which help children and adolescents effectively deal with the challenges of everyday life.

Gender equality

Evaluation studies are beginning to support community interventions that aim to prevent violence against women by promoting gender equality. For instance, evidence suggests that programmes that combine microfinance with gender equity training can reduce intimate partner violence. School-based programmes such as Safe Dates programme in the United States of America and the Youth Relationship Project in Canada have been found to be effective for reducing dating violence.

Cultural norms

Rules or expectations of behaviour – norms – within a cultural or social group can encourage violence. Interventions that challenge cultural and social norms supportive of violence can prevent acts of violence and have been widely used, but the evidence base for their effectiveness is currently weak. The effectiveness of interventions addressing dating violence and sexual abuse among teenagers and young adults by challenging social and cultural norms related to gender is supported by some evidence.

Support programmes

Interventions to identify victims of interpersonal violence and provide effective care and support are critical for protecting health and breaking cycles of violence from one generation to the next. Examples for which evidence of effectiveness is emerging includes: screening tools to identify victims of intimate partner violence and refer them to appropriate services; psychosocial interventions – such as trauma-focused cognitive behavioural therapy – to reduce mental health problems associated with violence, including post-traumatic stress disorder; and protection orders, which prohibit a perpetrator from contacting the victim, to reduce repeat victimization among victims of intimate partner violence.

Collective violence

Not surprisingly, scientific evidence about the effectiveness of interventions to prevent collective violence is lacking. However, policies that facilitate reductions in poverty, that make decision-making more accountable, that reduce inequalities between groups, as well as policies that reduce access to biological, chemical, nuclear and other weapons have been recommended. When planning responses to violent conflicts, recommended approaches include assessing at an early stage who is most vulnerable and what their needs are, co-ordination of activities between various players and working towards global, national and local capabilities so as to deliver effective health services during the various stages of an emergency.

Criminal justice

One of the main functions of law is to regulate violence. Sociologist Max Weber stated that the state claims the monopoly of the legitimate use of force practised within the confines of a specific territory. Law enforcement is the main means of regulating nonmilitary violence in society. Governments regulate the use of violence through legal systems governing individuals and political authorities, including the police and military. Civil societies authorize some amount of violence, exercised through the police power, to maintain the status quo and enforce laws.

However, German political theorist Hannah Arendt noted: "Violence can be justifiable, but it never will be legitimate ... Its justification loses in plausibility the farther its intended end recedes into the future. No one questions the use of violence in self-defence, because the danger is not only clear but also present, and the end justifying the means is immediate". Arendt made a clear distinction between violence and power. Most political theorists regarded violence as an extreme manifestation of power whereas Arendt regarded the two concepts as opposites. In the 20th century in acts of democide governments may have killed more than 260 million of their own people through police brutality, execution, massacre, slave labour camps, and sometimes through intentional famine.

Violent acts that are not carried out by the military or police and that are not in self-defense are usually classified as crimes, although not all crimes are violent crimes. Damage to property is classified as violent crime in some jurisdictions but not in all. The Federal Bureau of Investigation (FBI) classifies violence resulting in homicide into criminal homicide and justifiable homicide (e.g. self-defense).

The criminal justice approach sees its main task as enforcing laws that proscribe violence and ensuring that "justice is done". The notions of individual blame, responsibility, guilt, and culpability are central to criminal justice's approach to violence and one of the criminal justice system's main tasks is to "do justice", i.e. to ensure that offenders are properly identified, that the degree of their guilt is as accurately ascertained as possible, and that they are punished appropriately. To prevent and respond to violence, the criminal justice approach relies primarily on deterrence, incarceration and the punishment and rehabilitation of perpetrators.

The criminal justice approach, beyond justice and punishment, has traditionally emphasized indicated interventions, aimed at those who have already been involved in violence, either as victims or as perpetrators. One of the main reasons offenders are arrested, prosecuted, and convicted is to prevent further crimes – through deterrence (threatening potential offenders with criminal sanctions if they commit crimes), incapacitation (physically preventing offenders from committing further crimes by locking them up) and through rehabilitation (using time spent under state supervision to develop skills or change one's psychological make-up to reduce the likelihood of future offences).

In recent decades in many countries in the world, the criminal justice system has taken an increasing interest in preventing violence before it occurs. For instance, much of community and problem-oriented policing aims to reduce crime and violence by altering the conditions that foster it – and not to increase the number of arrests. Indeed, some police leaders have gone so far as to say the police should primarily be a crime prevention agency. Juvenile justice systems – an important component of criminal justice systems – are largely based on the belief in rehabilitation and prevention. In the US, the criminal justice system has, for instance, funded school- and community-based initiatives to reduce children's access to guns and teach conflict resolution. In 1974, the US Department of Justice assumed primary responsibility for delinquency prevention programmes and created the Office of Juvenile Justice and Delinquency Prevention, which has supported the "Blueprints for violence prevention" programme at the University of Colorado Boulder.

Public health

The public health approach is a science-driven, population-based, interdisciplinary, intersectoral approach based on the ecological model which emphasizes primary prevention. Rather than focusing on individuals, the public health approach aims to provide the maximum benefit for the largest number of people, and to extend better care and safety to entire populations. The public health approach is interdisciplinary, drawing upon knowledge from many disciplines including medicine, epidemiology, sociology, psychology, criminology, education and economics. Because all forms of violence are multi-faceted problems, the public health approach emphasizes a multi-sectoral response. It has been proved time and again that cooperative efforts from such diverse sectors as health, education, social welfare, and criminal justice are often necessary to solve what are usually assumed to be purely "criminal" or "medical" problems. The public health approach considers that violence, rather than being the result of any single factor, is the outcome of multiple risk factors and causes, interacting at four levels of a nested hierarchy (individual, close relationship/family, community and wider society) of the Social ecological model.

From a public health perspective, prevention strategies can be classified into three types:

Primary prevention – approaches that aim to prevent violence before it occurs.

Secondary prevention – approaches that focus on the more immediate responses to violence, such as pre-hospital care, emergency services or treatment for sexually transmitted infections following a rape.

Tertiary prevention – approaches that focus on long-term care in the wake of violence, such as rehabilitation and reintegration, and attempt to lessen trauma or reduce long-term disability associated with violence.

A public health approach emphasizes the primary prevention of violence, i.e. stopping them from occurring in the first place. Until recently, this approach has been relatively neglected in the field, with the majority of resources directed towards secondary or tertiary prevention. Perhaps the most critical element of a public health approach to prevention is the ability to identify underlying causes rather than focusing upon more visible "symptoms". This allows for the development and testing of effective approaches to address the underlying causes and so improve health.

The public health approach is an evidence-based and systematic process involving the following four steps:

Defining the problem conceptually and numerically, using statistics that accurately describe the nature and scale of violence, the characteristics of those most affected, the geographical distribution of incidents, and the consequences of exposure to such violence.

Investigating why the problem occurs by determining its causes and correlates, the factors that increase or decrease the risk of its occurrence (risk and protective factors) and the factors that might be modifiable through intervention.

Exploring ways to prevent the problem by using the above information and designing, monitoring and rigorously assessing the effectiveness of programmes through outcome evaluations.

Disseminating information on the effectiveness of programmes and increasing the scale of proven effective programmes. Approaches to prevent violence, whether targeted at individuals or entire communities, must be properly evaluated for their effectiveness and the results shared. This step also includes adapting programmes to local contexts and subjecting them to rigorous re-evaluation to ensure their effectiveness in the new setting.

In many countries, violence prevention is still a new or emerging field in public health. The public health community has started only recently to realize the contributions it can make to reducing violence and mitigating its consequences. In 1949, Gordon called for injury prevention efforts to be based on the understanding of causes, in a similar way to prevention efforts for communicable and other diseases. In 1962, Gomez, referring to the WHO definition of health, stated that it is obvious that violence does not contribute to "extending life" or to a "complete state of well-being". He defined violence as an issue that public health experts needed to address and stated that it should not be the primary domain of lawyers, military personnel, or politicians.

However, it is only in the last 30 years that public health has begun to address violence, and only in the last fifteen has it done so at the global level. This is a much shorter period of time than public health has been tackling other health problems of comparable magnitude and with similarly severe lifelong consequences.

The global public health response to interpersonal violence began in earnest in the mid-1990s. In 1996, the World Health Assembly adopted Resolution WHA49.25 which declared violence "a leading worldwide public health problem" and requested that the World Health Organization (WHO) initiate public health activities to (1) document and characterize the burden of violence, (2) assess the effectiveness of programmes, with particular attention to women and children and community-based initiatives, and (3) promote activities to tackle the problem at the international and national levels. The World Health Organization's initial response to this resolution was to create the Department of Violence and Injury Prevention and Disability and to publish the World report on violence and health (2002).

The case for the public health sector addressing interpersonal violence rests on four main arguments. First, the significant amount of time health care professionals dedicate to caring for victims and perpetrators of violence has made them familiar with the problem and has led many, particularly in emergency departments, to mobilize to address it. The information, resources, and infrastructures the health care sector has at its disposal are an important asset for research and prevention work. Second, the magnitude of the problem and its potentially severe lifelong consequences and high costs to individuals and wider society call for population-level interventions typical of the public health approach. Third, the criminal justice approach, the other main approach to addressing violence (link to entry above), has traditionally been more geared towards violence that occurs between male youths and adults in the street and other public places – which makes up the bulk of homicides in most countries – than towards violence occurring in private settings such as child maltreatment, intimate partner violence and elder abuse – which makes up the largest share of non-fatal violence. Fourth, evidence is beginning to accumulate that a science-based public health approach is effective at preventing interpersonal violence.

Human rights

The human rights approach is based on the obligations of states to respect, protect and fulfill human rights and therefore to prevent, eradicate and punish violence. It recognizes violence as a violation of many human rights: the rights to life, liberty, autonomy and security of the person; the rights to equality and non-discrimination; the rights to be free from torture and cruel, inhuman and degrading treatment or punishment; the right to privacy; and the right to the highest attainable standard of health. These human rights are enshrined in international and regional treaties and national constitutions and laws, which stipulate the obligations of states, and include mechanisms to hold states accountable. The Convention on the Elimination of All Forms of Discrimination Against Women, for example, requires that countries party to the Convention take all appropriate steps to end violence against women. The Convention on the Rights of the Child in its Article 19 states that States Parties shall take all appropriate legislative, administrative, social and educational measures to protect the child from all forms of physical or mental violence, injury or abuse, neglect or negligent treatment, maltreatment or exploitation, including sexual abuse, while in the care of parent(s), legal guardian(s) or any other person who has the care of the child.

Geographical context

Violence, as defined in the dictionary of human geography, "appears whenever power is in jeopardy" and "in and of itself stands emptied of strength and purpose: it is part of a larger matrix of socio-political power struggles". Violence can be broadly divided into three broad categories – direct violence, structural violence and cultural violence. Thus defined and delineated, it is of note, as Hyndman says, that "geography came late to theorizing violence" in comparison to other social sciences. Social and human geography, rooted in the humanist, Marxist, and feminist subfields that emerged following the early positivist approaches and subsequent behavioral turn, have long been concerned with social and spatial justice. Along with critical geographers and political geographers, it is these groupings of geographers that most often interact with violence. Keeping this idea of social/spatial justice via geography in mind, it is worthwhile to look at geographical approaches to violence in the context of politics.

Derek Gregory and Alan Pred assembled the influential edited collection Violent Geographies: Fear, Terror, and Political Violence, which demonstrates how place, space, and landscape are foremost factors in the real and imagined practices of organized violence both historically and in the present. Evidently, political violence often gives a part for the state to play. When "modern states not only claim a monopoly of the legitimate means of violence; they also routinely use the threat of violence to enforce the rule of law", the law not only becomes a form of violence but is violence. Philosopher Giorgio Agamben's concepts of state of exception and homo sacer are useful to consider within a geography of violence. The state, in the grip of a perceived, potential crisis (whether legitimate or not) takes preventative legal measures, such as a suspension of rights (it is in this climate, as Agamben demonstrates, that the formation of the Social Democratic and Nazi government's lager or concentration camp can occur). However, when this "in limbo" reality is designed to be in place "until further notice…the state of exception thus ceases to be referred to as an external and provisional state of factual danger and comes to be confused with juridical rule itself". For Agamben, the physical space of the camp "is a piece of land placed outside the normal juridical order, but it is nevertheless not simply an external space". At the scale of the body, in the state of exception, a person is so removed from their rights by "juridical procedures and deployments of power" that "no act committed against them could appear any longer as a crime"; in other words, people become only homo sacer. Guantanamo Bay could also be said to represent the physicality of the state of exception in space, and can just as easily draw man as homo sacer.

In the 1970s, genocides in Cambodia under the Khmer Rouge and Pol Pot resulted in the deaths of over two million Cambodians (which was 25% of the Cambodian population), forming one of the many contemporary examples of state-sponsored violence. About fourteen thousand of these murders occurred at Choeung Ek, which is the best-known of the extermination camps referred to as the Killing Fields. The killings were arbitrary; for example, a person could be killed for wearing glasses, since that was seen as associating them with intellectuals and therefore as making them part of the enemy. People were murdered with impunity because it was no crime; Cambodians were made homo sacer in a condition of bare life. The Killing Fields—manifestations of Agamben's concept of camps beyond the normal rule of law—featured the state of exception. As part of Pol Pot's "ideological intent...to create a purely agrarian society or cooperative", he "dismantled the country's existing economic infrastructure and depopulated every urban area". Forced movement, such as this forced movement applied by Pol Pot, is a clear display of structural violence. When "symbols of Cambodian society were equally disrupted, social institutions of every kind...were purged or torn down", cultural violence (defined as when "any aspect of culture such as language, religion, ideology, art, or cosmology is used to legitimize direct or structural violence") is added to the structural violence of forced movement and to the direct violence, such as murder, at the Killing Fields. Vietnam eventually intervened and the genocide officially ended. However, ten million landmines left by opposing guerillas in the 1970s continue to create a violent landscape in Cambodia.

Human geography, though coming late to the theorizing table, has tackled violence through many lenses, including anarchist geography, feminist geography, Marxist geography, political geography, and critical geography. However, Adriana Cavarero notes that, "as violence spreads and assumes unheard-of forms, it becomes difficult to name in contemporary language". Cavarero proposes that, in facing such a truth, it is prudent to reconsider violence as "horrorism"; that is, "as though ideally all the...victims, instead of their killers, ought to determine the name". With geography often adding the forgotten spatial aspect to theories of social science, rather than creating them solely within the discipline, it seems that the self-reflexive contemporary geography of today may have an extremely important place in this current (re) imaging of violence, exemplified by Cavarero.

Epidemiology

As of 2010, all forms of violence resulted in about 1.34 million deaths up from about 1 million in 1990. Suicide accounts for about 883,000, interpersonal violence for 456,000 and collective violence for 18,000. Deaths due to collective violence have decreased from 64,000 in 1990.

By way of comparison, the 1.5 millions deaths a year due to violence is greater than the number of deaths due to tuberculosis (1.34 million), road traffic injuries (1.21 million), and malaria (830'000), but slightly less than the number of people who die from HIV/AIDS (1.77 million).

For every death due to violence, there are numerous nonfatal injuries. In 2008, over 16 million cases of non-fatal violence-related injuries were severe enough to require medical attention. Beyond deaths and injuries, forms of violence such as child maltreatment, intimate partner violence, and elder maltreatment have been found to be highly prevalent.

Self-directed violence

In the last 45 years, suicide rates have increased by 60% worldwide. Suicide is among the three leading causes of death among those aged 15–44 years in some countries, and the second leading cause of death in the 10–24 years age group. These figures do not include suicide attempts which are up to 20 times more frequent than completed suicide. Suicide was the 16th leading cause of death worldwide in 2004 and is projected to increase to the 12th in 2030. Although suicide rates have traditionally been highest among the male elderly, rates among young people have been increasing to such an extent that they are now the group at highest risk in a third of countries, in both developed and developing countries.

Interpersonal violence

Rates and patterns of violent death vary by country and region. In recent years, homicide rates have been highest in developing countries in Sub-Saharan Africa and Latin America and the Caribbean and lowest in East Asia, the western Pacific, and some countries in northern Africa. Studies show a strong, inverse relationship between homicide rates and both economic development and economic equality. Poorer countries, especially those with large gaps between the rich and the poor, tend to have higher rates of homicide than wealthier countries. Homicide rates differ markedly by age and sex. Gender differences are least marked for children. For the 15 to 29 age group, male rates were nearly six times those for female rates; for the remaining age groups, male rates were from two to four times those for females.

Studies in a number of countries show that, for every homicide among young people age 10 to 24, 20 to 40 other young people receive hospital treatment for a violent injury.

Forms of violence such as child maltreatment and intimate partner violence are highly prevalent. Approximately 20% of women and 5–10% of men report being sexually abused as children, while 25–50% of all children report being physically abused. A WHO multi-country study found that between 15–71% of women reported experiencing physical and/or sexual violence by an intimate partner at some point in their lives.

Collective violence

Wars grab headlines, but the individual risk of dying violently in an armed conflict is today relatively low—much lower than the risk of violent death in many countries that are not suffering from an armed conflict. For example, between 1976 and 2008, African Americans were victims of 329,825 homicides. Although there is a widespread perception that war is the most dangerous form of armed violence in the world, the average person living in a conflict-affected country had a risk of dying violently in the conflict of about 2.0 per 100,000 population between 2004 and 2007. This can be compared to the average world homicide rate of 7.6 per 100,000 people. This illustration highlights the value of accounting for all forms of armed violence rather than an exclusive focus on conflict related violence. Certainly, there are huge variations in the risk of dying from armed conflict at the national and subnational level, and the risk of dying violently in a conflict in specific countries remains extremely high. In

Iraq, for example, the direct conflict death rate for 2004–07 was 65 per 100,000 people per year and, in Somalia, 24 per 100,000 people. This rate even reached peaks of 91 per 100,000 in Iraq in 2006 and 74 per 100,000 in Somalia in 2007.

Right-wing terrorism

Right-wing terrorism or far-right terrorism is terrorism that is motivated by a variety of different right-wing and far-right ideologies, most prominently by neo-Nazism, neo-fascism, white nationalism and anti-government patriot/ sovereign citizen beliefs and occasionally by anti-abortion and tax resistance. Modern right-wing terrorism first emerged in North America during the Reconstruction era (1863-1877) and it later emerged in Western and Central Europe in the 1970s, and following the dissolution of the Soviet Union in 1991, it emerged in Eastern Europe.

Right-wing terrorists aim to overthrow governments and replace them with nationalist and/or fascist regimes. Although they often take inspiration from Fascist Italy and Nazi Germany with some exceptions, right-wing terrorist groups frequently lack a rigid ideology.

Role of the media

Social media

Social media platforms have been one of the principal means by which right-wing extremist ideas and hate speech have been shared and promulgated, leading to extensive debate about the limits of free speech and its impact on terrorist action and hate crimes. In 2018, researchers in the US identified the YouTube recommendation system as promoting a range of political positions from mainstream libertarianism and conservatism to overt white nationalism. Many other online discussion groups and forums are used for online right-wing radicalization. Robert Bowers the perpetrator of the Pittsburgh synagogue shooting at Tree of Life - Or L'Simcha Congregation in Pittsburgh, Pennsylvania was a regular verified user on Gab a "free speech" alternative to Twitter and spread anti-Semitic, neo-Nazi and Holocauat denial propaganda as well as interacting or reposting 5 alt-right figures: Brad "Hunter Wallace" Griffin of Occidental Dissent and League of the South (LS), Daniel "Jack Corbin" McMahon a self-described "Antifa Hunter" "fascist", former California Republican Patrick Little, Jared Wyand of Project Purge and Daniel "Grandpa Lampshade" Kenneth Jeffreys of The Daily Stormer and Radio Aryan. Twitter was found to be offering advertisements targeted to 168,000 users in a white genocide conspiracy theory category, which they removed shortly after being contacted by journalists in the wake of the Pittsburgh synagogue shooting. After a Brooklyn synagogue was vandalized with death threats, the term "Kill all Jews" was listed as a trending topic on Twitter.

Australia-born terrorist Brenton Harrison Tarrant the perpetrator of the Christchurch mosque shootings at Al Noor Mosque and Linwood Islamic Centre in Christchurch, New Zealand recorded a video of the attacks on Facebook Live which was shared extensively on social media as well as spreading his manifesto The Great Replacement on his Facebook and Twitter accounts and on 8chan /pol/ where he would announce the attacks and prior to this the social media of Brenton Harrison Tarrant was filled with white nationalist, anti-Islamic and neo-fascist material and his profile picture was "The Australian Shitposter" an image of a tanned, blonde-haired Akubra hat wearing man from Australia used to represent users on 4chan and 8chan as well as the alt-right subculture "The Dingoes". The government of New Zealand already had laws in place relating to terrorism under which people sharing the video can be prosecuted, and it was announced that this would be vigorously pursued. Prime Minister Jacinda Ardern also vowed to investigate the role played by social media in the attack and take action, possibly alongside other countries, against the sites that broadcast the video. Facebook and Twitter became more active in banning extremists from their platform in the wake of the tragedy. Facebook pages associated with Future Now Australia had been removed from the platform, including their main page, Stop the Mosques and Save Australia. Far-right activist leaders in Australia urged their supporters to follow them on Gab after being banned from Twitter and Facebook. On March 28, 2019, Facebook announced that they have banned white nationalist and white separatist content along with white supremacy.

Mass media

Owen Jones wrote in The Guardian about how the press in Britain can play a role in helping to radicalise far right terrorists, quoting Neil Basu, Britain's counter-terrorism chief. Basu cited the Daily Mail and Daily Mirror as particular culprits, while Jones also give examples from The Times', The Telegraph, The Spectator and others, with articles bemoaning so-called cultural Marxism and misleading headlines such as "1 in 5 Brit Muslims" having sympathy with jihadists (The Sun).

Mass media exposure may be a primary goal of those carrying out terrorism, to expose issues that would otherwise be ignored by the media. Some consider this to be manipulation and exploitation of the media.

The Internet has created a new channel for groups to spread their messages. This has created a cycle of measures and counter measures by groups in support of and in opposition to terrorist movements. The United Nations has created its own online counter-terrorism resource.

The mass media will, on occasion, censor organizations involved in terrorism (through self-restraint or regulation) to discourage further terrorism. This may encourage organizations to perform more extreme acts of terrorism to be shown in the mass media. Conversely James F. Pastor explains the significant relationship between terrorism and the media, and the underlying benefit each receives from the other.

There is always a point at which the terrorist ceases to manipulate the media gestalt. A point at which the violence may well escalate, but beyond which the terrorist has become symptomatic of the media gestalt itself. Terrorism as we ordinarily understand it is innately media-related.

Former British Prime Minister Margaret Thatcher famously spoke of the close connection between terrorism and the media, calling publicity 'the oxygen of terrorism'.

The first level of interaction and mutual influence of mass media and international terrorism, first, is characteristic for electronic media. The reason for this not well-founded interest is the absence of the desire to satisfy the mass tastes. Nevertheless, the problem of violence, crime and terrorism, indicates V.N. Dremin, is one of the most popular topics in the media. According to V.N. Dremin, this popularity is connected primarily to crimes eccentricity and demand for viewer's and reader's information on crimes and explains the features of the human psychics. This creates the appearance of crime, which volume and content does not coincide with the real situation. Thus, the media reproduce and exaggerate the problem of terrorism.

In pursuit of the most vivid and exclusive story, the media are making passive cooperation with terrorists, becoming an instrument in the implementation of terror. Thus, mass media reproduce and hyperbolize the problem of terrorism.

International terrorism has turned into an industry that includes selection, ideological and psychological training, and professional training of personnel, especially suicide bombers. Implementation of a terrorist action requires a multi-million financing. This new type of violence is significantly different from other forms of organized crime. The violence of traditional organized crime is aimed at achieving financial benefits, whereas terrorist actions are always aimed at achieving political goals.

The paradox is that the goals of terrorists and the media coincide, although the attitude towards the victims is exactly the opposite. The media prioritized coverage of the OAS (Organisation armée secrete, or Secret Army Organisation) terror in the 1960s in France; in the 1970s. "Red Brigades" in Italy, the kidnapping and murder of Aldo Moro, the explosions at railway stations, museums, theatres and restaurants, murders of politicians, bankers, police officers. The terrorist war in Northern Ireland and on the streets of British cities, the occupation terror of Nagorno-Karabakh, Transnistria, Abkhazia and Ossetia, the Crimea and the east of Ukraine lasts for decades. Palestinian terrorism declared itself at the Munich Olympics. Basque terrorists ETA, Libyan terrorism, aircraft seizures, Japanese extremists, undeclared war in Chechnya, Moscow explosions, Volgodonsk, Buinaksk. September 11, 2001 in New York-all, these are modern terrorism.

Even in the Middle Ages, announcements of executions were widely distributed through heralds in squares and bazaars. Now the terrorists, after hostage taking, in the first place need the media to declare their demands. Reports are broadcasted, and the media does not prevent this from happening. Many terrorist organizations are trying to take over responsibility for an attack, even if they are not to be blamed for it. "Red Brigades" in Italy have tried to carry out terrorist attacks on Saturday in order the reports on them were published in the Sunday papers. Large terrorist organizations have their own media-newspapers, radio and television programs. According to this need, in the context of globalization, international terrorism must be seen not only as a threat to the individual states, but also a challenge to the whole humanity. This predetermined number of fundamentally new characteristics of the terror in the era of globalization in the most developed countries.

For a comprehensive analysis of the links between terrorism and the media in the information age, T.R. Korotkiy considers it expedient to single out several basic levels: firstly, the use of the media as a means of terror; secondly, the influence of the media on the coverage of the operational situation during the conduct of the terrorist act and their role in negotiating with terrorists; thirdly, the media importance in shaping public opinion about terror.

Prioritizing Prevention of Terrorism

Value of Prevention

It is obvious that violence has become a glaring reality of contemporary human society. Does that mean we give up on the prospects of peace and a secure life on this planet? Is doom and gloom perspective acceptable to human beings many of whom claim to be the 'most intelligent' of all known species? Is it acceptable to explore some alternatives to a life stricken by anger, hostility, hatred, and despair? A belief in the finality and irreversibility of evil implies a refusal to accept responsibility to act and look for good in human nature to eliminate evil. By focusing occasionally on a sense of doom and gloom,1we tend to deteriorate our courage and creativity to resolve the problem through a calm and constructive pragmatism of 'hope' and 'civility.'

By the 19th century, scholars started recognizing the value of each individual and of life. That perspective led to saving people's lives by advocating steps for preventing destructive behaviors based on psychological and social disturbances. Preventing problems through proactive planning is a rational activity and has become a priority in the area of violence across the globe. The so-called 'science of prevention' provides us tools for becoming prepared in meeting challenges of problems likely to occur in the future. It will contribute to the literature used by those trying to reduce the economic and social costs associated with threats and occurrences of violence. We will identify the worldwide implications of our study for making an impact on the societal ability to learn from terrorist incidents along with continuing a struggle for future prevention.

Terrorist occurrences have been on the rise during the past thirty or so years more than ever before in almost every corner of our planet. The potential for as well as incidents of terrorism in today's world have not only increased but have also become relatively more global, often conducted by transnational and non-state actors. These individuals are well-financed, difficult to penetrate, and have increased access to creative technology and all sorts of weapons of destruction.3Prevention may help reduce the surprise element in serious forms of violence enabling us to cope and endure consequences at a tolerable level.

We particularly need preventing strategies that may have long range impacts rather than ban-aid approaches providing short term solutions. However, it is disappointing that the United Nations in its 2005 Summit on Peace Building "neglected to establish the responsibility to prevent terrorism." It is important that we go beyond politics of decision making in world bodies and explicitly advocate and establish public's concern with the ability to predict and prevent violent deaths in the future through timely actions. We need to reaffirm professional interests of sociologists, criminologists, psychologists, and investigators from other fields to prevent deadly violence.5Empirical studies are needed that could have implications for legislators, law enforcement agencies, and pro-active leaders by identifying ways of early identification and prevention of possible terroristic threats in the future. Studies need to reflect on how and why terrorist individuals and groups become 'marginalized' and 'isolated' through their unreasonable use of violence.

Barriers to Prevention

Preventing problems before they occur often is not as easy as it sounds. There are many difficulties and obstacles before plans for prevention may be made and implemented. Some of the examples of barriers facing preventive measures are stated below.

First, preventing problems such as terrorism is a serious and complex process. We have to consider identifying the major factors related to or affecting the occurrence of terrorist incidents. That will require timely and systematic research as well as aggressively involved intelligence or investigating agencies to gather information on when, how, and where terrorist incidents are likely to happen. If that research is thorough, we may then have to decide how we can intercept and stop the incidents from happening. Realizing that an interception may or may not be the 'right' one, careful planning and its implementation will have to be required. In addition, all agencies collecting and organizing intelligence information on possible terrorist incidents have to share various pieces of information and coordinate their efforts in order to be effective in implementing preventive measure. However, many agents as well as agencies are often territorial and autonomous about their operations, particularly based in cross-national settings, and may not always coordinate preventive efforts with each other.

Second, terrorism is too complex and fluid phenomenon to prevent. News media make the situation even more complex as multiple stories and interpretations of terrorist events circulate, often causing confusion and ambivalence about what really happened. People with vested interests in the event contribute to either secrecy or circulating misinformation in the media.

Third, there often are people who deny access to information on a terrorist event. Some also refuse to acknowledge the realities of terrorist organizations and plans for political reasons. Some just do not want to be involved.

We therefore, have a number of reasons blocking open communication in hostile situations. Some of the reasons may include ignorance, fears of reprisals, guilt, irrationality, and name-calling. For example, naming and labeling separatist and religious groups may become counter-productive in opening international dialogues for prevention. Selfless leadership is often lacking because of complexity of international economic political situations causing delays in developing open and truthful communication on terrorist issues. Terrorist issues are not only complex but they involve sensitive matters related to territoriality or sovereignty, religious and political autonomy, and economic or business interests that may create obstacles for discussing terrorist problems, particularly at the international level.

Fourth, many political leaders prefer to work on short-range remedial solutions and shy away from idealistically conceptualized curative ideologies such as secularism and non-violence. I will be providing additional comments on those later in this chapter and the next one.

Levels of Prevention

Primary Prevention.

It is a serious form of prevention and is oriented toward a comprehensive understanding of the terrorism problems in order to develop long-term and curative (not band-aid) programs for prevention. This approach likes to go to the depth of the problem rather than seeking peripheral information on it. It would investigate and address the major sources of the issues involved and seek long-lasting means or resources for attacking the roots of the problem. It would increase awareness of the problem through media, and identify risks and benefits of prevention. It would also be transparent in providing continual evaluation of any program implementation for prevention for accountability purpose.

Secondary/Tertiary Prevention.

It is sort of 'something is better than nothing' strategy. It is needed particularly in the short run to investigate a terrorist problem, intervene as much as possible for corrective actions, treat injuries, repair damage caused by violent episode, provide compensation/protection to victims, seek changes in policies for security, consider changing legal ways, increase opportunities for survivors in the future, and reorganize/regroup for future attacks.

Conclusions and Directions for Further Research

1. Since terrorists use the media to achieve their goals, countering terrorism must also include a strategy for the media: the arena of a modern antiterrorist war can be both a television screen and a real battlefield.

2. Media, journalistic, publishing and broadcasting organizations, academic institutions and other structures of civil society should take measures to expand their ability to professionally report on terrorism and promote tolerance, including through training and providing opportunities for discussing ethical issues related to the coverage of terrorism.

3. An effective strategy for the media is an essential element in international measures against terrorism. The challenge from the part of terrorism of the 21

century is as follows: how the media in an atmosphere of fierce competition will be able to preserve democratic responsibility and at the same time provide the public with comprehensive information without turning into a worldwide propaganda tribune of terrorists to express their hatred.

4. Thus, international efforts against terrorism require, along with the coordination of media strategies among the governments of countrie's that are fighting against terrorism, also the participation of global media that understand their democratic responsibility. Objective and critical coverage of events does not contradict the duty to protect those rights and freedoms that the terrorists are trying to destroy. An effective media strategy aimed at combating terrorism should guarantee those freedoms, which countries with a democratic structure want to protect and which will not be destroyed through their efforts to combat terrorism.

5. The most acceptable form remains self-censorship. In addition, it is necessary to create groups to manage the coverage of terrorism in the media.

6. Actions of a (self) restrictive nature should be global and comprehensive, since non-compliance by at least one of the key players on the information field will lead to the refusal by the rest from the proposed rules.

7. In many countries, "press codes" have been adopted, but not always, they are mandatory. Therefore, now, alas, there is no common opinion in solving the problem. In order to develop common guidelines for reporting on terrorism, it is necessary to carefully analyse the role of the media in these events.

8. For the media, it is important: to have access to the sources of information originating from both terrorists and employees of special services, and direct victims of the terrorist act, their relatives and friends; operational scope, that is, the ability to record and transmit information; data verification sources.

9. We believe that the criterion for working in the proposed research direction is the formation of a complex antiterrorist communication environment, which is referred by certain analysts as counter-terrorist. It is within this effective atmosphere that the actions of the media and authorities will be closely linked with each other, and the role of civil society, which will create a special cognitive background for perceptions of terrorist attacks, will increase immeasurably.

4

The Palestine Question and Al Qaeda

Introduction

The Western media pays little attention to their almost predictable rants and threats, and even the Arab media shows much less interest than in the past. Even worse, growing dissatisfaction with al-Qaeda's mode of operations and its responsibility for the killing of numerous Muslims has led to a noticeable decline in its image through-out the Muslim world.

Something bad is happening to al-Qaeda. Although it is achieving considerable successes, along with its local allies, on its current main fronts in Afghanistan and Pakistan, its campaign in the highly prized Iraqi arena, where it took the lead, is collapsing. Moreover, al-Qaeda has failed to carry out any high-profile attacks against 'Western crusaders' in the United States or Europe in four years. Limited in their ability to operate, al-Qaeda's leaders have saturated jihadi forums with recorded statements but found that they can barely break out of this relatively small pool of sympathisers.

While its ability to operate in the heart of the Middle East is in decline, al-Qaeda has issued increasing numbers of statements dedicated to the Palestinian issue, in which it expresses support for the Palestinians, identifies with their plight, and accuses Arab regimes of abandoning their Palestinian brethren for cooperation with Israel. Many statements also attack Hamas's positions and ask Palestinians to prepare for the arrival of their jihadi brothers. The increased attention is not coincidental. In distress, al-Qaeda is seeking to use the Palestinian question to improve its image by presenting itself as the true defender of the Palestinian people.

Al-Qaeda operates as a network of Islamic extremists and Salafist jihadists. The organization has been designated as a terrorist group by the

United Nations Security Council, the North Atlantic Treaty Organization (NATO), the European Union, the United States, the United Kingdom, Russia, India, and various other countries (see below). Al-Qaeda has mounted attacks on non-military and military targets in various countries, including the 1998 United States embassy bombings, the September 11 attacks, and the 2002 Bali bombings. The United States government responded to the September 11 attacks by launching the "War on Terror", which sought to undermine al-Qaeda and its allies. The deaths of key leaders, including that of Osama bin Laden, have led al-Qaeda's operations to shift from the top down organization and planning of attacks, to the planning of attacks which are carried out by associated groups and lone-wolf operators. Al-Qaeda characteristically employs attacks which include suicide attacks and the simultaneous bombing of several targets. Activities which are ascribed to al-Qaeda involve the actions of those who have made a pledge of loyalty to bin Laden, or to the actions of "al-Qaeda-linked" individuals who have undergone training in one of its camps in Afghanistan, Pakistan, Iraq or Sudan. Al-Qaeda ideologues envision the removal of all foreign influences in Muslim countries, and the creation of a new caliphate ruling over the entire Muslim world.

Among the beliefs ascribed to al-Qaeda members is the conviction that a Christian–Jewish alliance is conspiring to destroy Islam. As Salafist jihadists, members of al-Qaeda believe that the killing of non-combatants is religiously sanctioned. This belief ignores the aspects of religious scripture which forbid the murder of non-combatants and internecine fighting. Al-Qaeda also opposes what it regards as man-made laws, and wants to replace them with a strict form of sharia law.

Al-Qaeda has carried out many attacks on targets which it considers kafir. Al-Qaeda is also responsible for instigating sectarian violence among Muslims. Al-Qaeda's leaders regard liberal Muslims, Shias, Sufis and other sects as heretical and its members and sympathizers have attacked their mosques and gatherings. Examples of sectarian attacks include the Yazidi community bombings, the Sadr City bombings, the Ashoura massacre and the April 2007 Baghdad bombings.

Following the death of bin Laden in 2011, the group has been led by Egyptian Ayman al-Zawahiri.

Organization

Al-Qaeda's philosophy calls for the centralization of decision making, while allowing for the decentralization of execution. However, after the War on Terror, al-Qaeda's leadership has become isolated. As a result, the leadership has become decentralized, and the organization has become regionalized into several al-Qaeda groups.

Many terrorism experts do not believe that the global jihadist movement is driven at every level by al-Qaeda's leadership. However, bin Laden held considerable ideological sway over some Muslim extremists before his death. Experts argue that al-Qaeda has fragmented into a number of disparate regional movements, and that these groups bear little connection with one another.

This view mirrors the account given by Osama bin Laden in his October 2001 interview with Tayseer Allouni: this matter isn't about any specific person and... is not about the al-Qa'idah Organization. We are the children of an Islamic Nation, with Prophet Muhammad as its leader, our Lord is one... and all the true believers [mu'mineen] are brothers. So the situation isn't like the West portrays it, that there is an 'organization' with a specific name (such as 'al-Qa'idah') and so on. That particular name is very old. It was born without any intention from us. Brother Abu Ubaida... created a military base to train the young men to fight against the vicious, arrogant, brutal, terrorizing Soviet empire... So this place was called 'The Base' ['Al-Qa'idah'], as in a training base, so this name grew and became. We aren't separated from this nation. We are the children of a nation, and we are an inseparable part of it, and from those public *** which spread from the far east, from the Philippines, to Indonesia, to Malaysia, to India, to Pakistan, reaching Mauritania... and so we discuss the conscience of this nation.

Bruce Hoffman, however, sees al-Qaeda as a cohesive network that is strongly led from the Pakistani tribal areas.

Leadership

Osama bin Laden (1988 – May 2011)

Osama bin Laden was the Senior Operations Chief of al-Qaeda prior to his assassination by US forces on May 1, 2011. Atiyah Abd al-Rahman was alleged to be second in command prior to his death on August 22, 2011.

Bin Laden was advised by a Shura Council, which consists of senior al-Qaeda members. The group was estimated to consist of 20–30 people. One such member is thought to have been Sayed Tayib al-Madani.

After May 2011

Ayman al-Zawahiri had been al-Qaeda's Deputy Operations Chief and assumed the role of commander after bin Laden's death. Al-Zawahiri replaced Saif al-Adel, who had served as interim commander.

On June 5, 2012, Pakistani intelligence officials announced that al-Rahman's alleged successor Abu Yahya al-Libi had been killed in Pakistan.

Nasir al-Wuhayshi was said to have become second in command in 2013. He was the leader of al-Qaeda in the Arabian Peninsula (AQAP), until he was killed in a US airstrike in June 2015.

Al-Qaeda's network was built from scratch as a conspiratorial network which drew upon the leadership of a number of regional nodes. The organization divided itself into several committees, which include:

The Military Committee, which is responsible for training operatives, acquiring weapons, and planning attacks.

The Money/Business Committee, which funds the recruitment and training of operatives through the hawala banking system. US-led efforts to eradicate the sources of "terrorist financing" were most successful in the year immediately following the September 11 attacks. Al-Qaeda continues to operate through unregulated banks, such as the 1,000 or so hawaladars in Pakistan, some of which can handle deals of up to US$10 million. The committee also procures false passports, pays al-Qaeda members, and oversees profit-driven businesses. In the 9/11 Commission Report, it was estimated that al-Qaeda required $30 million-per-year to conduct its operations.

The Law Committee reviews Sharia law, and decides upon courses of action conform to it.

The Islamic Study/Fatwah Committee issues religious edicts, such as an edict in 1998 telling Muslims to kill Americans.

The Media Committee ran the now-defunct newspaper Nashrat al Akhbar (English: Newscast) and handled public relations.

In 2005, al-Qaeda formed As-Sahab, a media production house, to supply its video and audio materials.

Command structure

Al-Qaeda is not operationally managed by Ayman al-Zawahiri. Several operational groups exist, which consult with the leadership in situations where attacks are in preparation.

When asked in 2005 about the possibility of al-Qaeda's connection to the July 7, 2005 London bombings, Metropolitan Police Commissioner Sir Ian Blair said: "Al-Qaeda is not an organization. Al-Qaeda is a way of working... but this has the hallmark of that approach... al-Qaeda clearly has the ability to provide training... to provide expertise... and I think that is what has occurred here." On August 13, 2005, The Independent newspaper, reported that the July 7 bombers had acted independently of an al-Qaeda mastermind.

Nasser al-Bahri, who was Osama bin Laden's bodyguard for four years in the run-up to 9/11 wrote in his memoir a highly detailed description of how the group functioned at that time. Al-Bahri described al-Qaeda's formal administrative structure and vast arsenal. However, author Adam Curtis argued that the idea of al-Qaeda as a formal organization is primarily an American invention. Curtis contended the name "al-Qaeda" was first brought to the attention of the public in the 2001 trial of bin Laden and the four men accused of the 1998 US embassy bombings in East Africa. Curtis wrote:

The reality was that bin Laden and Ayman al-Zawahiri had become the focus of a loose association of disillusioned Islamist militants who were attracted by the new strategy. But there was no organization. These were militants who mostly planned their own operations and looked to bin Laden for funding and assistance. He was not their commander. There is also no evidence that bin Laden used the term "al-Qaeda" to refer to the name of a group until after September 11 attacks, when he realized that this was the term the Americans had given it.

During the 2001 trial, the US Department of Justice needed to show that bin Laden was the leader of a criminal organization in order to charge him in absentia under the Racketeer Influenced and Corrupt Organizations Act. The name of the organization and details of its structure were provided in the testimony of Jamal al-Fadl, who said he was a founding member of the group and a former employee of bin Laden. Questions about the reliability of al-Fadl's testimony have been raised by a number of sources because of his history of dishonesty, and because he was delivering it as part of a plea bargain agreement after being convicted of conspiring to attack US military establishments. Sam Schmidt, a defense attorney who defended al-Fadl said:

There were selective portions of al-Fadl's testimony that I believe was false, to help support the picture that he helped the Americans join together. I think he lied in a number of specific testimony about a unified image of what this organization was. It made al-Qaeda the new Mafia or the new Communists. It made them identifiable as a group and therefore made it easier to prosecute any person associated with al-Qaeda for any acts or statements made by bin Laden.

Field operatives

The number of individuals in the group who have undergone proper military training, and are capable of commanding insurgent forces, is largely unknown. Documents captured in the raid on bin Laden's compound in 2011 show that the core al-Qaeda membership in 2002 was 170. In 2006, it was estimated that al-Qaeda had several thousand commanders embedded in 40 different countries. As of 2009, it was believed that no more than 200–300 members were still active commanders.

According to the 2004 BBC documentary The Power of Nightmares, al-Qaeda was so weakly linked together that it was hard to say it existed apart from bin Laden and a small clique of close associates. The lack of any significant numbers of convicted al-Qaeda members, despite a large number of arrests on terrorism charges, was cited by the documentary as a reason to doubt whether a widespread entity that met the description of al-Qaeda existed.

Insurgent forces

According to author Robert Cassidy, al-Qaeda maintains two separate forces which are deployed alongside insurgents in Iraq and Pakistan. The first, numbering in the tens of thousands, was "organized, trained, and equipped as insurgent combat forces" in the Soviet–Afghan war. The force was composed primarily of foreign mujahideen from Saudi Arabia and Yemen. Many of these fighters went on to fight in Bosnia and Somalia for global jihad. Another group, which numbered 10,000 in 2006, live in the West and have received rudimentary combat training.

Other analysts have described al-Qaeda's rank and file as being "predominantly Arab" in its first years of operation, but that the organization also includes "other peoples" as of 2007. It has been estimated that 62% of al-Qaeda members have university education.

Financing

In the 1990s, financing for al-Qaeda came partly from the personal wealth of Osama bin Laden. Other sources of income included the heroin trade and donations from supporters in Kuwait, Saudi Arabia and other Islamic Gulf states. A WikiLeaks-released 2009 internal US government cable stated that "terrorist funding emanating from Saudi Arabia remains a serious concern".

Among the first pieces of evidence regarding Saudi Arabia's support for al-Qaeda was the so-called "Golden Chain", a list of early al-Qaeda funders seized during a 2002 raid in Sarajevo by Bosnian police. The hand-written list was validated by al-Qaeda defector Jamal al-Fadl, and included the names of both donors and beneficiaries. Osama bin-Laden's name appeared seven times among the beneficiaries, while 20 Saudi and Gulf-based businessmen and politicians were listed among the donors. Notable donors included Adel Batterjee, and Wael Hamza Julaidan. Batterjee was designated as a terror financier by the US Department of the Treasury in 2004, and Julaidan is recognized as one of al-Qaeda's founders.

Documents seized during the 2002 Bosnia raid showed that al-Qaeda widely exploited charities to channel financial and material support to its operatives across the globe. Notably, this activity exploited the International Islamic Relief Organization (IIRO) and the Muslim World League (MWL). The IIRO had ties with al-Qaeda associates worldwide, including al-Qaeda's deputy Ayman al Zawahiri. Zawahiri's brother worked for the IIRO in Albania and had actively recruited on behalf of al-Qaeda. The MWL was openly identified by al-Qaeda's leader as one of the three charities al-Qaeda primarily relied upon for funding sources.

Allegations of Qatari support

Several Qatari citizens have been accused of funding al-Qaeda. This includes Abd Al-Rahman al-Nuaimi, a Qatari citizen and a human-rights activist who founded the Swiss-based non-governmental organization (NGO) Alkarama. On December 18, 2013, the US Treasury designated Nuaimi as a terrorist for his activities supporting al-Qaeda. The US Treasury has stated that Nuaimi "has facilitated significant financial support to al-Qaeda in Iraq, and served as an interlocutor between al-Qaeda in Iraq and Qatar-based donors".

Nuaimi was accused of overseeing a $2 million monthly transfer to al-Qaeda in Iraq as part of his role as mediator between Iraq-based al-Qaeda senior officers and Qatari citizens. Nuaimi allegedly entertained relationships with Abu-Khalid al-Suri, al-Qaeda's top envoy in Syria, who processed a $600,000 transfer to al-Qaeda in 2013. Nuaimi is also known to be associated with Abd al-Wahhab Muhammad 'Abd al-Rahman al-Humayqani, a Yemeni politician and founding member of Alkarama, who was listed as a Specially Designated Global Terrorist (SDGT) by the US Treasury in 2013. The US authorities claimed that Humayqani exploited his role in Alkarama to fundraise on behalf of al-Qaeda in the Arabian Peninsula (AQAP). A prominent figure in AQAP, Nuaimi was also reported to have facilitated the flow of funding to AQAP affiliates based in Yemen. Nuaimi was also accused of investing funds in the charity directed by Humayqani to ultimately fund AQAP. About ten months after being sanctioned by the US Treasury, Nuaimi was also restrained from doing business in the UK.

Another Qatari citizen, Kalifa Mohammed Turki Subayi, was sanctioned by the US Treasury on June 5, 2008, for his activities as a "Gulf-based al-Qaeda financier". Subayi's name was added to the UN Security Council's Sanctions List in 2008 on charges of providing financial and material support to al-Qaeda senior leadership. Subayi allegedly moved al-Qaeda recruits to South Asia-based training camps. He also financially supported Khalid Sheikh Mohammed, a Pakistani national and senior al-Qaeda officer who is believed to be the mastermind behind the September 11 attack according to the September 11 Commission report.

Qataris provided support to al-Qaeda through the country's largest NGO, the Qatar Charity. Al-Qaeda defector al-Fadl, who was a former member of Qatar Charity, testified in court that Abdullah Mohammed Yusef, who served as Qatar Charity's director, was affiliated to al-Qaeda and simultaneously to the National Islamic Front, a political group that gave al-Qaeda leader Osama Bin Laden harbor in Sudan in the early 1990s.

Legal proceedings from the trial United States vs. Enaam M. Arnaout revealed that Qatar Charity was cited by Bin Laden in 1993 as one of the charities used to channel financial support to al-Qaeda operatives overseas. The same documents also report Bin Laden's complaint that the failed assassination attempt of Egyptian President Hosni Mubarak had compromised the ability of al-Qaeda to exploit charities to support its operatives to the extent that it was capable of before 1995. It is alleged that the Qatar Charity gave financial support to members of al-Qaeda in Chechnya. This accusation was publicly denied by Hamad bin Nasser al-Thani. Qatar Charity is among the NGOs allegedly channelling funds to Ansar Dine in North Mali, according to French military intelligence reports from France's intervention in the country in early 2013.

Qatar finances al-Qaeda's enterprises through al-Qaeda's affiliate in Syria, Jabhat al-Nusra. The funding is primarily channeled through kidnapping for ransom. The Consortium Against Terrorist Finance (CATF) reported that the Gulf country has funded al-Nusra since 2013. Al-Awsat estimated that Qatar disbursed $25 million in support of al-Nusra through kidnapping for ransom. In addition, Qatar has launched fundraising campaigns on behalf of al-Nusra. Al-Nusra acknowledged a Qatar-sponsored campaign "as one of the preferred conduits for donations intended for the group".

Religious compatibility

Abdel Bari Atwan wrote that:

While the leadership's own theological platform is essentially Salafi, the organization's umbrella is sufficiently wide to encompass various schools of thought and political leanings. Al-Qaeda counts among its members and supporters people associated with Wahhabism, Shafi'ism, Malikism, and

Hanafism. There are even some Al-Qaeda members whose beliefs and practices are directly at odds with Salafism, such as Yunis Khalis, one of the leaders of the Afghan mujahedin. He was a mystic who visited the tombs of saints and sought their blessings – practices inimical to bin Laden's Wahhabi-Salafi school of thought. The only exception to this pan-Islamic policy is Shi'ism. Al-Qaeda seems implacably opposed to it, as it holds Shi'ism to be heresy. In Iraq it has openly declared war on the Badr Brigades, who have fully cooperated with the US, and now considers even Shi'i civilians to be legitimate targets for acts of violence.

History of al-Qaeda

The Guardian in 2009 described five distinct phases in the development of al-Qaeda: its beginnings in the late 1980s, a "wilderness" period in 1990–1996, its "heyday" in 1996–2001, a network period from 2001 to 2005, and a period of fragmentation from 2005 to 2009.

Jihad in Afghanistan

CIA-funded and ISI-trained Afghan mujahideen fighters crossing the Durand Line border to fight Soviet forces and the Soviet-backed Afghan government in 1985.

The origins of al-Qaeda can be traced to the Soviet War in Afghanistan (December 1979 – February 1989). The United States viewed the conflict in Afghanistan in terms of the Cold War, with Marxists on one side and the native Afghan mujahideen on the other. This view led to a CIA program called Operation Cyclone, which channeled funds through Pakistan's Inter-Services Intelligence agency to the Afghan Mujahideen. The US government provided substantial financial support to the Afghan Islamic militants. Aid to Gulbuddin Hekmatyar, an Afghan mujahideen leader and founder of the Hezb-e Islami, amounted to more than $600 million. In addition to American aid, Hekmatyar was the recipient of Saudi aid. In the early 1990s, after the US had withdrawn support, Hekmatyar "worked closely" with bin Laden.

At the same time, a growing number of Arab mujahideen joined the jihad against the Afghan Marxist regime, which was facilitated by international Muslim organizations, particularly the Maktab al-Khidamat (MAK). In 1984, MAK was established in Peshawar, Pakistan, by bin Laden and Abdullah Yusuf Azzam, a Palestinian Islamic scholar and member of the Muslim Brotherhood. MAK organized guest houses in Peshawar, near the Afghan border, and gathered supplies for the construction of paramilitary training camps to prepare foreign recruits for the Afghan war front. MAK was funded by the Saudi government as well as by individual Muslims including Saudi businessmen. Bin Laden also became a major financier of the mujahideen, spending his own money and using his connections to influence public opinion about the war.

From 1986, MAK began to set up a network of recruiting offices in the US, the hub of which was the Al Kifah Refugee Center at the Farouq Mosque on Brooklyn's Atlantic Avenue. Among notable figures at the Brooklyn center were "double agent" Ali Mohamed, whom FBI special agent Jack Cloonan called "bin Laden's first trainer", and "Blind Sheikh" Omar Abdel-Rahman, a leading recruiter of mujahideen for Afghanistan. Azzam and bin Laden began to establish camps in Afghanistan in 1987.

MAK and foreign mujahideen volunteers, or "Afghan Arabs", did not play a major role in the war. While over 250,000 Afghan mujahideen fought the Soviets and the communist Afghan government, it is estimated that were never more than 2,000 foreign mujahideen on the field at any one time. Nonetheless, foreign mujahideen volunteers came from 43 countries, and the total number that participated in the Afghan movement between 1982 and 1992 is reported to have been 35,000. Bin Laden played a central role in organizing training camps for the foreign Muslim volunteers.

The Soviet Union withdrew from Afghanistan in 1989. Mohammad Najibullah's Communist Afghan government lasted for three more years, before it was overrun by elements of the mujahideen.

Expanding operations

Toward the end of the Soviet military mission in Afghanistan, some foreign mujahideen wanted to expand their operations to include Islamist struggles in other parts of the world, such as Palestine and Kashmir. A number of overlapping and interrelated organizations were formed, to further those aspirations. One of these was the organization that would eventually be called al-Qaeda.

Research suggests that al-Qaeda was formed on August 11, 1988, when a meeting between leaders of Egyptian Islamic Jihad, Abdullah Azzam, and bin Laden took place. An agreement was reached to link bin Laden's money with the expertise of the Islamic Jihad organization and take up the jihadist cause elsewhere after the Soviets withdrew from Afghanistan.

Notes indicate al-Qaeda was a formal group by August 20, 1988. A list of requirements for membership itemized the following: listening ability, good manners, obedience, and making a pledge (bayat) to follow one's superiors. In his memoir, bin Laden's former bodyguard, Nasser al-Bahri, gives the only publicly available description of the ritual of giving bayat when he swore his allegiance to the al-Qaeda chief. According to Wright, the group's real name wasn't used in public pronouncements because "its existence was still a closely held secret."

After Azzam was assassinated in 1989 and MAK broke up, significant numbers of MAK followers joined bin Laden's new organization.

In November 1989, Ali Mohamed, a former special forces sergeant stationed at Fort Bragg, North Carolina, left military service and moved to California. He traveled to Afghanistan and Pakistan and became "deeply involved with bin Laden's plans." In 1991, Ali Mohammed is said to have helped orchestrate bin Laden's relocation to Sudan.

Gulf War and the start of US enmity

Following the Soviet Union's withdrawal from Afghanistan in February 1989, bin Laden returned to Saudi Arabia. The Iraqi invasion of Kuwait in August 1990 had put the Kingdom and its ruling House of Saud at risk. The world's most valuable oil fields were within striking distance of Iraqi forces in Kuwait, and Saddam's call to pan-Arab/Islamism could potentially rally internal dissent.

In the face of a seemingly massive Iraqi military presence, Saudi Arabia's own forces were outnumbered. Bin Laden offered the services of his mujahideen to King Fahd to protect Saudi Arabia from the Iraqi army. The Saudi monarch refused bin Laden's offer, opting instead to allow US and allied forces to deploy troops into Saudi territory.

The deployment angered bin Laden, as he believed the presence of foreign troops in the "land of the two mosques" (Mecca and Medina) profaned sacred soil. After speaking publicly against the Saudi government for harboring American troops, he was banished and forced to live in exile in Sudan.

Sudan

From around 1992 to 1996, al-Qaeda and bin Laden based themselves in Sudan at the invitation of Islamist theoretician Hassan al-Turabi. The move followed an Islamist coup d'état in Sudan, led by Colonel Omar al-Bashir, who professed a commitment to reordering Muslim political values. During this time, bin Laden assisted the Sudanese government, bought or set up various business enterprises, and established training camps.

A key turning point for bin Laden occurred in 1993 when Saudi Arabia gave support for the Oslo Accords, which set a path for peace between Israel and Palestinians. Due to bin Laden's continuous verbal assault on King Fahd of Saudi Arabia, Fahd sent an emissary to Sudan on March 5, 1994 demanding bin Laden's passport. Bin Laden's Saudi citizenship was also revoked. His family was persuaded to cut off his stipend, $7 million a year, and his Saudi assets were frozen. His family publicly disowned him. There is controversy as to what extent bin Laden continued to garner support from members afterwards.

In 1993, a young schoolgirl was killed in an unsuccessful attempt on the life of the Egyptian prime minister, Atef Sedki. Egyptian public opinion turned against Islamist bombings, and the police arrested 280 of al-Jihad's members and executed 6. In June 1995, an attempt to assassinate Egyptian president Mubarak led to the expulsion of Egyptian Islamic Jihad (EIJ), and in May 1996, of bin Laden from Sudan.

According to Pakistani-American businessman Mansoor Ijaz, the Sudanese government offered the Clinton Administration numerous opportunities to arrest bin Laden. Ijaz's claims appeared in numerous op-ed pieces, including one in the Los Angeles Times and one in The Washington Post co-written with former Ambassador to Sudan Timothy M. Carney. Similar allegations have been made by Vanity Fair contributing editor David Rose, and Richard Miniter, author of Losing bin Laden, in a November 2003 interview with World.

Several sources dispute Ijaz's claim, including the 9/11 Commission, which concluded in part:

Sudan's minister of defense, Fatih Erwa, has claimed that Sudan offered to hand Bin Ladin over to the US. The Commission has found no credible evidence that this was so. Ambassador Carney had instructions only to push the Sudanese to expel Bin Ladin. Ambassador Carney had no legal basis to ask for more from the Sudanese since, at the time, there was no indictment out-standing.

Refuge in Afghanistan

After the fall of the Afghan communist regime in 1992, Afghanistan was effectively ungoverned for four years and plagued by constant infighting between various mujahideen groups. This situation allowed the Taliban to organize. The Taliban also garnered support from graduates of Islamic schools, which are called madrassa. According to Ahmed Rashid, five leaders of the Taliban were graduates of Darul Uloom Haqqania, a madrassa in the small town of Akora Khattak. The town is situated near Peshawar in Pakistan, but the school is largely attended by Afghan refugees. This institution reflected Salafi beliefs in its teachings, and much of its funding came from private donations from wealthy Arabs. Four of the Taliban's leaders attended a similarly funded and influenced madrassa in Kandahar. Bin Laden's contacts were laundering donations to these schools, and Islamic banks were used to transfer money to an "array" of charities which served as front groups for al-Qaeda.

Many of the mujahideen who later joined the Taliban fought alongside Afghan warlord Mohammad Nabi Mohammadi's Harkat i Inqilabi group at the time of the Russian invasion. This group also enjoyed the loyalty of most Afghan Arab fighters.

The continuing lawlessness enabled the growing and well-disciplined Taliban to expand their control over territory in Afghanistan, and it came to establish an enclave which it called the Islamic Emirate of Afghanistan. In 1994, it captured the regional center of Kandahar, and after making rapid territorial gains thereafter, the Taliban captured the capital city Kabul in September 1996.

In 1996, Taliban-controlled Afghanistan provided a perfect staging ground for al-Qaeda. While not officially working together, Al-Qaeda enjoyed the Taliban's protection and supported the regime in such a strong symbiotic relationship that many Western observers dubbed the Taliban's Islamic Emirate of Afghanistan as, "the world's first terrorist-sponsored state." However, at this time, only Pakistan, Saudi Arabia, and the United Arab Emirates recognized the Taliban as the legitimate government of Afghanistan.

While in Afghanistan, the Taliban government tasked al-Qaeda with the training of Brigade 055, an elite element of the Taliban's army. The Brigade mostly consisted of foreign fighters, veterans from the Soviet Invasion, and adherents to the ideology of the mujahideen. In November 2001, as Operation Enduring Freedom had toppled the Taliban government, many Brigade 055 fighters were captured or killed, and those that survived were thought to have escaped into Pakistan along with bin Laden.

By the end of 2008, some sources reported that the Taliban had severed any remaining ties with al-Qaeda, however, there is reason to doubt this. According to senior US military intelligence officials, there were fewer than 100 members of al-Qaeda remaining in Afghanistan in 2009.

Call for global Salafi jihadism

In 1994, the Salafi groups waging Salafi jihadism in Bosnia entered into decline, and groups such as the Egyptian Islamic Jihad began to drift away from the Salafi cause in Europe. Al-Qaeda stepped in and assumed control of around 80% of non-state armed cells in Bosnia in late 1995. At the same time, al-Qaeda ideologues instructed the network's recruiters to look for Jihadi international Muslims who believed that extremist-jihad must be fought on a global level. Al-Qaeda also sought to open the "offensive phase" of the global Salafi jihad. Bosnian Islamists in 2006 called for "solidarity with Islamic causes around the world", supporting the insurgents in Kashmir and Iraq as well as the groups fighting for a Palestinian state.

Fatwas

In 1996, al-Qaeda announced its jihad to expel foreign troops and interests from what they considered Islamic lands. Bin Laden issued a fatwa, which amounted to a public declaration of war against the US and its allies, and began to refocus al-Qaeda's resources on large-scale, propagandist strikes.

On February 23, 1998, bin Laden and Ayman al-Zawahiri, a leader of Egyptian Islamic Jihad, along with three other Islamist leaders, co-signed and issued a fatwa calling on Muslims to kill Americans and their allies. Under the banner of the World Islamic Front for Combat Against the Jews and Crusaders, they declared:

[T]he ruling to kill the Americans and their allies – civilians and military – is an individual duty for every Muslim who can do it in any country in which it is possible to do it, in order to liberate the al-Aqsa Mosque [in Jerusalem] and the holy mosque [in Mecca] from their grip, and in order for their armies to move out of all the lands of Islam, defeated and unable to threaten any Muslim. This is in accordance with the words of Almighty Allah, 'and fight the pagans all together as they fight you all together,' and 'fight them until there is no more tumult or oppression, and there prevail justice and faith in Allah'.

Neither bin Laden nor al-Zawahiri possessed the traditional Islamic scholarly qualifications to issue a fatwa. However, they rejected the authority of the contemporary ulema (which they saw as the paid servants of jahiliyya rulers), and took it upon themselves.

Iraq

Al-Qaeda has launched attacks against the Iraqi Shia majority in an attempt to incite sectarian violence. Al-Zarqawi purportedly declared an all-out war on Shiites while claiming responsibility for Shiite mosque bombings. The same month, a statement claiming to be from Al-Qaeda in Iraq was rejected as a "fake". In a December 2007 video, al-Zawahiri defended the Islamic State in

Iraq, but distanced himself from the attacks against civilians, which he deemed to be perpetrated by "hypocrites and traitors existing among the ranks".

US and Iraqi officials accused Al-Qaeda in Iraq of trying to slide Iraq into a full-scale civil war between Iraq's Shiite population and Sunni Arabs. This was done through an orchestrated campaign of civilian massacres and a number of provocative attacks against high-profile religious targets. With attacks including the 2003 Imam Ali Mosque bombing, the 2004 Day of Ashura and Karbala and Najaf bombings, the 2006 first al-Askari Mosque bombing in Samarra, the deadly single-day series of bombings in which at least 215 people were killed in Baghdad's Shiite district of Sadr City, and the second al-Askari bombing in 2007, Al-Qaeda in Iraq provoked Shiite militias to unleash a wave of retaliatory attacks, resulting in death squad-style killings and further sectarian violence which escalated in 2006. In 2008, sectarian bombings blamed on al-Qaeda in Iraq killed at least 42 people at the Imam Husayn Shrine in Karbala in March, and at least 51 people at a bus stop in Baghdad in June.

In February 2014, after a prolonged dispute with al-Qaeda in Iraq's successor organisation, the Islamic State of Iraq and the Levant (ISIS), al-Qaeda publicly announced it was cutting all ties with the group, reportedly for its brutality and "notorious intractability".

Somalia and Yemen

In Somalia, al-Qaeda agents had been collaborating closely with its Somali wing, which was created from the al-Shabaab group. In February 2012, al-Shabaab officially joined al-Qaeda, declaring loyalty in a video. Somalian al-Qaeda recruited children for suicide-bomber training, recruited young people to participate in militant actions against Americans.

The percentage of attacks in the First World originating from the Afghanistan–Pakistan (AfPak) border declined starting in 2007, as al-Qaeda shifted to Somalia and Yemen. While al-Qaeda leaders were hiding in the tribal areas along the AfPak border, middle-tier leaders heightened activity in Somalia and Yemen.

In January 2009, al-Qaeda's division in Saudi Arabia merged with its Yemeni wing to form al-Qaeda in the Arabian Peninsula (AQAP). Centered in Yemen, the group takes advantage of the country's poor economy, demography and domestic security. In August 2009, the group made an assassination attempt against a member of the Saudi royal family. President Obama asked Ali Abdullah Saleh to ensure closer cooperation with the US in the struggle against the growing activity of al-Qaeda in Yemen, and promised to send additional aid. The wars in Iraq and Afghanistan, drew US attention from Somalia and Yemen. In December 2011, US Secretary of Defense Leon Panetta said that the US operations against al-Qaeda "are now concentrating on key groups in Yemen, Somalia and North Africa." Al-Qaeda in the Arabian Peninsula claimed responsibility for the 2009 bombing attack on Northwest Airlines Flight 253 by Umar Farouk Abdulmutallab. The AQAP declared the Al-Qaeda Emirate in Yemen in March 31, 2011, after capturing the most of the Abyan Governorate.

As the Saudi-led military intervention in Yemen escalated in July 2015, 50 civilians were killed, and 20 million were in need of aid. In February 2016, al-Qaeda forces and Saudi Arabian-led coalition forces were both seen fighting Houthi rebels in the same battle. In August 2018, Al Jazeera reported that "A military coalition battling Houthi rebels secured secret deals with al-Qaeda in Yemen and recruited hundreds of the group's fighters. ... Key figures in the deal-making said the United States was aware of the arrangements and held off on drone attacks against the armed group, which was created by Osama bin Laden in 1988."

United States operations

In December 1998, the Director of the CIA Counterterrorism Center reported to President Bill Clinton that al-Qaeda was preparing to launch attacks in the United States, and that the group was training personnel to hijack aircraft. On September 11, 2001, al-Qaeda attacked the United States, hijacking four airliners within the country and deliberately crashing two into the twin towers of the World Trade Center in New York City. The third plane crashed into the western side of the Pentagon in Arlington County, Virginia. The fourth plane was crashed into a field in Shanksville, Pennsylvania. In total, the attackers killed 2,977 victims and injured more than 6,000 others.

US officials noted that Anwar al-Awlaki had considerable reach within the US. A former FBI agent identified Awlaki as a known "senior recruiter for al-Qaeda", and a spiritual motivator. Awlaki's sermons in the US were attended by three of the 9/11 hijackers, and accused Fort Hood shooter Nidal Malik Hasan. US intelligence intercepted emails from Hasan to Awlaki between December 2008 and early 2009. On his website, Awlaki has praised Hasan's actions in the Fort Hood shooting.

An unnamed official claimed there was good reason to believe Awlaki "has been involved in very serious terrorist activities since leaving the US [in 2002], including plotting attacks against America and our allies." US President Barack Obama approved the targeted killing of al-Awlaki by April 2010, making al-Awlaki the first US citizen ever placed on the CIA target list. That required the consent of the US National Security Council, and officials argued that the attack was appropriate because the individual posed an imminent danger to national security. In May 2010, Faisal Shahzad, who pleaded guilty to the 2010 Times Square car bombing attempt, told interrogators he was "inspired by" al-Awlaki, and sources said Shahzad had made contact with al-Awlaki over the Internet. Representative Jane Harman called him "terrorist number one", and Investor's Business Daily called him "the world's most dangerous man". In July 2010, the US Treasury Department added him to its list of Specially Designated Global Terrorists, and the UN added him to its list of individuals associated with al-Qaeda. In August 2010, al-Awlaki's father initiated a lawsuit against the US government with the American Civil Liberties Union, challenging its order to kill al-Awlaki. In October 2010, US and UK officials linked al-Awlaki to the 2010 cargo plane bomb plot. In September 2011, al-

Awlaki was killed in a targeted killing drone attack in Yemen. On March 16, 2012, it was reported that Osama bin Laden plotted to kill US President Barack Obama.

Death of Osama bin Laden

On May 1, 2011, US President Barack Obama announced that Osama bin Laden had been killed by "a small team of Americans" acting under direct orders, in a covert operation in Abbottabad, Pakistan. The action took place 50 km (31 mi) north of Islamabad. According to US officials, a team of 20–25 US Navy SEALs under the command of the Joint Special Operations Command stormed bin Laden's compound with two helicopters. Bin Laden and those with him were killed during a firefight in which US forces experienced no casualties. According to one US official the attack was carried out without the knowledge or consent of the Pakistani authorities. In Pakistan some people were reported to be shocked at the unauthorized incursion by US armed forces. The site is a few miles from the Pakistan Military Academy in Kakul. In his broadcast announcement President Obama said that US forces "took care to avoid civilian casualties." Details soon emerged that three men and a woman were killed along with bin Laden, the woman being killed when she was "used as a shield by a male combatant". DNA from bin Laden's body, compared with DNA samples on record from his dead sister, confirmed bin Laden's identity. The body was recovered by the US military and was in its custody until, according to one US official, his body was buried at sea according to Islamic traditions. One US official stated that "finding a country willing to accept the remains of the world's most wanted terrorist would have been difficult." US State Department issued a "Worldwide caution" for Americans following bin Laden's death and US diplomatic facilities everywhere were placed on high alert, a senior US official said. Crowds gathered outside the White House and in New York City's Times Square to celebrate bin Laden's death.

Syria

In 2003, President Bashar al-Assad revealed in an interview with a Kuwaiti newspaper that he doubted that al-Qaeda even existed. He was quoted as saying, "Is there really an entity called al-Qaeda? Was it in Afghanistan? Does it exist now?" He went on further to remark about bin Laden, commenting "[he] cannot talk on the phone or use the Internet, but he can direct communications to the four corners of the world? This is illogical."

Following the mass protests that took place in 2011, which demanded the resignation of al-Assad, al-Qaeda affiliated groups and Sunni sympathizers soon began to constitute an effective fighting force against al-Assad. Before the Syrian Civil War, al-Qaeda's presence in Syria was negligible, but its growth thereafter was rapid. Groups such as the al-Nusra Front and the Islamic State of Iraq and the Levant have recruited many foreign Mujahideen to train and fight in what has gradually become a highly sectarian war. Ideologically, the Syrian Civil War has served the interests of al-Qaeda as it pits a mainly Sunni opposition against a Shia government. Al-Qaeda and other fundamentalist

Sunni militant groups have invested heavily in the civil conflict, actively backing and supporting the Syrian Opposition.

On February 2, 2014, al-Qaeda distanced itself from ISIS and its actions in Syria, however during 2014–15, ISIS and the al-Qaeda-linked al-Nusra Front were still able to occasionally cooperate in their fight against the Syrian government. Al-Nusra (backed by Saudi Arabia and Turkey as part of the Army of Conquest during 2015–2017) launched many attacks and bombings, mostly against targets affiliated with or supportive of the Syrian government. From October 2015, Russian air strikes targeted positions held by al-Nusra Front, as well as other Islamist and non-Islamist rebels, while the US also targeted al-Nusra with airstrikes. In early 2016, a leading ISIL ideologue described al-Qaeda as the "Jews of jihad".

India

In September 2014 al-Zawahiri announced al-Qaeda was establishing a front in India to "wage jihad against its enemies, to liberate its land, to restore its sovereignty, and to revive its Caliphate." Al-Zawahiri nominated India as a beachhead for regional jihad taking in neighboring countries such as Myanmar and Bangladesh. The motivation for the video was questioned, as it appeared the militant group was struggling to remain relevant in light of the emerging prominence of ISIS. The new wing was to be known as "Qaedat al-Jihad fi'shibhi al-qarrat al-Hindiya" or al-Qaida in the Indian Subcontinent (AQIS). Leaders of several Indian Muslim organizations rejected al-Zawahiri's pronouncement, saying they could see no good coming from it, and viewed it as a threat to Muslim youth in the country.

In 2014 Zee News reported that Bruce Riede (a former CIA analyst and National Security Council official for South Asia) accused the Pakistan military intelligence—Inter-Services Intelligence (ISI)—of organising and assisting Al-Qaeda to organise in India, that Pakistan ought to be warned that it will be placed on the list of State Sponsors of Terrorism, and wrote that "Zawahiri made the tape in his hideout in Pakistan, no doubt, and many Indians suspect the ISI is helping to protect him".

War on Terror

In the immediate aftermath of the 9/11 attacks, the US government responded, and began to prepare its armed forces to overthrow the Taliban, which it believed was harboring al-Qaeda. The US offered Taliban leader Mullah Omar a chance to surrender bin Laden and his top associates. The first forces to be inserted into Afghanistan were paramilitary officers from the CIA's elite Special Activities Division (SAD).

The Taliban offered to turn over bin Laden to a neutral country for trial if the US would provide evidence of bin Laden's complicity in the attacks. US President George W. Bush responded by saying: "We know he's guilty. Turn him over", and British Prime Minister Tony Blair warned the Taliban regime: "Surrender bin Laden, or surrender power".

Soon thereafter the US and its allies invaded Afghanistan, and together with the Afghan Northern Alliance removed the Taliban government as part of the war in Afghanistan. As a result of the US special forces and air support for the Northern Alliance ground forces, a number of Taliban and al-Qaeda training camps were destroyed, and much of the operating structure of al-Qaeda is believed to have been disrupted. After being driven from their key positions in the Tora Bora area of Afghanistan, many al-Qaeda fighters tried to regroup in the rugged Gardez region of the nation.

By early 2002, al-Qaeda had been dealt a serious blow to its operational capacity, and the Afghan invasion appeared to be a success. Nevertheless, a significant Taliban insurgency remained in Afghanistan.

Debate continued regarding the nature of al-Qaeda's role in the 9/11 attacks. The US State Department released a videotape showing bin Laden speaking with a small group of associates somewhere in Afghanistan shortly before the Taliban was removed from power. Although its authenticity has been questioned by a couple of people, the tape definitively implicates bin Laden and al-Qaeda in the September 11 attacks. The tape was aired on many television channels, with an accompanying English translation provided by the US Defense Department.

In September 2004, the 9/11 Commission officially concluded that the attacks were conceived and implemented by al-Qaeda operatives. In October 2004, bin Laden appeared to claim responsibility for the attacks in a videotape released through Al Jazeera, saying he was inspired by Israeli attacks on high-rises in the 1982 invasion of Lebanon: "As I looked at those demolished towers in Lebanon, it entered my mind that we should punish the oppressor in kind and that we should destroy towers in America in order that they taste some of what we tasted and so that they be deterred from killing our women and children."

By the end of 2004, the US government proclaimed that two-thirds of the most senior al-Qaeda figures from 2001 had been captured and interrogated by the CIA: Abu Zubaydah, Ramzi bin al-Shibh and Abd al-Rahim al-Nashiri in 2002; Khalid Sheikh Mohammed in 2003; and Saif al Islam el Masry in 2004. Mohammed Atef and several others were killed. The West was criticized for not being able to handle Al-Qaida despite a decade of the war.

When al-Qaeda invited journalists and the people at large to direct questions by internet to al-Qaeda's second-in-command, Dr. Ayman al-Zawahiri, one of the most frequent questions was: "Why does al-Qaeda not launch operations in Palestine?" Al-Zawahiri responded with an audio message published on al-Sahab, the media wing of al-Qaeda, threatening Israel and Jewish interests. He endorsed "every operation against Jewish interests" and promised to "strive as much as we can to deal blows to the Jews inside Israel and outside it, with Allah's help and guidance." Al-Zawahiri also advised "the people of Palestine to perform jihad, jihad and jihad." He added, "I expect the jihadi influence to spread after the Americans' exit from Iraq and to move toward Jerusalem" (Al-Sharq al-Awsat, April 4).

The Palestinian issue has been a big challenge for the propaganda of al-Qaeda. Most Muslims around the world look at Israel as a hostile occupier and sympathize with the Palestinians. At any level of the Israeli-Palestinian conflict, Muslims obviously consider Israel as their enemy, yet al-Qaeda activity within Israel has been strikingly non-existent.

Al-Qaeda Front in Gaza?

In early March Israel ended a week-long offensive in Gaza in an attempt to stop Palestinian militants from firing rockets against the nearby Israeli cities of Ashkelon and Sderot. The Israeli assault killed more than 120 people, including many civilians. Three Israelis were also killed (al-Jazeera, March 13; AP, March 24). During the weeks following the operation, al-Qaeda released two audiotapes by bin Laden, one of which addressed the situation in Gaza and the Palestinians (al-Jazeera, March 20). Al-Zawahiri also appeared in an audiotape, which arrived shortly after bin Laden's March 20 release:

Today there is no room for he who says that we should only fight the Jews in Palestine. Let us strike their interests everywhere, just like they gathered against us from everywhere... Let [the Americans] know that they will get blood for every dollar they spend in the killing of the Muslims, and for every bullet they fire at us, a volcano will turn back on them...They cannot expect to support Israel, then live in peace while the Jews are killing our fugitive and besieged people (al-Sahab, March 24).

Bin Laden called for the use of "iron and fire to end the siege of Gaza" and accused what he called the "Zionist-Crusader alliance" of implementing the siege on Gaza, which came on the heels of the U.S.-hosted November 2007 Annapolis Conference, intended to revive the peace process in the Middle East. "This killing siege has started after the support of the Arabs of Annapolis to America and the Zionist entity (Israel); by that support they are partners in committing this horrible crime." Bin Laden identified jihad as the only way to support the Palestinian people, but urged Muslims to join "the mujahideen brothers in Iraq" to support the Palestinians rather than going to Palestine to fight:

Iraq is the perfect base to set up the jihad to liberate Palestine... Palestine and its people have been suffering from too much bitterness for almost a century now at the hands of the Christians and the Jews. And both parties didn't take Palestine from us by negotiations and dialogue, but with arms and fire, and this is the only way to take it back (Al-Jazeera, March 20).

After Hamas took over Gaza and drove out rival Fatah fighters and security services, the Palestinian president and leader of Fatah, Mahmoud Abbas, accused Hamas of protecting al-Qaeda and allowing it to gain a foothold in Gaza (Haaretz, July 10, 2007). Abbas renewed his accusations this year, alleging that al-Qaeda militants had infiltrated the Gaza strip and were receiving assistance from Hamas to establish a base of operations there. He also declared that an alliance had formed between al-Qaeda and Hamas (al-Hayat, February 25). Hamas denied the accusations, but interestingly it seems that Hamas used the specter of al-Qaeda in Gaza during their talks with Egypt right before taking over Gaza. Khalid Meshaal, the head of the political bureau of Hamas, told the Egyptians that if Hamas lost its battle with Fatah over Gaza, "al-Qaeda will be your neighbor." The delegation told the Egyptians clearly that only Hamas was capable of securing the borders and curbing the cells of al-Qaeda. In retrospect it appears Meshaal wanted to neutralize Egypt before his approaching battle with Fatah in Gaza (Masrawy, June 18, 2007).

New Extremist Groups Emerge in Gaza

The propaganda of jihad has been spreading for years among the youth in Gaza, with stores making big profits selling the recordings of bin Laden and Abu Musab al-Zarqawi, the late leader of al-Qaeda in Iraq—killed by a U.S. air strike in June 2006. The Gaza strip borders with Israel and Egypt and is approximately 25 miles long and 6 miles wide. It is populated by only about 1.3 million Palestinians, most of whom live in poverty and suffer from both unemployment and neglect—an ideal environment for extreme ideologies to spread. Gaza has been a stronghold of the Muslim Brotherhood-rooted Hamas since its formation in the late 1980s.

After the Israeli withdrawal from Gaza in 2005, Gaza became a land of political confusion and lawlessness. The conflict between Hamas and Fatah elements was escalating and under these circumstances the name of al-Qaeda appeared in Gaza. On May 8, 2006, a group called al-Jaysh al-Quds al-Islami (The Islamic Army of Jerusalem) announced its formation: "With Allah's help the Islamic Army of al-Quds (Jerusalem), which follows the organization of al-Qaeda in the land of Ribat (i.e., Palestine), has been formed, basing [itself] on the words of Shaykh Osama bin Laden, Shaykh Ayman al-Zawahiri and Shaykh Abu Musab al-Zarqawi." The group added that it would target every enemy of Islam: "We will explode with our bodies all of their locations and shake the land under their feet" (Al-Watan, May 24, 2006).

Later in 2006 another allegedly Palestinian group released a videotape. Calling itself Qaedat al-Jihad Wilayat Palestine (The Base of Jihad – Palestine region), the group started the tape with an excerpt from bin Laden's well known speech that followed the 9/11 attacks: "To America, I say to it and its people: I swear by God, who has elevated the skies without pillars, neither America nor the people who live in it will dream of security before we live in Palestine" (al-Jazeera, October 7, 2001). The video also included al-Zarqawi saying: "We fight in Iraq with our eyes on Jerusalem which cannot be regained without the sword" (al-Asr, November 2, 2006).

A Gaza group called Suyuf al-Haq (The Swords of Righteousness) proclaimed its existence with attacks on Internet cafes, music stores and women not wearing Islamic dress. Churches and Christian book shops were also targeted. The group did not introduce itself as part of al-Qaeda but seemed to have similar Salafist beliefs. Khalid Abu Hilal, spokesman of the Palestinian Ministry of the Interior, said that he did not believe there was a link between the Palestinian extremists and the international organization of al-Qaeda, but a security source said that some al-Qaeda-affiliated extremists might have succeeded in entering Gaza through the border with Egypt the previous year (al-Naba, June 6, 2006).

On March 12, 2007, BBC reporter Alan Johnston—the only Western journalist based in Gaza—was kidnapped. A group called Jaysh al-Islam (Army of Islam) claimed responsibility and released a video of Johnston. The group demanded the release of Abu Kutada, who is believed to be al-Qaeda's spiritual leader in Europe and is currently jailed in Britain. After Hamas took power in Gaza, Johnston was turned over to Hamas forces (BBC, October 25, 2007).

The Jaysh al-Islam, which is believed to be headed by Mumtaz Daghmash, was also linked to the kidnapping of Israeli soldier Gilad Schalit. In an operation launched on June 25, 2006, Jaysh al-Islam joined with two other groups: the Izz al-Din al-Kassam brigades—the military wing of Hamas—and the Salah al-Din brigades, who are closer to Fatah. Three Israeli soldiers were killed in the operation and corporal Schalit captured. The statement of the Army of Islam garnered a lot of attention; it was their first appearance and the operation indicated the organization's ability to coordinate with other active armed groups or with extremist elements within them, creating new strategic possibilities in the Israeli-Palestinian conflict (al-Arabia, July 7, 2006).

Al-Qaeda's growing pains

Long a champion of war against the US-led 'Zionist–crusaders' alliance, al-Qaeda has had little to show its sympathisers in recent years. It succeeded in dragging the United States and NATO into what seems like an unwinnable war in Afghanistan and was instrumental in spreading instability in Pakistan. It also bled US forces in Iraq. But al-Qaeda has played mostly a supporting role in the Afghan and Pakistani arenas, with the Taliban taking the lead, and botched its campaign in Iraq. Its loss in Iraq is particularly disappointing for an organisation that values the establishment of a base in the heart of the Middle East even more than success in Central Asia.

There was a time when al-Qaeda believed that victory was at hand, and had begun to prepare for the post-US period. Today, its Iraq campaign is in shambles. Moreover, al-Qaeda's 'bread and butter', attacks in 'crusader' countries, have been largely absent. For eight years it has failed to penetrate the American security wall, and has not carried out a significant operation on a Western target outside the Middle East since the 2005 London bombings. In addition, a series of operations in Middle Eastern countries from 2003 failed to erode local regimes' hold on power, but resulted in the killing of numerous Muslim civilians in Saudi Arabia, Morocco, Jordan and Algeria, undermining the sympathy of an important constituency: Muslims who do not necessarily support al-Qaeda's goals but share its hostility to the United States and oppressive Middle Eastern regimes. The bombing of three hotels in Amman in November 2005 was particularly damaging to al-Qaeda's reputation and resulted in a steep decline in its image throughout the Muslim world. Even within jihadi circles, al-Qaeda's stature suffered when it attempted, with severe brutality, to coerce all Islamic Sunni insurgency groups in Iraq to unite under its leadership within the framework of the 'Islamic State of Iraq'.

The confrontation with Israel is a serious challenge for al-Qaeda. Prior to 11 September 2001, the organisation showed little interest in the Palestinian question. Palestine was listed among Osama bin Laden's grievances against the West and the Middle Eastern regimes, along with other Muslim territories allegedly occupied by non-Muslims; it received even slightly greater weight due to Jerusalem's unique religious importance. But bin Laden and al-Zawahiri were clearly more interested in their homelands of Saudi Arabia and Egypt. When al-Qaeda referred to the Palestinian problem, it was often in support of its propaganda efforts. For instance, bin Laden used the 'abandonment of Palestine' as an example of the poor condition of the umma following the destruction of the Ottoman Caliphate and its replacement by a host of 'tyrant' leaders.

There have been indications that al-Qaeda's long-term plan includes the Palestinian arena. In 2005, the newspaper al-Quds al-Arabi serialised a book on al-Zarqawi written by Fuad Hussein, a Jordanian author close to jihadi circles. Hussein argues that al-Qaeda has marked out the removal of Israel as one of its main goals. In addition to the intrinsic appeal of this objective, attacking Israel is expected to weaken the Arab regimes, win al-Qaeda cred-ibility among Muslims, prove its eligibility to lead the umma, and win it recruits as well as financial and moral support. To some extent, from the organisation's perspective, beating Israel, the spearhead of the West planted in the heart of the Islamic world, is a key to the success of the entire jihadi project.

An essay written by an al-Qaeda ideologue using the pseudonym 'Asad al-Jihad2' and posted to a jihadi website at the beginning of 2008 repeated the parts of this plan that pertain to the Palestinian front. It claimed that by the end of 2009, al-Qaeda would complete the long preparations for jihad in Palestine (the base for these preparations being Iraq). Then, fierce battle would take place in the fourth stage, between the years 2010 and 2013. The author proceeded to advise Palestinians on how to prepare for the arrival of foreign fighters and for the upcoming jihad, by practicing martial arts, building bombs and rockets, acquiring weapons, storing food, and learning ways to bring in and protect the Muhajirun (foreign fighters).

ut despite abundant motivation, al-Qaeda does not have the capability to shift its operations to the Palestinian arena and transform Palestinian territories into bases from which to attack Israel. As al-Qaeda members lament, entry into the Palestinian territories requires traversing Arab countries – Lebanon, Syria, Jordan and Egypt – that are hostile to al-Qaeda. Moreover, access to the West Bank requires operatives to cross Israel, and to reach Gaza they must slip through Egyptian security. Even if successful, turning the Palestinian territories into an al-Qaeda base hinges on the reception the foreign jihadis receive from the local authorities; both Fatah and Hamas, however, view al-Qaeda's presence as a threat and will not welcome the new arrivals.

Al-Qaeda's Hamas problem

Operational limitations are not the only factor constraining al-Qaeda's desire to join the Palestinian front. In recent years its relationship with Hamas has grown increasingly sour, finally developing into a full-blown rivalry. It was not always this way. Contrary to its negative view of the Palestinian Authority, which it deemed an apostate regime, al-Qaeda initially held a positive opinion of Hamas and its (late) leader Sheikh Ahmad Yasin. Although the two movements had ideological differences, al-Qaeda saw Hamas as a fellow jihadi group, rather than as the Palestinian branch of the Muslim Brotherhood, especially in the first few years of the second Palestinian intifada. Al-Qaeda approved of Hamas's refusal to join the political system of the Palestinian Authority and its leading role in attack-ing Israel. Its regular use of suicide bombing demonstrated tactical affinity with al-Qaeda and rendered this tactic more legitimate in the eyes of many Muslims. Al-Qaeda must have been unhappy with Hamas's attempts to distance itself from al-Qaeda following 11 September 2001, but it still identified with Hamas's struggle.

But when Hamas began to reconsider its strategy in the Palestinian arena and its approach to Israel, the ideological gap between the two movements widened, eventually producing a war of words. Loyal to the view that the Palestinian question is primarily a Muslim, not a Palestinian, affair, al-Qaeda is unwilling to show deference to the Palestinian movements; it sees itself as fulfilling a responsibility to the umma by offering advice and sounding alarm bells about the misguided actions of the Palestinian groups.16 Moreover, al-Qaeda doctrine specifies that Palestine is not an isolated conflict but part of a broader war between Islam and the West. Therefore, the struggle requires expansion beyond a narrow nationalistic perspective17 and is intrinsically linked to al-Qaeda's war against the US-led camp.

Specifically, three major Hamas decisions drew al-Qaeda's ire: its participation in the elections for the Palestinian legislative council (January 2006), its power-sharing agreement with Fatah (February 2007), and its refusal to impose sharia after ousting Fatah loyalists from the Gaza Strip (June 2007). At every step, outspoken al-Qaeda leaders offered advice and then responded with harsh criticism when Hamas rejected their positions. Al-Qaeda's statements underscored differences regarding the obligation to liberate an Islamic land, the best way to con-front Israel, the role of democracy, the relationship between nationalism and Islam, and even the status of Shi'ites. Expressing general disappointment, al-Zawahiri concluded that Hamas had transformed from 'a mujahid movement to part of the Arab consensus which surrenders to America, the Arab consensus which sells the lands of the Muslims'.

Al-Qaeda accuses Hamas of recognising Israel indirectly. Recognition, al-Zawahiri has argued, takes various forms. Because the UN is based on the principle of aspiring to peaceful relations among all member states, as well as respect for their sovereignty and the integrity of their territories, participating in a Palestinian government with recognised status in the UN amounts to recognising Israel.23 Hamas's acceptance of the legitimacy of the Palestinian Authority, founded on the Oslo Accords in which the Palestine Liberation Organisation accepted Israel's right to exist, is also considered an implied recognition of Israel. When Hamas, in an attempt to break inter-national isolation, declared that it would respect international resolutions despite its refusal to recognise Israel's right to exist, al-Zawahiri character-ised the difference between the two formulations as semantic. If anything, al-Zawahiri argued, 'respect' shows higher esteem than 'recognition'.

The intensity of the exchange between the two movements fluctuated until suddenly reaching a peak in February 2008, when al-Baghdadi ratcheted up al-Qaeda's attack on Hamas to new levels. Al-Baghdadi's statement was unusual; normally his messages were restricted to the situation in Iraq. Not this time. In an audio message dedicated to events in Palestine and titled 'The Religion is the Advice', al-Baghdadi accused Hamas's leaders of betraying their religion and the umma. He repeated al-Qaeda's charges against Hamas but then crossed a red line by directly challenging Hamas's control over the Gaza Strip, first by calling on Palestinians to establish Salafi groups to guide the Palestinian people in preparation for the arrival of foreign jihadis, and then, more importantly, by calling on members of Hamas's military wing, the al-Qassam brigades, to split from Hamas and isolate its leadership.

Al-Qaeda's Palestinian dilemma

Subjected to harsh criticism throughout the Muslim world, al-Qaeda is seeking to salvage its reputation and gain new recruits to save its collapsing effort in Iraq. Becoming the knight of the Palestinian cause, particularly by targeting Israel, could provide it a lifeline and a possible way out of its predicament. For this scenario to materialise, al-Qaeda would need greater presence in the Palestinian territories, but operational limitations do not allow the sending of significant numbers of foreign jihadis into either the West Bank or the Gaza Strip. In Gaza, even if its operatives were to succeed in infiltrating the border, the tight clan-based nature of the strip would make it virtually impossible to operate without being detected by Hamas.

Theoretically, al-Qaeda could draw on local Salafi sympathisers, including Palestinians who trained in its camps in Afghanistan and Pakistan's tribal areas, to lead local Palestinian cells on its behalf. A few such attempts have been documented, but in general these efforts have had no significant impact. The formation in recent years of Gazan Salafi groups that identify with al-Qaeda35 (although denying any organisational ties with the group) has been equally futile. Some such groups represent families who, in the struggle for resources, found the Salafi stream an available and useful niche. Jaish al-Islam, responsible for the March 2007 kidnapping of British journal-ist Alan Johnston, is the most prominent among these groups. It has some genuine Salafis in its ranks, but its core comprises members of the Dugmush clan, known for many years for its criminal activities and inclination to shift alliances. As part of Hamas's efforts to consolidate its position in Gaza, in 2008 it clamped down on Jaish al-Islam, sending a strong signal that it would not tolerate challenges to its rule.

In the face of these difficulties, al-Qaeda chose a riskier strategy that is guaranteed to alienate Hamas even further. It has opted for the 'off-the-shelf' option – converting Hamas forces into a jihadi outfit by encouraging members of Hamas's military wing to switch sides to al-Qaeda, providing an already-trained force within the Palestinian territories. Al-Qaeda is aware of the internal schism within Hamas and its radical wing's dissatisfaction with the movement's willingness to suspend or reduce the resistance to Israel while consolidating its control of Gaza and pushing to take over the Palestinian Authority in the West Bank. Al-Qaeda believes this conflict may make some among Hamas's military wing amenable to defection to maintain the violent struggle. Moreover, experience from other fronts reveals that many young fighters, untrained for other, respectable jobs, are attached to the continuation of conflict, which offers them a source of income and social status.

Palestinian political violence

Palestinian political violence refers to acts of violence or terror motivated by Palestinian nationalism. These political objectives include self-determination in and sovereignty over Palestine, the "liberation of Palestine" and recognition of a Palestinian state, either in place of both Israel and the Palestinian territories, or solely in the Palestinian territories. Periodically directed toward more limited goals such as the release of Palestinian prisoners in Israel, another key aim is to advance the Palestinian right of return.

Palestinian groups that have been involved in politically motivated violence include the Palestinian Liberation Organization (PLO), Fatah, the Popular Front for the Liberation of Palestine (PFLP), the Popular Front for the Liberation of Palestine – General Command (PFLP-GC), the Democratic Front for the Liberation of Palestine, the Abu Nidal Organization, the Palestinian Islamic Jihad, and Hamas. The PLO officially renounced terrorism in 1988, and Fatah says it no longer engages in terrorism, although the Authority continues to incentivize terrorism by awarding large stipends to the families of Palestinians killed or arrested while committing acts of terrorism via the Palestinian Authority Martyr's Fund, payouts that absorb 7% of the Authority's national budget. The PFLP-GC has been internationally inactive. The Abu Nidal organization all but dissolved on his death and exists only in name.

Tactics have included hostage taking, plane hijackings, stone throwing, stabbing, shootings, and bombings. Several of these groups are considered terrorist organizations by the United States government, Canada and the European Union.

Palestinian political violence has targeted Israelis, Palestinians, Lebanese, Jordanians, Egyptians, Americans and citizens of other countries. The attacks have taken place within and outside Israel and have been directed at both military and civilian targets. Israeli statistics state that 3,500 Israelis have been killed and 25,000 have been wounded as a result of Palestinian violence since the establishment of the state of Israel in 1948. These figures include soldiers as well as civilians, including those killed in exchanges of gunfire. Israeli statistics listing 'hostile terrorist attacks' also include incidents in which stones are thrown. Suicide bombings constituted just 0.5% of Palestinian attacks against Israelis in the first two years of the Al Aqsa Intifada, though this percentage accounted for half of the Israelis killed in that period.

History

Overview and context

In protest against the Balfour Declaration, which proposed Palestine as a homeland for the Jewish people, and its implementation under a League of Nations Mandate for Great Britain, Palestinians, both Muslim and Christian, from November 1918 onwards, began to organize in opposition to Zionism. By the end of Ottoman rule, the Jewish population of Palestine was 56,000 or one-sixth of the population. Hostility to Jewish immigration led to incidents, such as the riots of April 1920, the Jaffa riots of 1921, the 1929 Palestine riots, until a general Arab revolt broke out for three years, in 1936–1939, which was crushed, with the loss of 5,000 lives, by the British army. After the passing of the United Nations Partition Plan for Palestine in 1947 which called for the establishment of independent Arab and Jewish States, a Palestinian Civil War broke out. On the declaration of the state of Israel, 15 May 1948, a full-scale war, involving also the intervention of neighbouring Arab states, took place, with casualties of 6,000 Israelis and, according to the 1958 survey by Arif al-Arif, 13,000 Palestinians and the exodus, through expulsion, or panicked flight, of approximately 700,000 Arab Palestinians who subsequently became refugees. In the Six-Day War, a further 280,000–360,000 Palestinians became refugees, and the remaining Palestinian territories were also occupied from Jordan and from Egypt, and later began to be settled by Jewish and Israeli settlers, while the Palestinians were placed under military administration. While historically, Palestinian militancy was fragmented into several groups, the PLO led, and eventually united, most factions, while conducting military campaigns that varied from airplane hijackings, militant operations and civil protest. In 1987, a mass revolt, of predominantly civil resistance, called the First Intifada, exploded, leading to the Madrid Conference of 1991, and subsequently to the Oslo I Accord, which produced an interim understanding allowing a new Palestinian authority, the Palestinian National Authority (PNA) to exercise limited autonomy in 3% (later 17%) of the West Bank, and parts of the Gaza Strip not used or earmarked for Israeli settlement. Frustration over the perceived failure of the peace talks to yield a Palestinian state led to the outbreak of the Al Aqsa Intifada in September 2000, which ended in 2005, coincident with the Israeli withdrawal from Gaza. The rise of Hamas, the use of Palestinian rocketry and Israel's control of Gaza's borders, has led to further chronic violence, culminating in a further two conflicts, the Gaza War of 2008–09 and Operation Pillar of Defense in 2012. It is estimated that since 1920, when the first riots against Jews broke out, 90,785 Arabs including Palestinians have died, and some 67,602 been wounded in all wars and conflicts between Israel and its neighbors. On the other hand, 24,841 Jews and Israelis have died and 35,356 have been wounded during the same period. Since 1967, some reports estimate that some 40% of the male population of the West Bank and Gaza have been arrested or detained in Israeli prisons for political or military reasons.

UN Partition Plan to establishment of PLO (1947–1964)

Around 400 Palestinian 'infiltrators' were killed by Israeli Security Forces each year in 1951, 1952 and 1953; a similar number and probably far more were killed in 1950. 1,000 or more were killed in 1949. At least 100 were killed during 1954–1956. In total upward of 2,700 and possibly as many as 5,000 'infiltrators' were killed by the IDF, police, and civilians along Israel's borders between 1949 and 1956. Most of the people in question were refugees attempting to return to their homes, take back possessions that had been left behind during the war and to gather crops from their former fields and orchards inside the new Israeli state. Meron Benivasti states that the fact that the "infiltrators" were for the most part former inhabitants of the land returning for personal, economic and sentimental reasons was suppressed in Israel as it was feared that this may lead to an understanding of their motives and to the justification of their actions.

Throughout the period 1949–56 the Egyptian government opposed the movement of refugees from the Gaza strip into Israel, but following the IDF's Gaza Raid on February 28, 1955, the Egyptian authorities facilitated militant infiltration but still continued to oppose civilian infiltration. At first, Palestinians were trying to go back to their houses or to retrieve property but after 1950 these acts became much more violent and included killings of civilians in nearby cities.

After Israel's Operation Black Arrow in 1955 which came as a result of a series of massacres in the city of Rehovot, the Palestinian fedayeen were incorporated into an Egyptian unit. John Bagot Glubb, a high-ranking British army general who worked with the Arab Legion, explained in his autobiographical history of the period how he convinced the Legion to arm and train the fedayeen for free. The Israeli government cites dozens of these attacks as "Major Arab Terrorist Attacks against Israelis prior to the 1967 Six-Day War". Between 1951 and 1956, 400 Israelis were killed and 900 wounded by fedayeen attacks.; according to the Anti-Defamation League "[i]n 1955 alone, 260 Israeli citizens were killed or wounded by fedayeen".

Black September

Various clashes between the fedayeen and the army occurred between the years 1968–1970. The situation climaxed in September 1970, when several attempts to assassinate king Hussein failed. On September 7, 1970, in the series of Dawson's Field hijackings, three planes were hijacked by PFLP: a SwissAir and a TWA that were landed in Azraq area and a Pan Am that was landed in

Cairo. Then on September 9, a BOAC flight from Bahrain was also hijacked to Zarqa. The PFLP announced that the hijackings were intended "to pay special attention to the Palestinian problem". After all hostages were removed, the planes were dramatically blown up in front of TV cameras.

A bitterly fought 10-day civil war known as Black September ensued, drawing involvement by Syria and Iraq, and sparking troop movements by Israel and the United States Navy. The number of people killed on all sides were estimated as high as 3,500, other sources claiming it to be as high as 20,000.

Battles between Palestinian guerrilla forces and the Jordanian army continued during the closing months of 1970 and the first six months of 1971. In November 1971, members of the Palestinian Black September group, who took their name from the civil war, assassinated Jordanian Prime Minister Wasfi al-Tal in Cairo. In December the group made an unsuccessful attempt to assassinate the Jordanian ambassador in Britain.

Relocation to Lebanon and Lebanese Civil War

In the aftermath of Black September in Jordan, many Palestinians arrived in Lebanon, among them Yasser Arafat and the Palestinian Liberation Organization (PLO). In the early 1970s their presence exacerbated an already tense situation in Lebanon, and in 1975 the Lebanese Civil War broke out. Beginning with street fighting in Beirut between Christian Phalangists and Palestinian militiamen, the war quickly deteriorated into a conflict between two loosely defined factions: the side wishing to preserve the status quo, consisting primarily of Maronite militias, and the side seeking change, which included a variety of militias from leftist organizations and guerrillas from rejectionist Palestinian (nonmainstream PLO) organizations. The Lebanese civil war lasted until 1990 and resulted in an estimated 130,000 to 250,000 civilian fatalities and one million wounded.

After Black September, the PLO and its offshoots waged an international campaign against Israelis. Notable events were the Munich Olympics massacre (1972), the hijacking of several civilian airliners (some were thwarted, see for example: Entebbe Operation), the Savoy Hotel attack, the Zion Square explosive refrigerator and the Coastal Road massacre. During the 1970s and the early 1980s, Israel suffered attacks from PLO bases in Lebanon, such as the Avivim school bus massacre in 1970, the Maalot massacre in 1974 (where Palestinian militants massacred 21 school children) and the Nahariya attack led by Samir Kuntar in 1979, as well as a terrorist bombing by Ziad Abu Ein that killed two Israeli 16-year-olds and left 36 other youths wounded during the Lag BaOmer cerebration in Tiberias. Following the 1982 Israeli invasion of Lebanon, called "Operation Peace for Galilee" by the IDF, and the exile of the PLO to Tunis, Israel had a relatively quiet decade.

International terrorism and internal struggles in 1980s

Mass internal executions of members of the Abu Nidal Organization and their families were conducted by Abu Nidal and his key associates in 1987–

1988. The number of executed is estimated at 600 people, mostly Palestinians, done in several separate locations in Syria, Lebanon and Libya.

First Intifada (1987–1993)

Palestinian rioters in Qalandiya throw rocks from behind an ambulance during a riot as part of the "Nakba" protests.

The First Intifada was characterized more by grassroots and non-violent political actions from among the population in the Israeli occupied Palestinian territories. A total of 160 Israelis and 2,162 Palestinians were killed, including 1,000 Palestinians killed by other Palestinians under the accusation of being collaborators. The Intifada lasted five years and ended with the signing of the Oslo Accords. The strategy of non-violence, though widespread among Palestinians, was not always adhered to, and there were youth who threw molotov cocktails and stones, with such violence generally directed against Israeli soldiers and settlers.

There were two attacks that represented new developments in terms of political violence inside Israel in this period. The first Palestinian suicide attack took place on July 6, 1989, when a member of the Palestinian Islamic Jihad boarded the Tel Aviv Jerusalem bus 405. He walked up to the driver and pulled the wheel to the right, driving the vehicle into a ravine, killing 16 people. The end of the intifada also saw the first use of suicide bombing as a tactic by Palestinian militants. On April 16, 1993, Hamas carried out the Mehola Junction bombing, in which operative Saher Tamam al-Nabulsi detonated his explosives-laden car between two buses. One person, a Palestinian, other than the attacker was killed, and 21 were wounded.

Oslo Accords to Camp David Summit (1993–2000)

The years between the intifadas were marked by intense diplomatic activity between Israel and Palestinians as well as the creation of the Palestinian National Authority. In this period, suicide bombings of Israeli buses and crowded spaces as a regular tactic, particularly by Hamas and Islamic Jihad. Attacks during this period include the Beit Lid massacre, a double-suicide bombing at a crowded junction that killed 21 people, and the Dizengoff Center massacre, a suicide bombing outside a Tel Aviv shopping mall that killed 13 people.

Second Intifada (2000–2005)

According to B'Tselem, as of July 10, 2005, over 400 members of the Israeli Security forces, and 821 Israeli civilians have been killed by Palestinians since the signing of the Oslo Accords in 1993, 553 of whom were killed within the 1949 Armistice lines, mainly by suicide bombings. Targets of attacks included buses, Israeli checkpoint, restaurants, discothèques, shopping malls, a university, and civilian homes. During the Second Intifada alone 1,137 Israelis were killed by Palestinians, according to the Israeli Ministry of Foreign Affairs (counted since September 29, 2000, retrieved at December 26, 2007).

In October 2000 a Palestinian mob lynched two non-combatant Israel

Defense Forces reservists, Vadim Nurzhitz (sometimes spelled as Norzhich) and Yossi Avrahami (or Yosef Avrahami), who had accidentally entered the Palestinian Authority-controlled city of Ramallah in the West Bank. The brutality of the event, captured in a photo of a Palestinian rioter proudly waving his blood-stained hands to the crowd below, sparked international outrage and further intensified the ongoing conflict between Israeli and Palestinian forces.

A spate of suicide bombings and attacks, aimed mostly at civilians (such as the Dolphinarium discotheque suicide bombing), was launched against Israel and elicited a military response. A suicide bombing dubbed the Passover Massacre (30 Israeli civilians were killed at Park hotel, Netanya) climaxed a bloody month of March 2002, in which more than 130 Israelis, mostly civilians, were killed in attacks. Israel launched Operation Defensive Shield. The operation led to the apprehension of many members of militant groups, as well as their weaponry and equipment. 497 Palestinians and 30 Israelis were killed during Operation Defensive Shield.

In 2004, 31 people were killed and 159 others were wounded in a simultaneous attack against multiple tourist destinations in Egypt. Of the dead, 15 were Egyptians, 12 were from Israel, two from Italy, one from Russia, and one was an Israeli-American. According to the Egyptian government, the bombers were Palestinians led by Iyad Saleh, who had tried to enter Israel to carry out attacks there but were unsuccessful.

2005–present

In the mid-2000s Hamas started putting greater emphasis on its political characteristics and strengthened its popularity amongst Palestinians. In 2006 Palestinian legislative elections Hamas won a majority in the Palestinian Legislative Council, prompting the United States and many European countries to cut off all funds to Hamas and the Palestinian Authority, insisting that Hamas must recognize Israel, renounce violence and accept previous peace pacts.

After the Israel's unilateral disengagement plan in 2005 and the 2006 Palestinian legislative elections Hamas took control over all the Gaza Strip in June 2007 in a bloody coup. Palestinian militant groups in the Gaza strip increased the firing of Qassam rockets, mortars and Grad missiles on southern Israel. Attacks continued outside the Gaza strip perimeter, including the attack that resulted in the Israeli soldier Gilad Shalit being captured and held in the Gaza Strip for over five years.

Hamas has made use of guerrilla tactics in the Gaza Strip and to a lesser degree the West Bank. Hamas has adapted these techniques over the years since its inception. According to a 2006 report by rival Fatah party, Hamas had smuggled "between several hundred and 1,300 tons" of advanced rockets, along with other weaponry, into Gaza. Some Israelis and some Gazans both noted similarities in Hamas's military buildup to that of Hezbollah in the 2006 Israel-Hezbollah war.

Hamas has used IEDs and anti-tank rockets against the IDF in Gaza. The latter include standard RPG-7 warheads and home-made rockets such as the Al-Bana, Al-Batar and Al-Yasin. The IDF has a difficult, if not impossible time trying to find hidden weapons caches in Palestinian areas – this is due to the high local support base Hamas enjoys.

During the Gaza War (2008–09), Palestinian militant groups fired rockets aimed at civilian targets which struck the cities of Ashdod, Beersheba and Gedera. The military wing of Hamas said that after a week from the start, it had managed to fire 302 rockets, at an average of 44 rockets daily. 102 rockets and 35 mortars were fired by Fatah at Israel. Over 750 rockets and mortars were fired from Gaza into Israel during the conflict wounded 182 civilians, killing 3 people, and causing minor suffering to another 584 people suffering from shock and anxiety. Several rockets landed in schools and one fell close to a kindergarten, all located in residential areas. The UN fact finding mission stated that this constituted a deliberate attack against the civilian population and was unjustifiable in international law.

In 2012, terror attacks against Israelis in the West Bank increased compared to 2011. The number of terror attacks in the West Bank increased from 320 in 2011 to 578 in 2012. The attacks mainly involved rock throwing, Molotov cocktails, firearms and explosives.

In 2013, Hamas stated that the "kidnapping of IDF soldiers is at the heart of Palestinian culture."

Involvement of governments

Israeli officials and other political figures have harshly criticized what they regard as Palestinians inciting violence against Jews and Israel.

Palestinian Authority TV has been accused of glorifying terror. In 2011, Israeli PM Benyamin Netanyahu stated that the incitement promulgated by the Palestinian Authority was destroying Israel's confidence, and he condemned what he regarded as the glorification of the murderers of the Fogel family in Itamar on PA television. The perpetrator of the murders had been described as a "hero" and a "legend" by members of his family, during a weekly program.

Isi Leibler wrote in the Jerusalem Post that Mahmoud Abbas and his chief negotiator Saeb Erekat deny Israel's right to exist and promote vicious hatred against Jews, in statements made in Arabic. He claimed that the state-controlled Palestinian media praised the murders committed by Palestinians. Abbas al-Sayed who perpetrated the Passover suicide attack at the Park Hotel in Netanya which killed 30 civilians was described by Abbas as a "hero" and "symbol of the Palestinian Authority."

Following the Itamar massacre and a bombing in Jerusalem, 27 US senators sent a letter requesting the US Secretary of State to identify the administration's steps to end Palestinian incitement to violence against Jews and Israel that they said was occurring within the "Palestinian media, mosques and schools, and even by individuals or institutions affiliated with the Palestinian Authority."

The United Nations body UNESCO stopped funding a children's magazine sponsored by the Palestinian Authority that commended Hitler's killing of Jews. It deplored this publication as contrary to its principles of building tolerance and respect for human rights and human dignity.

Palestinian Media Watch reported that the Palestinian Authority spent more than $5 million a month paying salaries to Palestinians and Israeli Arabs imprisoned in Israel for terror crimes. They also stated that groups in a summer camp for children sponsored by PA Prime Minister Salam Fayyad were named after militants: Dalal Mughrabi, who led the Coastal Road Massacre; Salah Khalaf, head of Black September that carried out the Munich Massacre; and Abu Ali Mustafa, the general secretary of the Popular Front for the Liberation of Palestine who perpetrated many attacks. Saddam Hussein, the leader of Iraq, donated $25,000 to the families of suicide bombers, and $10,000 to the families of Palestinian civilians killed by the Israeli military.

After Israel agreed to hand over the bodies of dead Palestinian suicide bombers and other militants as part of what the Israeli Government described as 'a humanitarian gesture' to PA chairman Mahmoud Abbas to help the peace process, the Palestinian Authority planned a national rally to honour them and to provide full military funerals. The bodies included the suicide bombers that perpetrated the bus bombing in Jerusalem's Shmuel Hanavi neighborhood which killed twenty-three people, many of them children, and the attacker in the Cafe Hillel bombing. Israel will also return the remains of the bombers that committed the bombings on two buses in Beersheba in 2004 killing 16 people, the Stage night club bombing, the attack on the open-air Hadera market as well as the attackers of the Savoy Hotel in Tel Aviv who killed eight hostages. The Palestinian Authority and Hamas both planned official ceremonies and PA president Abbas attended a ceremony at his Muqataa compound. Prisoners Affairs Minister Qaraqi called on Palestinians for a day of celebration. The rally in honor of the dead will be attended by PA President Mahmoud Abbas, PLO leaders, and families of the dead militants. The dead are considered martyrs by Palestinians, but viewed as terrorists by Israelis.

Violence against civilians

According to B'Tselem, the Israeli Information Center for Human Rights in the Occupied Territories, 500 Israeli civilians were killed by Palestinians from September 29, 2000, to March 31, 2012, in Israel, and another 254 Israeli civilians were killed in the Gaza Strip and the West Bank.

B'tselem reported that the main argument used to justify violence against civilians is that "all means are legitimate in fighting for independence against a foreign occupation". B'Tselem criticized this argument, saying it is completely baseless, and contradicts the fundamental principle of international humanitarian law.

"According to this principle, civilians are to be protected from the consequences of warfare, and any attack must discriminate between civilians and military targets. This principle is part of international customary law; as such, it applies to every state, organization, and person, even those who are not party to any relevant convention."

B'Tselem further noted that Palestinian spokespersons distinguish between attacks inside Israel proper and attacks directed at settlers in the Occupied Territories, stating that since the settlements are illegal and many settlers belong to Israel's security forces, settlers are not entitled to the international law protections granted to civilians. Human rights group B'tselem rejected this argument, and stated:

"The illegality of the settlements has no effect at all on the status of their civilian residents. The settlers constitute a distinctly civilian population, which is entitled to all the protections granted civilians by international law. The Israeli security forces' use of land in the settlements or the membership of some settlers in the Israeli security forces does not affect the status of the other residents living among them, and certainly does not make them proper targets of attack. B'Tselem strongly opposes the attempts to justify attacks against Israeli civilians by using distorted interpretations of international law. Furthermore, B'Tselem demands that the Palestinian Authority do everything within its power to prevent future attacks and to prosecute the individuals involved in past attacks."

Rocket attacks within the green line

Palestinian rocket and mortar attacks on Israel from the Gaza Strip have occurred since 2001. Between 2001 and January 2009, over 8,600 rockets had been launched, leading to 28 deaths and several hundred injuries, as well as widespread psychological trauma and disruption of daily life.

The weapons, often generically referred to as Qassams, were initially crude and short-range, mainly affecting the Israeli city of Sderot and other communities bordering the Gaza Strip. However, in 2006 more sophisticated rockets began to be deployed, reaching the larger coastal city of Ashkelon, and by early 2009 major cities Ashdod and Beersheba had been hit by Katyusha and Grad rockets.

Attacks have been carried out by all Palestinian armed groups, and, prior to the 2008–2009 Gaza War, were consistently supported by most Palestinians, although the stated goals have been mixed. The attacks, widely condemned for targeting civilians, have been described as terrorism by United Nations, European Union and Israeli officials, and are defined as war crimes by human rights groups Amnesty International and Human Rights Watch.

Defenses constructed specifically to deal with the weapons include fortifications for schools and bus stops as well as an alarm system named Red Color. Iron Dome, a system to intercept short-range rockets, was developed by Israel and first deployed in the spring of 2011 to protect Beersheba and Ashkelon, but officials and experts warned that it would not be completely effective. Shortly thereafter, it intercepted a Palestinian Grad rocket for the first time.

The attacks were a stated cause of the Gaza blockade, the Gaza War (Dec 27, 2008 – Jan 21, 2009) and other Israeli military operations in the Gaza Strip, including Operation Rainbow (May 2004), Operation Days of Penitence (2004), the 2006 Israel-Gaza conflict, Operation Autumn Clouds (2006), and Operation Hot Winter (2008).

Attacks began in 2001. Since then, nearly 4,800 rockets have hit southern Israel, just over 4,000 of them since Israel withdrew from the Gaza Strip in August 2005. The range of the rockets has increased over time. The original Qassam rocket has a range of about 10 km (6.2 mi) but more advanced rockets, including versions of the old Soviet Grad or Katyusha have hit Israeli targets 40 km (25 mi) from Gaza.

Some analysts see the attacks as a shift away from reliance on suicide bombing, which was previously Hamas's main method of attacking Israel, and an adoption of the rocket tactics used by Lebanese militant group Hezbollah.

Denial of service attacks on the emergency services

There have been a number of reports in the Israeli press about denial of service attacks by Palestinians on the Magen David Adom and other emergency call lines. A spokesman said that they had received up to 2400 harassing calls per day to the Beersheba MDA office deputy Mayor of Sderot said that after investigation that Palestinians were blocking the ability of citizens to seek for help after mortar and missile attacks. According to the MDA director in the Negev some callers identified themselves as Palestinians and said that they had been paid to make the calls. The director said the calls were intended to block the MDA's ability to provide emergency services particularly during major events such as mortar attacks. As of 2006 filtering systems had been developed and deployed to handle with this type of calls, according to MDA 2008 report one filtering system recognized more than 129,000 phone calls as abusive calls.

Threats of using Chemical and Biological weapons

In a testimony given to the congress, it had been reported that Hamas was seeking to acquire chemical and biological weapons during 1990–1993.

In a statement by Director of Central Intelligence George J. Tenet before the Senate Select Committee on Intelligence on The Worldwide Threat in 2000: Global Realities of Our National Security, it was stated that Hamas was pursuing a capability to conduct attacks with toxic chemicals.

The plot for Passover massacre included the use of Cyanide. 4 kilos of Cyanide had been bought and prepared for a chemical attack.

In 2003, one report by the CSIS stated The Palestinian terrorist group that allegedly recruited a Canadian to carry out attacks in North America may be developing chemical weapons.

On 26 June 2006, Yedioth Ahronot published a report stating that Fatah's armed wing said it had developed biological, chemical weapons, which would be used if Israel invaded Gaza. 'We say to Olmert, Peretz: Your threats of invasion do not frighten us. We will surprise you with new weapons you have not faced until now,' Al-Aqsa Brigades says.

On June 29, 2006, the al-Aqsa Martyrs Brigades, claimed to have launched a single rocket with a chemical warhead against the southern part of Israel. An Israeli military spokeswoman said the army had not detected that any such rocket was fired, nor was there any report of such a weapon hitting Israel.

Israeli news reports have stated that chemical weapons, and missiles with chemical warheads from Libya have been transferred to Palestinians in Gaza, with some allegedly transferred via Sudan, although Sudanese officials have denied the accusations.

Palestinian stone-throwing

Palestinian stone-throwing is a violent political statement celebrated in the literature of the Palestinian national liberation movement. Stone throwing was the primary tactic of the First Intifada (1997 - 1993.) It encompasses the practice of throwing stones by hand and using powerful slings variously aimed at Israel security personnel, Israeli civilians, and at both civilian and military vehicles. It has resulted in the death of both Israelis and Arabs unknowingly targeted by stone-throwers.

Internal violence

B'Tselem reports that from September 29, 2000, to March 31, 2012, there were 669 Palestinians killed by Palestinians. Of those, 134 were killed for suspected collaboration with Israel.

Concerning the killing of Palestinians by other Palestinians, a January 2003 Humanist magazine article reports:

For over a decade the PA has violated Palestinian human rights and civil liberties by routinely killing civilians—including collaborators, demonstrators, journalists, and others—without charge or fair trial. Of the total number of Palestinian civilians killed during this period by both Israeli and Palestinian security forces, 16 percent were the victims of Palestinian security forces.

... According to Freedom House's annual survey of political rights and civil liberties, Freedom in the World 2001–2002, the chaotic nature of the Intifada along with strong Israeli reprisals has resulted in a deterioration of living conditions for Palestinians in Israeli-administered areas. The survey states:

"Civil liberties declined due to: shooting deaths of Palestinian civilians by Palestinian security personnel; the summary trial and executions of alleged collaborators by the Palestinian Authority (PA); extra-judicial killings of suspected collaborators by militias; and the apparent official encouragement of Palestinian youth to confront Israeli soldiers, thus placing them directly in harm's way."

Internal Palestinian violence has been called an Intrafada.

Designations of Terrorism

The United States and European Union have designated the Abu Nidal Organisation, Al-Aqsa Martyrs Brigades, Hamas, Islamic Jihad, Palestine

Liberation Front, the PFLP and PFLP-GC as terrorist organisations. A United States Congress decision from 1987 also described the PLO as a terrorist organization

The military wing of Hamas is also designated as a terrorist organization by Israel, Canada, Germany, Japan, Jordan, the United Kingdom and Australia.

According to an Israeli NGO, if the Palestinian Authority is accepted into the International Criminal Court (ICC), it will become liable to lawsuits. In anticipation, the civil rights NGO Shurat HaDin Law Center, is collecting thousands of testimonies from Israeli victims of Palestinian terror attacks to present at the ICC. The stated aim of the campaign is to prevent the Palestinian Authority from suing Israelis for alleged war crimes at the ICC in The Hague.

Palestinian attitudes towards political violence

1995–2000

A study conducted by Mkhaimer Abusada of Al-Azhar University explored attitudes towards the use of political violence. Four questions were posed on the subject of political violence to over a thousand respondents randomly selected from localities in the West Bank and Gaza Strip. The first question was: "Do you support the continuing resort of some Palestinian factions to armed operations against Israeli targets in Gaza and Jericho?" Overall, 56% of respondents responded negatively. Those affiliated with leftist groups showed the highest levels of support for armed attacks against Israelis (74%), while those affiliated with parties supporting the peace process showed the lowest levels (24%). The Islamic opposition was split, with slightly over half in favor, and slightly less than half opposed.

In September 1995, survey participants were asked whether they supported, opposed or had no opinion with regard to "armed attacks against Israeli army targets," "armed attacks against Israeli settlers," and "armed attacks against Israeli civilian targets." The majority supported the use of armed attacks against Israeli military targets and settlers in the West Bank and Gaza Strip. Support crossed all party lines and groups, and was highest among the Islamic opposition (91% and 84%) and the leftists (90% and 89%), though a significant majority of those who supported the peace process also supported armed attacks on military targets and settlers (69% and 73%). To explain the apparent paradox in the latter position, Abusada quotes Shikaki (1996) who, "contends that Palestinian support for the use of armed attacks against Israeli military targets and settlers does not indicate 'opposition to the peace process but Palestinian insistence that the process entails an end to occupation and settlements.'" Palestinian support for armed attacks against Israeli civilian targets in Israel was 20% overall, with support being highest among those affiliated with the Islamic opposition (42%) and the leftists (32%), and lowest among supporters of the peace process (12%) and the National Independents (10%).

2000–04

A July 2001 poll conducted by the Palestinian Center for Policy & Survey Research (PSR) found that 58 percent of Palestinians supported armed attacks against Israeli civilians inside Israel and 92 percent supported armed confrontations against the Israeli army in the West Bank and the Gaza Strip. A May 2002 poll by the center found that support for bombings of civilians inside Israel dropped to 52%, but support for armed attacks against Israeli settlers remained "very high" at 89 percent. Support for armed attacks against soldiers stood at 92 percent. A poll after the 2003 Maxim restaurant suicide bombing, in which 20 Israelis were killed, found that 75 percent of Palestinians supported the attack, with support higher, "in the Gaza Strip (82%) compared to the West Bank (70%), in refugee camps (84%) compared to towns and villages (69%), among women (79%) compared to men (71%), among the young (78%) compared to the old (66%), among students (81%) compared to professionals (33%), and among supporters of Hamas (92%) compared to supporters of Fateh (69%)."

The firing of rockets from Beit Hanoun into Israel was acceptable to about three quarters of the Palestinian public in the occupied territories, and was higher in the West Bank (78%) compared to the Gaza Strip (71%), among students (83%) compared to merchants (63%), and among supporters of Hamas (86%) compared to supporters of Fatah (73%). While firing rockets from Beit Hanoun was supported by a majority of Palestinians (75%), 59% of the residents of Beit Hanoun rejected this practice. 83% of Palestinians favored a mutual cessation of violence.

A report by the Jerusalem Media and Communication Center, a Palestinian organization, showing trends based on polls conducted since 1997, indicated that Palestinian support for military operations against Israeli targets stood at 34–40 percent in 1997–1999, climbed to 65–85 percent in 2000–2004, and dropped back to 41 percent at the end of 2004. "Military operations" were defined as including shootings, car bombs and mortar rocket attacks, but not suicide bombings. A 2005 poll by the center indicated that 53 percent of Palestinians supported "the continuation of [the] Al-Aqsa Intifada, 50 percent supported "suicide bombings against Israeli civilians", and 36 percent supported "the resumption of military operations against Israeli targets".

A 2004 study by Victoroff et al. was conducted on a group of 52 boys, all 14 years old, from the al-Shati camp in Gaza. Forty-three percent of the boys reported that a family member had been wounded or killed by the IDF, and half lived in households where the father's employment was lost following the outbreak of the Second Intifada. "Sympathy for terrorism" was found to be correlated with depression and anxiety scores, as well as with the level of "perceived oppression," and "emotional distress". Of those who felt subject to unjust treatment, 77 percent expressed sympathy for terrorism.

2005–present

A March 2008 report by Palestinian Center for Policy & Survey Research

(PSR) noted that the level of support for armed attack against Israeli civilians inside Israel increased significantly with 67% supporting and 31% opposed, compared to support by 40% in 2005 and 55% in 2006. A February 2008 suicide bombing that killed one Israeli woman in Dimona was supported by 77% and opposed by 19%. An overwhelming majority of 84 percent supported the March 2008 Mercaz HaRav massacre, in which a Palestinian gunman killed eight students and wounded eleven in a Jerusalem school. Support for the attack was 91 percent in the Gaza Strip compared to 79 percent in the West Bank. Similar suicide attacks in 2005 had been less widely supported, with 29% support for a suicide attack that took place in Tel Aviv, and 37% support for another one in Beersheba.

The 2009 Hamas political violence took place in the Gaza Strip during and after the 2009 Gaza War. A series of violent acts, ranging from physical assaults, torture, and executions of Palestinians suspected of collaboration with the Israel Defense Forces, as well as members of the Fatah political party, occurred. According to Human Rights Watch, at least 32 people were killed by these attacks: 18 during the conflict and 14 afterward, and several dozen more were maimed, many by shots to the legs.

In 2012, the number of militant attacks in the West Bank rose from 320 in 2011 to 578 in 2012. During that same year, 282 attacks were carried out in Jerusalem, compared to 191 in 2011. According to an annual Shin Bet report, the increase is due in part to a 68% rise of attacks using molotov cocktails. However, the number of attacks involving firearms and explosives also grew by 42%—37 compared to 26 in 2011.

Palestinian groups involved in political violence

Hamas

Founded in 1987 by Ahmed Yassin and Mohammad Taha as an outgrowth of the Muslim Brotherhood, Hamas' goal is the establishment of a Palestinian state.

Armed wing is the Izz ad-Din al-Qassam Brigades; the sole target of its suicide bombings and missile attacks is Israel.

Took part in 2006 elections and won. After the 2007 Battle of Gaza the Hamas government was disbanded by Mahmoud Abbas but remained de facto rulers of the Gaza Strip.

- Currently led by Khaled Mashaal and Ismail Haniyeh
- Palestinian Islamic Jihad (PIJ) (founded 1970s)
- Formed by Fathi Shaqaqi as a branch of Egyptian Islamic Jihad
- Goal is the destruction of the state of Israel and replacement with an Islamist state
- Armed wing is the Al-Quds Brigades (Jerusalem brigades)
- Currently led by Ramadan Shallah, the Secretary General and Abd Al Aziz Awda

The Popular Resistance Committees

Islamist

- Founded in 2000 by Jamal Abu Samhadana who led the group until he was killed in 2006.
- Hamas linked group, based in the Gaza Strip
- Palestine Liberation Organization (PLO) (founded June 1964)
- Formed as the political representation of the Palestinian people
- Currently led by Mahmoud Abbas
- Sub-groups of the PLO
- Popular Front for the Liberation of Palestine (PFLP) (founded 1967)

Left-wing

Joined the PLO in 1968 and became the second-largest PLO faction, after Arafat's al-Fatah, but withdrew in 1974, accusing the group of moving away from the goal of abolishing the State of Israel. It was led by Abu Ali Mustapha until his assassination in 2001.

- Armed wing is the Abu Ali Mustapha Brigades and Jihad Jibril Brigades
- Currently led by Ahmad Sa'adat
- Democratic Front for the Liberation of Palestine (DFLP) (founded 1969)

Marxist-Leninist group that believes Palestinian national goals can be achieved only through revolution of the masses. Split into two factions in 1991; Nayif Hawatmah leads the majority and more hard-line faction, which continue to dominate the group. Joined with other rejectionist groups to form the Alliance of Palestinian Forces (APF) to oppose the Declaration of Principles signed in 1993. Broke from the APF – along with the PFLP – over ideological differences. Has made limited moves towards merging with the PFLP since the mid-1990s.

Abu Nidal organization (ANO), also known as Fatah - the Revolutionary Council (FRC), (founded 1974)

Split from PLO; part of the so-called rejectionist front, the ANO is a secular, nationalist group. Was led by Abu Nidal, widely regarded as the most ruthless of the Palestinian leaders, until his death in August 2002. According to Kameel Nasr, Arab and Israeli Terrorism, The group was infiltrated and influenced by Israeli security.

Palestine Liberation Front (PLF)

- Minor Left wing faction
- Founded in 196 by Ahmed Jibril and Shafiq al-Hout, re established in 1977 by Abu Abbas
- Arab Liberation Front (ALF)
- Minor faction tied to the Iraqi Ba'ath Party
- Founded in 1969, first leader was Zeid Heidar

Currently led by Rakad Salem

- As-Sa'iqa (VPLW)
- Palestinian branch of the Syrian Ba'ath Party
- Founded in 1966 as alternative to Fatah, organisation boycotts Palestinian National Authority and is opposed to Oslo Accords
- Organisation was not active during the Second Intifada

Currently led by Farhan Abu Al-Hayja.

- Palestinian Popular Struggle Front (PPSF)
- Minor Socialist faction formerly led by Samir Ghawshah
- Palestinian Arab Front (PAF)
- Minor Arab Nationalist faction
- Originally part of the ALF, split from the ALF in 1993
- Supports the Palestinian right of return and creation of Palestinian state within 1967 borders

Currently led by Jameel Shihadeh.

- Fatah (founded early 1960s)
- Palestinian nationalist political party
- Reverse acronym for "Harekat at-Tahrir al-Wataniyyeh al-Falastiniyyeh" ("Palestinian National Liberation Movement" in Arabic)
- Also known as the Movement for the National Liberation of Palestine
- Founded by Yasser Arafat in 1959. Took control of the PLO in 1968, with Arafat as chairman.

Currently led by Mahmoud Abbas

- Groups associated with Fatah
- Tanzim (founded 1995)
- Means "organization" in Arabic
- Loosely organized Fatah militia
- Led by Marwan Barghouti until his arrest in 2002.
- Force 17 (early 1970s–2007)
- Elite unit of the PLO once under Yasser Arafat's direct guidance.
- Acts as a versatile unit for combat and intelligence-gathering.
- Dismantled in 2007 and incorporated into the Palestinian Presidential Guard.
- Fatah Special Operations Group (Fatah-SOG)
- Founded in the early 1970s by Col. Abdullah Abd al-Hamid Labib
- Also known as the Martyrs of Tel Al Za'atar, Hawari, and Amn Araissi.
- Recently inactive (as of 2004)
- Ahmed Abu Reish Brigade
- Extremist offshoot of Fatah.

- Was involved in July 17, 2004 kidnappings in the Gaza Strip.
- Possibly linked to the Popular Resistance Committees
- Led by Ahmed Abu Reish
- Al Aqsa Martyrs Brigade

Responsible for many suicide bombings and shootings of Israeli civilians

Responsible for executing suspected conspirators and leaders of opposition against Arafat

Funded by Fatah and the Palestinian Authority

Offshoot of this group, Fatah Hawks, has carried out guerrilla attacks against Israeli military personnel in the Gaza Strip.

Black September Organization (1970–1973)

Began as a small cell of Fatah men determined to take revenge upon King Hussein and the Jordanian army for Black September in Jordan. Recruits from the PFLP, as-Sa'iqa, and other groups also joined.

Carried out Munich Massacre.

- Carried out Attack on the Saudi embassy in Khartoum
- Splinter groups of the PLO
- Popular Front for the Liberation of Palestine - General Command (PFLP-GC) (founded 1968)
- Splinter group from the PFLP, founded by Ahmed Jibril. Declared its focus would be military, not political. Was a member of the PLO, but left in 1974 for the same reasons as PFLP.
- al-Qaeda linked groups
- Army of Islam (Jaysh al-Islam)
- Also known as the Tawhid and Jihad Brigades and al-Qaeda in Palestine
- The group are an armed Gaza clan named Doghmush who are affiliated with al-Qaeda and Abu Qatada
- Abdullah Azzam Brigades
- Jund Ansar Allah (2008–)
- al-Qaeda-affiliated group in the Gaza Strip, founded in November 2008 by Abdel Latif Moussa
- In August 2009, the group proclaimed the creation of an Islamic emirate in Gaza and led an armed rebellion against Hamas.
- The group's leader Abdel Latif Moussa was killed during that rebellion.

Fatah al-Islam (2006–) al-Qaeda-affiliated group involved in a conflict with the Lebanese army in 2007 over control of Palestinian refugee camps, which caused the death of nearly 500 people.

The group was established in 2006 by Shaker al-Abssi who led the group until killed by Lebanese forces in 2007.

- Abu Mohamad Awad succeeded al-Abbsi as the group's leader.
- Jund al-Sham (1999–2008)
- Radical Islamist group set up by Palestinians and Syrians which operated in different areas of the Middle East.
- The group's leader Abu Youssef Sharqieh was captured by Lebanese forces during the 2007 conflict in Palestinian refugee camps.
- The group was disbanded in 2008 as its members joined Lebanese al-Qaeda affiliated group Osbat al-Ansar.
- Jaljalat (2006–)
- A Hamas-splinter organisation founded in 2006 by Mahmoud Taleb, a former al-Qassam Brigades commander, after he opposed Hamas joining the 2006 elections
- The group is affiliated with both Jund Ansar Allah and al-Qaeda
- Jahafil Al-Tawhid Wal-Jihad fi Filastin (2008–)
- al-Qaeda-affiliated group in the Gaza Strip, founded in November 2008 by Abu al-Walid al-Maqdisi
- Iran linked groups
- Sabireen Movement (2014-)
- Leadership converted to Shiism
- At odds with both Hamas and Palestinian Islamic Jihad
- Openly supports Hezbollah and Iran as well as their intervention on behalf of the Syrian Government

Al-Qaeda involvement in Asia

Al Qaeda involvement in Asia. It is believed that members of Al-Qaeda are in hiding along the border of Afghanistan and northwest sections of Pakistan. In Iraq, elements loosely associated with al-Qaeda, in the Jama'at al-Tawhid wal-Jihad organization commanded by Abu Musab al-Zarqawi, have played a key role in the War in Iraq.

Iraq

Osama bin Laden first took interest in Iraq when the country invaded Kuwait in 1990, raising concerns the secular Baathist government of Iraq might next set its sights on Saudi Arabia. In a letter sent to King Fahd, he offered to send an army of mujahedeen to defend Saudi Arabia, but the offer was rebuffed.

In November 2001, a month after the 11 September attacks, Mubarak al-Duri was contacted by Sudanese intelligence services who informed him that the FBI had sent Jack Cloonan and several other agents, to speak with a number of people known to have ties to Bin Laden. al-Duri and another Iraqi colleague agreed to meet with Cloonan in a safe house overseen by the intelligence service. They were asked whether there was any possible connection between Saddam Hussein and al-Qaeda, and laughed stating that Bin Laden hated the dictator who he believed was a "Scotch-drinking, woman-chasing apostate."

Links between Saddam's regime and al-Qaeda, as claimed by the Bush Administration (which formed a crucial part of the WMD justification for the Iraq invasion), were non-existent or exaggerated, according to the report of both the United States Government's 9/11 Commission and the Pentagon; despite these conclusions, Vice President Dick Cheney has continued to publicly assert an Iraqi–al-Qaeda link. Recently, the US has acknowledged that the role of al-Qaeda in post-invasion violence in Iraq was overstated. The US also claimed that al-Qaeda was in contact with the Kurdish Islamist group Ansar al-Islam from its inception in 1999; however, Ansar al-Islam's founder, Mullah Krekar, has staunchly denied any such link.

Since the 2003 invasion of Iraq, elements at first loosely associated with al-Qaeda, commanded by Abu Musab al-Zarqawi, have supported local resistance to the occupying coalition forces and the emerging government, particularly targeting Iraq's Shia majority. They have been implicated in the bombing of the United Nations headquarters in Iraq, as well as hundreds of other small and large scale attacks on the military and civilian targets. Eventually, al-Zarqawi claimed allegiance to bin Laden in October 2004.

Al-Zarqawi was killed by U.S. air strikes on a safe house near Baqubah on 7 June 2006. Before his death, he was allegedly trying to use Iraq as a launching pad for international terrorism, most notably dispatching suicide bombers to attack hotels and government targets in Jordan. Since the killing of al-Zarqawi, it was believed that Abu Ayyub al-Masri took over as head of "al-Qaeda in Iraq". On 3 September 2006 the second-in-command of "al-Qaeda in Iraq", Hamed Jumaa Farid al-Saeedi (also known as Abu Humam or Abu Rana), was arrested north of Baghdad, along with a group of his aides and followers.

In a 39-page document retrieved in November and a 16-page document retrieved in October gives insight on how Al-Qaeda in Iraq is in panic and fear. The documents reveal how local fighters are being mistreated by the foreign fighters and labeled as "scoundrels, sectarians, and non-believers." Abu-Tariq, states that the number of fighters has dwindled from 600 to 20 fighters.

Israel and Palestine

Bin Laden's and Ayman al-Zawahiri's repeatedly refer to the Palestinian cause in their manifestos and interviews.

Jund Ansar Allah, a group which claims to be inspired by Al-Qaeda, is active in the Gaza Strip.

Members of an al-Qaeda cell were convicted of the 2009 Murder of Yafim Weinstein near Nazareth.

Lebanon

Shakir al-Abssi, a former associate of al-Qaeda in Iraq, recruited Palestinian refugees in Lebanon into Fatah al-Islam and rose against the government. The exact nature of the group's al-Qaeda links remains a matter of controversy.

On 9 May 2008, the media outlet Presstv alleges that Al-Qaeda declared war on Hezbollah.

Saudi Arabia

On February 3, 2009, the government of Saudi Arabia published a list of 85 suspected terrorists. One key aspect of its international involvement has been to make alliances, which are often "underutilized.".

The Saudi government believed that all of these men were living outside of Saudi Arabia, and encouraged them to surrender themselves at the closest Saudi Embassy. Many of those named on the list were believed to be in Asia.

Yemen

Al-Qaeda was responsible for the USS Cole bombing was a suicide bombing attack against the U.S. Navy destroyer USS Cole (DDG 67) on 12 October 2000 while it was harbored in the Yemeni port of Aden Seventeen American sailors were killed.

Activities of Al-Qaeda

Africa

Al-Qaeda involvement in Africa has included a number of bombing attacks in North Africa, while supporting parties in civil wars in Eritrea and Somalia. From 1991 to 1996, bin Laden and other al-Qaeda leaders were based in Sudan.

Islamist rebels in the Sahara calling themselves al-Qaeda in the Islamic Maghreb have stepped up their violence in recent years. French officials say the rebels have no real links to the al-Qaeda leadership, but this has been disputed. It seems likely that bin Laden approved the group's name in late 2006, and the rebels "took on the al Qaeda franchise label", almost a year before the violence began to escalate.

In Mali, the Ansar Dine faction was also reported as an ally of al-Qaeda in 2013. The Ansar al Dine faction aligned themselves with the AQIM.

Following the Libyan Civil War, the removal of Gaddafi and the ensuing period of post-civil war violence in Libya, various Islamist militant groups affiliated with al-Qaeda were able to expand their operations in the region. The 2012 Benghazi attack, which resulted in the death of US Ambassador J. Christopher Stevens and three other Americans, is suspected of having been carried out by various Jihadist networks, such as Al-Qaeda in the Islamic Maghreb, Ansar al-Sharia and several other Al-Qaeda affiliated groups. The capture of Nazih Abdul-Hamed al-Ruqai, a senior al-Qaeda operative wanted by the United States for his involvement in the 1998 United States embassy bombings, on October 5, 2013, by US Navy Seals, FBI and CIA agents illustrates the importance the US and other Western allies have placed on North Africa.

Europe

Prior to the September 11 attacks, al-Qaeda was present in Bosnia and Herzegovina, and its members were mostly veterans of the El Mudžahid detachment of the Bosnian Muslim Army of the Republic of Bosnia and Herzegovina. Three al-Qaeda operatives carried out the Mostar car bombing in 1997. The operatives were closely linked to and financed by the Saudi High Commission for Relief of Bosnia and Herzegovina founded by then-prince King Salman of Saudi Arabia.

Before the 9/11 attacks and the US invasion of Afghanistan, westerners who had been recruits at al-Qaeda training camps were sought after by al-Qaeda's military wing. Language skills and knowledge of Western culture were generally found among recruits from Europe, such was the case with Mohamed Atta, an Egyptian national studying in Germany at the time of his training, and other members of the Hamburg Cell. Osama bin Laden and Mohammed Atef would later designate Atta as the ringleader of the 9/11 hijackers. Following the attacks, Western intelligence agencies determined that al-Qaeda cells operating in Europe had aided the hijackers with financing and communications with the central leadership based in Afghanistan.

In 2003, Islamists carried out a series of bombings in Istanbul killing fifty-seven people and injuring seven hundred. Seventy-four people were charged by the Turkish authorities. Some had previously met bin Laden, and though they specifically declined to pledge allegiance to al-Qaeda they asked for its blessing and help.

In 2009, three Londoners, Tanvir Hussain, Assad Sarwar and Ahmed Abdullah Ali, were convicted of conspiring to detonate bombs disguised as soft drinks on seven airplanes bound for Canada and the US The MI5 investigation regarding the plot involved more than a year of surveillance work conducted by over two hundred officers. British and US officials said the plot – unlike many similar homegrown European Islamic militant plots – was directly linked to al-Qaeda and guided by senior al-Qaeda members in Pakistan.

In 2012, Russian Intelligence indicated that al-Qaeda had given a call for "forest jihad" and has been starting massive forest fires as part of a strategy of "thousand cuts".

Arab world

Following Yemeni unification in 1990, Wahhabi networks began moving missionaries into the country. Although it is unlikely that bin Laden or Saudi al-Qaeda were directly involved, the personal connections they made would be established over the next decade and used in the USS Cole bombing. Concerns grew over Al Qaeda's group in Yemen.

In Iraq, al-Qaeda forces loosely associated with the leadership were embedded in the Jama'at al-Tawhid wal-Jihad group commanded by Abu Musab al-Zarqawi. Specializing in suicide operations, they have been a "key driver" of the Sunni insurgency. Although they played a small part in the overall insurgency, between 30% and 42% of all suicide bombings which took place in the early years were claimed by Zarqawi's group. Reports have indicated that oversights such as the failure to control access to the Qa'qaa munitions factory in Yusufiyah have allowed large quantities of munitions to fall into the hands of al-Qaida. In November 2010, the militant group Islamic State of Iraq, which is linked to al-Qaeda in Iraq, threatened to "exterminate all Iraqi Christians".

Al-Qaeda did not begin training Palestinians until the late 1990s. Large groups such as Hamas and Palestinian Islamic Jihad have rejected an alliance with al-Qaeda, fearing that al-Qaeda will co-opt their cells. This may have changed recently. The Israeli security and intelligence services believe that al-Qaeda has managed to infiltrate operatives from the Occupied Territories into Israel, and is waiting for an opportunity to attack.

As of 2015, Saudi Arabia, Qatar and Turkey are openly supporting the Army of Conquest, an umbrella rebel group fighting in the Syrian Civil War against the Syrian government that reportedly includes an al-Qaeda linked al-Nusra Front and another Salafi coalition known as Ahrar al-Sham.

Kashmir

Bin Laden and Ayman al-Zawahiri consider India to be a part of an alleged Crusader-Zionist-Hindu conspiracy against the Islamic world. According to a 2005 report by the Congressional Research Service, bin Laden was involved in training militants for Jihad in Kashmir while living in Sudan in the early 1990s. By 2001, Kashmiri militant group Harkat-ul-Mujahideen had become a part of the al-Qaeda coalition. According to the United Nations High Commissioner for Refugees (UNHCR), al-Qaeda was thought to have established bases in Pakistan administered Kashmir (in Azad Kashmir, and to some extent in Gilgit–Baltistan) during the 1999 Kargil War and continued to operate there with tacit approval of Pakistan's Intelligence services.

Many of the militants active in Kashmir were trained in the same madrasahs as Taliban and al-Qaeda. Fazlur Rehman Khalil of Kashmiri militant group Harkat-ul-Mujahideen was a signatory of al-Qaeda's 1998 declaration of Jihad against America and its allies. In a 'Letter to American People' (2002), bin Laden wrote that one of the reasons he was fighting America was because of its support to India on the Kashmir issue. In November 2001, Kathmandu airport went on high alert after threats that bin Laden planned to hijack a plane and crash it into a target in New Delhi. In 2002, US Secretary of Defense Donald Rumsfeld, on a trip to Delhi, suggested that al-Qaeda was active in Kashmir though he did not have any evidence. Rumsfeld proposed hi-tech ground sensors along the Line of Control to prevent militants from infiltrating into Indian-administered Kashmir. An investigation in 2002 found evidence that al-Qaeda and its affiliates were prospering in Pakistan-administered Kashmir with tacit approval of Pakistan's Inter-Services Intelligence. In 2002, a special team of Special Air Service and Delta Force was sent into Indian-Administered Kashmir to hunt for bin Laden after receiving reports that he was being sheltered by Kashmiri militant group Harkat-ul-Mujahideen, which had been responsible for kidnapping western tourists in Kashmir in 1995. Britain's highest-ranking al-Qaeda operative Rangzieb Ahmed had previously fought in Kashmir with the group Harkat-ul-Mujahideen and spent time in Indian prison after being captured in Kashmir.

US officials believe that al-Qaeda was helping organize attacks in Kashmir in order to provoke conflict between India and Pakistan. Their strategy was to force Pakistan to move its troops to the border with India, thereby relieving pressure on al-Qaeda elements hiding in northwestern Pakistan. In 2006 al-Qaeda claimed they had established a wing in Kashmir. However Indian Army General H.S. Panag argued that the army had ruled out the presence of al-Qaeda in Indian-administered Jammu and Kashmir. Panag also stated that al-Qaeda had strong ties with Kashmiri militant groups Lashkar-e-Taiba and Jaish-e-Mohammed based in Pakistan. It has been noted that Waziristan has become a battlefield for Kashmiri militants fighting NATO in support of al-Qaeda and Taliban. Dhiren Barot, who wrote the Army of Madinah in Kashmir and was an al-Qaeda operative convicted for involvement in the 2004 financial buildings plot, had received training in weapons and explosives at a militant training camp in Kashmir.

Maulana Masood Azhar, the founder of Kashmiri group Jaish-e-Mohammed, is believed to have met bin Laden several times and received funding from him. In 2002, Jaish-e-Mohammed organized the kidnapping and murder of Daniel Pearl in an operation run in conjunction with al-Qaeda and funded by bin Laden. According to American counter-terrorism expert Bruce Riedel, al-Qaeda and Taliban were closely involved in the 1999 hijacking of Indian Airlines Flight 814 to Kandahar which led to the release of Maulana Masood Azhar and Ahmed Omar Saeed Sheikh from an Indian prison. This hijacking, Riedel stated, was rightly described by then Indian Foreign Minister Jaswant Singh as a 'dress rehearsal' for September 11 attacks. Bin Laden personally welcomed Azhar and threw a lavish party in his honor after his release. Ahmed Omar Saeed Sheikh, who had been in prison for his role in the 1994 kidnappings of Western tourists in India, went on to murder Daniel Pearl and was sentenced to death in Pakistan. Al-Qaeda operative Rashid Rauf, who was one of the accused in 2006 transatlantic aircraft plot, was related to Maulana Masood Azhar by marriage.

Lashkar-e-Taiba, a Kashmiri militant group which is thought to be behind 2008 Mumbai attacks, is also known to have strong ties to senior al-Qaeda leaders living in Pakistan. In Late 2002, top al-Qaeda operative Abu Zubaydah was arrested while being sheltered by Lashkar-e-Taiba in a safe house in Faisalabad. The FBI believes that al-Qaeda and Lashkar have been 'intertwined' for a long time while the CIA has said that al-Qaeda funds Lashkar-e-Taiba. Jean-Louis Bruguière told Reuters in 2009 that "Lashkar-e-Taiba is no longer a Pakistani movement with only a Kashmir political or military agenda. Lashkar-e-Taiba is a member of al-Qaeda."

In a video released in 2008, American-born senior al-Qaeda operative Adam Yahiye Gadahn stated that "victory in Kashmir has been delayed for years; it is the liberation of the jihad there from this interference which, Allah willing, will be the first step towards victory over the Hindu occupiers of that Islam land."

In September 2009, a US drone strike reportedly killed Ilyas Kashmiri who was the chief of Harkat-ul-Jihad al-Islami, a Kashmiri militant group associated with al-Qaeda. Kashmiri was described by Bruce Riedel as a 'prominent' al-Qaeda member while others have described him as head of military operations for al-Qaeda. Kashmiri was also charged by the US in a plot against Jyllands-Posten, the Danish newspaper which was at the center of Jyllands-Posten Muhammad cartoons controversy. US officials also believe that Kashmiri was involved in the Camp Chapman attack against the CIA. In January 2010, Indian authorities notified Britain of an al-Qaeda plot to hijack an Indian airlines or Air India plane and crash it into a British city. This information was uncovered from interrogation of Amjad Khwaja, an operative of Harkat-ul-Jihad al-Islami, who had been arrested in India.

In January 2010, US Defense secretary Robert Gates, while on a visit to Pakistan, stated that al-Qaeda was seeking to destabilize the region and planning to provoke a nuclear war between India and Pakistan.

Internet

Al-Qaeda and its successors have migrated online to escape detection in an atmosphere of increased international vigilance. The group's use of the Internet has grown more sophisticated, with online activities that include financing, recruitment, networking, mobilization, publicity, and information dissemination, gathering and sharing.

Abu Ayyub al-Masri's al-Qaeda movement in Iraq regularly releases short videos glorifying the activity of jihadist suicide bombers. In addition, both before and after the death of Abu Musab al-Zarqawi (the former leader of al-Qaeda in Iraq), the umbrella organization to which al-Qaeda in Iraq belongs, the Mujahideen Shura Council, has a regular presence on the Web.

The range of multimedia content includes guerrilla training clips, stills of victims about to be murdered, testimonials of suicide bombers, and videos that show participation in jihad through stylized portraits of mosques and musical scores. A website associated with al-Qaeda posted a video of captured American entrepreneur Nick Berg being decapitated in Iraq. Other decapitation videos and pictures, including those of Paul Johnson, Kim Sun-il, and Daniel Pearl, were first posted on jihadist websites.

In December 2004 an audio message claiming to be from bin Laden was posted directly to a website, rather than sending a copy to al Jazeera as he had done in the past. Al-Qaeda turned to the Internet for release of its videos in order to be certain they would be available unedited, rather than risk the possibility of al Jazeera editing out anything critical of the Saudi royal family.

Alneda.com and Jehad.net were perhaps the most significant al-Qaeda websites. Alneda was initially taken down by American Jon Messner, but the operators resisted by shifting the site to various servers and strategically shifting content.

The US government charged a British information technology specialist, Babar Ahmad, with terrorist offences related to his operating a network of English-language al-Qaeda websites, such as Azzam.com. He was convicted and sentenced to 12-and-a-half years in prison.

Online communications

In 2007, al-Qaeda released Mujahedeen Secrets, encryption software used for online and cellular communications. A later version, Mujahideen Secrets 2, was released in 2008.

Aviation network

Al-Qaeda is believed to be operating a clandestine aviation network including "several Boeing 727 aircraft", turboprops and executive jets, according to a 2010 Reuters story. Based on a US Department of Homeland Security report, the story said that al-Qaeda is possibly using aircraft to transport drugs and weapons from South America to various unstable countries in West Africa. A Boeing 727 can carry up to 10 tons of cargo. The drugs eventually are smuggled to Europe for distribution and sale, and the weapons are used in conflicts in Africa and possibly elsewhere. Gunmen with links to al-Qaeda have been increasingly kidnapping Europeans for ransom. The profits from the drug and weapon sales, and kidnappings can, in turn, fund more militant activities.

5

Tactics of Terrorism

The tactics of terrorism are diverse. As important as the actual attacks is the cultivation in the target population of the fear of such attacks, so that the threat of violence becomes as effective as actual violence.

While advancements in technology, modernization, and globalization have helped many states prosper over the course of history, they have also opened terrorist groups to new tactics and weaponry. The different tactics that terrorist groups utilize can be very simple to extremely complex. In his book, Why Terrorism Works: Understanding the Threat, Responding to the Challenge, Harvard Law Professor Alan M. Dershowitz states that before the dawn of dynamite and automatic weapons, killings conducted by terrorists had to be done on a one-on-one basis. Dershowitz also describes how the introduction of new weapons and technology has enabled terrorists to kill more efficiently and in greater numbers:

"The weapons of choice for earlier terrorists were the dagger, the noose, the sword, and the poison elixir. The introduction of the hand-thrown bomb and the pistol, and more recently the machine gun and plastic explosives, enabled terrorists to kill much more efficiently. Now weapons of mass, or 'wholesale,' destruction allow terrorists to 'leverage' their personnel, as proved by the events of September 11, 2001, in which a relatively small number of highly trained individuals armed with primitive box cutters and prepared to give up their own lives were able to use passenger jets as weapons of mass murder."

Terrorist tactics tend to favor attacks that avoid effective countermeasures and exploit vulnerabilities. As such, terrorist groups have the potential to utilize many different types of terrorism tactics depending on the circumstances and the perceived likelihood of success. Some tactics are more conventional and widely used in the operations of many terrorist groups. These tactics include shootings, hijackings, kidnappings, bombings, and suicide attacks. Other tactics are seen more unconventional and have only been used in a few instances, if at all. However, these unconventional tactics are perceived by government officials and experts alike as serious potential threats. Some types of unconventional terrorism tactics commonly recognized by terrorism experts are bioterrorism, agroterrorism, nuclear terrorism, and cyberterrorism.

Suicide attacks

Suicide terrorism is the most aggressive form of terrorism, pursuing coercion even at the expense of losing support among terrorists' own community. What distinguishes a suicide terrorist is that the attacker does not expect to survive a mission and often employs a method of attack that requires the attacker's death in order to succeed (such as planting a car bomb, wearing a suicide vest, or ramming an airplane into a building). In essence, a suicide terrorist kills others at the same time that he kills himself. Usually these tactics are used for a demonstrative purposes or to targeted assassinations. In most cases though, they target to kill a large number of people. Thus, while coercion is an element in all terrorism, coercion is the paramount objective of suicide terrorism.

The number of attacks using suicide tactics has grown from an average of fewer than five per year during the 1980s to 180 per year between 2000 and 2005, and from 81 suicide attacks in 2001 to 460 in 2005. These attacks have been aimed at diverse military and civilian targets, including in Sri Lanka, in Israel since July 6, 1989, in Iraq since the US-led invasion of that country in 2003, and in Pakistan and Afghanistan since 2005.

Between 1980 and 2000, the largest number of suicide attacks was carried out by separatist Liberation Tigers of Tamil Eelam of Sri Lanka. The number of attacks conducted by LTTE was almoust double that of nine other major extremist organizations.

In Israel, Gaza and the West Bank, suicide bombings are an anti-Israel strategy perpetrated generally by Islamist and occasionally by secular Palestinian groups including the PFLP.

Rocket and mortar attacks

The use of rocket and mortar attacks had been widely used from 1982–2012, in the example of the middle east rocket attacks against cities and settlements had been carried out by political entities such as Hizballa and Hamas (not counted as state terrorism) and to non political organization such as Islamic Jihad, Islamic Jihad Movement in Palestine, al-Qaeda and many others. Rocket-propelled grenades, especially RPG-7, and hand grenades, are in widespread use by terrorist groups.

The number of attacks using explosive projectiles has grown as can be seen in Palestinian rocket attacks on Israel, according to the reports somewhere between 800,000 people to million and a half are being in direct danger of mortar and missile range. In research published in 2011, 15,000 people had been treated or need treatment for PTSD and 1,000 people are being treated in psychometric facilities due to reasons directly to mortar (qassam) and rocket attacks (Grad).

Vehicle-based attacks

In the 2000s, there have been a number of vehicle-based attacks in which terrorists used earthmovers or other motor vehicles to run over pedestrians or to attack vehicles. Some examples of such attacks include the 2008 Jerusalem bulldozer attack and the Omeed Aziz Popal SUV rampage.

Compared to suicide-bomb attacks, using vehicles as weapons is easier to plan and carry out without detection. The tactic does not require acquiring explosives. The weapon, a standard street-legal vehicle, is readily available in the target country and can be used without raising suspicion. According to a report by Stratfor global intelligence, using a vehicle as a terrorist tactic is nearly as effective, yet not as destructive as a suicide bombing.

In 2016, two deadly terrorist vehicle-based attacks occurred in Europe: the July attack in Nice, France, that killed 86; and the December attack in Berlin, Germany, that killed 12. This was followed by five other similar attacks in 2017: one in Jerusalem in January that killed four, one in London in March that killed three, one in Stockholm in April that killed five, a second attack in London in June that killed three, and two in Barcelona and Cambrils in August that killed fourteen people. That same year, another similar attack occurred in the US, specifically New York City, in October, killing eight. Other terrorist attacks of a similar M.O. have occurred intermittently in Western countries since 2014, though these produced no fatalities.

Bombings

As a consequence of globalisation, the relative ease of access to the chemicals used to make explosives has made improvised explosive devices (IEDs) increasingly prominent. This has the dual effect of increasing the available firepower of terrorists who are generally far weaker than their targets as well as assuring the publicity necessary to attract sympathisers to their cause.

These may be implanted in automobiles to make a car bomb, planted on the roadside to detonate near target vehicles, or even strapped to the bodies of individuals for suicide attacks. From a tactical perspective, each of these methods have positives and drawback, for instance car bombs act as their own delivery mechanisms and can carry a relatively large amount of explosives with weights of up to and over 1000 pounds (450 kg), while a suicide vest has a much smaller payload but may allow the wearer access to spaces and individuals that vehicles cannot.

Aircraft attacks and hijackings

In the failed 2002 airliner attack, shoulder-launched surface-to-air missiles were fired at an airliner while taking off.

Aircraft hijacking is also employed as a terrorist tactic. On September 11, 2001, 19 al-Qaeda terrorists hijacked American Airlines Flight 11, United Airlines Flight 175, American Airlines Flight 77, and United Airlines Flight 93 and crashed them into the Twin Towers of the World Trade Center, the southwestern side of the Pentagon building, and Stonycreek Township near Shanksville, Pennsylvania in a terrorist attack, killing 2,977 victims, most of them American citizens.

Chemical and biological weapons

Bioterrorism is the deliberate release of viruses, bacteria, or other germs (agents) used to cause illness or death in people, animals, or plants. Biological agents are typically found in nature, but it is possible that they can be changed to increase their ability to cause disease, make them resident to current medicines, or to increase their ability to be spread into the environment. Biological agents in the hands of terrorists pose serious threats to states' security because they can be easily spread through the air, through water, and through food. Biological agents can also be difficult to detect and often do not cause illness for several hours to several days. A prominent example of a bioterrorist attack on the United States is the September 2001 anthrax attacks. On September 18, 2001, several letters containing anthrax were sent to media outlets and the U.S. Congressional offices of Senator Thomas Daschle and Senator Patrick Leahy. Five Americans died from anthrax inhalation as a result of contact with the contaminated mail. While the 2001 anthrax attacks were relatively small-scale, the United States government has taken several steps since to 2001 to pass legislation and initiatives aimed at better protecting the United States against biological attacks, improving the United States' public health system, and improving the United States ability to respond to biological attacks.

The use of chemical weapons includes that by Aum Shinrikyo, a Japanese "new religious movement", which in 1995 carried out the Sarin gas attack on the Tokyo subway. Ian Davison, a British white supremacist, and neo-Nazi who was arrested in 2009 for planning terrorist attacks involving ricin poison. In 2011 the United States government discovered information that terrorist groups were attempting to obtain large amounts of castor beans for weaponized ricin use.

Agro-terrorism

The ultimate goal of agroterrorism in killing livestock and plants and contaminating food is to cause economic crises in the agricultural and food industries, social unrest, and loss of confidence in the government. Many experts believe that the United States' agricultural sector and food supply are among the most vulnerable and least protected of all potential targets of attack, and they believe that terrorists have taken note of this. A subset of bioterrorism, agroterrorism refers to the deliberate introduction of an animal or plant disease for the purposes of generating fear, causing economic losses, or undermining social stability. After American and allied forces overran some Al-Qaeda's refuges in caves in eastern Afghanistan in 2002, they found U.S. agricultural documents and Al-Qaeda training manuals on targeting agriculture among thousands of other documents.

Analysts have identified a number of characteristics of the United States' agricultural system that make it very vulnerable to agroterrorism. Given that agriculture generally demands large expanses of land, farms are geographically dispersed in environments that are difficult to secure. Also, livestock are usually concentrated in confined locations, which allows diseases to infect more animals quickly. Although many experts believe the United States is susceptible to agroterrorism, they have never suffered from a large scale agroterrorism related attack. Many political scientists have identified the 1984 salmonella attack in The Dalles, Oregon as a small-scale example of an agroterrorism attack in the United States. A religious cult intentionally contaminated ten restaurant salad bars with salmonella in an attempt to influence a local election, sickening more than 750 people. Even though the United States has not experienced a large-scale agroterrorism attack to date, similar to its anti-bioterrorism initiatives, the United States government has passed several pieces of legislation and started initiatives over the past few decades to better secure its agricultural system and prepare for potential attacks.

Cyberterrorism

In the developing age Information Technology, many political scientists and prominent government officials have become increasingly concerned about the ability of terrorist groups to execute cyber attacks and states' vulnerabilities to these attacks. Cyberterrorism could potentially become an increasingly desirable tactic for terrorist groups given that they can be executed thousands of miles away from the target and are difficult to trace back to the perpetrator. In an October 2012 speech, United States Secretary of Defense Leon Panetta described the seriousness of a cyber attack on the United States: "A cyber attack perpetrated by nation states or violent extremists groups could be as destructive as the terrorist attack of 9/11.

Such a destructive cyber terrorist attack could paralyze the nation." The term "cyberterrorism" was first coined by Barry Collin, a senior research fellow at the Institute for Security and Intelligence in California, in the 1980s. The Center for Strategic and International Studies defines cyberterrorism as "the use of computer network tools to shut down critical national infrastructures (such as energy, transportation, government operations) or to coerce or intimidate a government or civilian population." Many experts believe that new vulnerabilities will be created as nations and their critical infrastructures become more dependent on computer networks for their operation.

While concern is growing, cyberterrorism attacks still largely remain hypothetical, especially in the United States. In his report for the Center for Strategic and International Studies, James A Lewis writes that so far cyberterrorism has meant little more than propaganda and intelligence collection, and that no critical infrastructures have ever been shut down by cyber terrorist attacks. Lewis also describes how terrorist groups like Al-Qaeda have made significant use of the Internet, but only as a tool for intra-group relations, fundraising, and public relations. An Al-Qaeda training manual entitled "Military Studies in the Jihad Against the Tyrants" explicates that explosives are the preferred weapon of terrorists because "explosives strike the enemy with sheer terror and fright." While explosions are dramatic, strike fear into the hearts of opponents, and do lasting damage, cyber attacks, like some other types of terrorism tactics, simply do not have the same dramatic and political effect that terrorists seek. Some political scientists, like Lewis, argue that terrorist organizations like Al-Qaeda might use cyber attacks to disrupt emergency services in order to reinforce and multiply the effect of a physical attack.

Nuclear weapons

Concerns have also been raised regarding attacks involving nuclear weapons. It is considered plausible that terrorists could acquire a nuclear weapon. In 2011, the British news agency, the Telegraph, received leaked documents regarding the Guantanamo Bay interrogations of Khalid Sheikh Mohammed. The documents cited Khalid saying that, if Osama Bin Laden is captured or killed by the Coalition of the Willing, an Al-Qaeda sleeper cell will detonate a "weapon of mass destruction" in a "secret location" in Europe, and promised it would be "a nuclear hellstorm".

While no terrorist group has ever successfully acquired and used a nuclear weapon, many political scientists and prominent government officials consider nuclear terrorism to be one of the single greatest threats in global security. There is strong evidence that terrorist groups like Al-Qaeda are actively seeking to acquire nuclear weapons, and the plutonium or highly enriched uranium (HEU) needed to produce them. Another serious concern is that weaknesses in many states' nuclear security apparatuses have left them susceptible to theft or loss of HEU or plutonium. According to the International Atomic Energy Agency's (IAEA) Illicit Trafficking Database (ITDB), there have been 18 incidents of theft or loss of HEU and plutonium reported in ITDB's participating states. Given these serious concerns, the United States, its allies, and international organizations like the United Nations have established several international agreements and initiatives to ensure that all states' nuclear security standards are adequate and effective, and to secure all vulnerable and unprotected nuclear stockpiles around the world over the next few years.

Cyberterrorism

In the developing age Information Technology, many political scientists and prominent government officials have become increasingly concerned about the ability of terrorist groups to execute cyber attacks and states' vulnerabilities to these attacks. Cyberterrorism could potentially become an increasingly desirable tactic for terrorist groups given that they can be executed thousands of miles away from the target and are difficult to trace back to the perpetrator. In an October 2012 speech, United States Secretary of Defense Leon Panetta described the seriousness of a cyber attack on the United States:

"A cyber attack perpetrated by nation states or violent extremists groups could be as destructive as the terrorist attack of 9/11. Such a destructive cyber terrorist attack could paralyze the nation."The term "cyberterrorism" was first coined by Barry Collin, a senior research fellow at the Institute for Security and Intelligence in California, in the 1980s.

The Center for Strategic and International Studies defines cyberterrorism as "the use of computer network tools to shut down critical national infrastructures (such as energy, transportation, government operations) or to coerce or intimidate a government or civilian population." Many experts believe that new vulnerabilities will be created as nations and their critical infrastructures become more dependent on computer networks for their operation. While concern is growing, cyberterrorism attacks still largely remain hypothetical, especially in the United States. In his report for the Center for Strategic and International Studies, James A Lewis writes that so far cyberterrorism has meant little more than propaganda and intelligence collection, and that no critical infrastructures have ever been shut down by cyber terrorist attacks. Lewis also describes how terrorist groups like Al-Qaeda have made significant use of the Internet, but only as a tool for intra-group relations, fundraising, and public relations. An Al-Qaeda training manual entitled "Military Studies in the Jihad Against the Tyrants" explicates that explosives are the preferred weapon of terrorists because "explosives strike the enemy with sheer terror and fright." While explosions are dramatic, strike fear into the hearts of opponents, and do lasting damage, cyber attacks, like some other types of terrorism tactics, simply do not have the same dramatic and political effect that terrorists seek. Some political scientists, like Lewis, argue that terrorist organizations like Al-Qaeda might use cyber attacks to disrupt emergency services in order to reinforce and multiply the effect of a physical attack.

Conventional firearms

The 2008 Mumbai terrorist attacks were done partly by guns and partly by bombs. Also, one Transportation Security Administration officer was killed and few others injured by a man with an assault rifle in the 2013 Los Angeles International Airport shooting. Despite the popular image of terrorism as bombings alone, and the large number of casualties and higher media impact associated with bombings, conventional firearms are as much if not more pervasive in their use. For example, in the second part of the 2011 Norway attacks 68 people were killed by Anders Breivik, a man armed with two guns. In 2015, Omar Mateen killed 50 people with firearms during Orlando nightclub shooting.

In 2004, the European Council recognized the "need to ensure terrorist organisations and groups are starved of the components of their trade," including "the need to ensure greater security of firearms, explosives, bomb-making equipment and technologies that contribute to the perpetration of terrorist outrages."

Designated Foreign Terrorist Organizations

This is a list of designated terrorist groups by national governments, former governments, and inter-governmental organizations, where the proscription has a significant effect on the group's activities. Many organizations that are accused of being a terrorist organization deny using terrorism as a military tactic to achieve their goals, and there is no international consensus on the legal definition of terrorism. Some organisations have multiple wings or components, one or more of which may be designated as terrorist while others are not.

This listing does not include unaffiliated individuals accused of terrorism, which are considered under lone wolf terrorism. This list also excludes groups which might be widely considered terrorist, but who are not officially so designated according to the criteria specified above. This list is not all inclusive. For more inclusive lists, including people, entities (corporations), and specific vehicles, refer to lists under Process of designation. There are near about 210 recognised terrorist organisations.

Process of designation

Among the countries that publish a list of designated terrorist organizations, some have a clear established procedure for listing and delisting, and some are opaque. The Berghof Foundation argues that opaque delisting conditions reduce the incentive for the organization to abandon terrorism, while fuelling radicalism.

Australia

Since 2002, the Australian Government maintains a list of terrorist organizations under the Security Legislation Amendment (Terrorism) Act 2002. Listing, de-listing and re-listing follows a protocol that mainly involves the Australian Security Intelligence Organisation and the Attorney-General's Department.

Canada

Since December 18, 2001, section 83.05 of the Canadian Criminal Code allows the Governor in Council to maintain a list of entities that are engaged in terrorism, facilitating it, or acting on behalf of such an entity.

Entities are reviewed by the Minister and the Chief Justice of the Federal Court, and finally published in the Canada Gazette. The list is also published on the website of Public Safety Canada.

European Union

The European Union has two lists of designated terrorist organisations that provide for different sanctions for the two groups. The first list is copied from the United Nations, and the second is an autonomous list.

Autonomous list

All other designated organizations. the freezing of all funds, other financial assets and economic resources. a ban on directly or indirectly making funds, other financial assets and economic resources available.

It is important to note that sanctions are only applicable to EU-external groups regardless of designation. For example, 47 groups are listed as terrorist organizations in the EU but sanctions are only applied to 27 of these. Member States do have an obligation to assist each other in preventing and combating terrorist acts but this is the only action that follows from the designation of an EU-internal organization.

European Union list of terrorist groups and individuals, 25 June 2012.

Listing process

- New organizations are added to the autonomous list following this process:
- "Designation": Member states and third party states tips about an organization. This state must have solid evidence and must the tip must be sent by the national authority.
- Scrutinity: The Presidency, or a delegation, gathers basic information, and might require more information from the tipping state.
- Consultations: Information is shared with other member states for discussion. Everything is still confidential. 15 days after, delegates of the states meet as the CP 931 Working Party, Europol is sometimes invited too.
- Recommendation: The CP 931 Working Party prepares the listing decision.
- Decision by EU Council: The council adopts the list. The decision must be unanimous, which means that every state has a veto right.
- Official Publishing: In the EU Official Journal
- Notification and Statement of Reason: The council secretariat notifies each designated organization via mail, together with instructions on how to get the decision to be reconsidered.

Delisting process

The EU has similar process to review the list, and to remove organizations for the list.

Under the Unlawful Activities (Prevention) Act, the Ministry of Home Affairs maintains a list of banned organizations: List of organisations banned by the Government of India.

The Democratic People's Republic of Korea outlawed the Aum Shinrikyo as a terrorist group.

The Republic of Korea, however, has not yet listed a number of designated terrorist groups. Such groups banned under the National Security Act include, for example, the Workers' Party of Korea (the ruling party of North Korea) and al-Qaeda.

Myanmar

In Myanmar (formerly Burma), the Anti-Terrorism Central Committee is responsible for designating terrorist organisations in accordance with the country's counter-terrorism law. Designations must be approved by the union government before being official. The only group on Myanmar's terror list is the Arakan Rohingya Salvation Army, declared on 25 August 2017 in accordance with the counter-terrorism law.

New Zealand

The New Zealand Police are responsible for coordinating any requests to the Prime Minister for designation as a terrorist entity. The designation of terrorist organizations is also guided by the Terrorism Suppression Act 2002. New Zealand also abides by several United Nations resolutions dealing with counter-terrorism including UN Resolutions 1267, 1989, 2253, 1988, and 1373.

Pakistan

Government of Pakistan under section 11-B of Anti Terrorism Act can declare an organization believed to be concerned with terrorism as a Proscribed Organization or put it under surveillance. Ministry of Interior issues the formal notification of proscription of an organization. National Counter Terrorism Authority is primarily concerned with monitoring for any signs of re-emergence through intelligence coordination, once an organization is proscribed.

People's Republic of China

The Ministry of Public Security maintains a list of terrorist organizations on its website mps.gov.cn. This list has been translated to English by the Embassy of the People's Republic of China in the US.

Philippines

The first group to be officially listed as a terrorist organization under the Human Security Act of 2007 is the Abu Sayyaf on September 10, 2015 by the Basilan provincial court.

In December 2017, President Rodrigo Duterte reportedly issued a proclamation declaring the Communist Party of the Philippines (CPP) and its armed wing, the New People's Army (NPA), as terrorist organizations. The proclamation was made in accordance with the Human Security Act and the Terrorism Financing Prevention and Suppression Act.

Historically the CPP-NPA has been considered as an "organized conspiracy" by the Philippines Government. The label was placed on the CPP's predecessor, the Partido Komunista ng Pilipinas-1930 and its armed group the Hukbalahap in 20 June 1957 through the Anti Subversion Act or Republic Act No. 1700. The law covered any succeeding organizations of the PKP-1930 and the Hukbalahap which includes the CPP-NPA. Being a member of groups covered by the law is considered illegal. On October 1992, Fidel Ramos signed a law repealing the Anti-Subversion law.

Russia

A single federal list of organizations recognized as terrorist is used by the Supreme Court of the Russian Federation. The National Anti-Terrorism Committee maintains a list of terrorist organizations on its website nac.gov.ru, named "Federal United list of Terrorist Organizations".

Serbia

Serbian authorities and their Yugoslav predecessors regard the Kosovo Liberation Army (KLA) as a terrorist group.

Tajikistan

In 2015, the Islamic Renaissance Party of Tajikistan was banned in Tajikistan as a terrorist organization.

Ukraine

In Ukraine, the Donetsk and Luhansk People's Republics are designated as terrorist organizations. Ukrainian authorities claim that the two organizations are made up of a rigid hierarchy, financing channels and supply of weapons with the purpose of deliberately propagating violence, seizing hostages, carrying out subversive activity, assassinations, and the intimidation of citizens.

United Nations

The United Nations does not have a general list of all terrorist organizations. Instead, it has several lists focusing on a particular context.

UN 1267 regime list

The UN 1267 regime list is focused on Al-Qaeda, the Taliban and their associates.

- prohibition of sale or transfer of arms and related materiel.
- the freezing of funds and other financial assets or resources.
- the prevention of entry onto or transit through the territories of member states.
- a prohibition on provision of technical assistance or training in military matters or in the manufacture or maintenance of arms and related materiel.

The EU provides exceptions to the implementation of relevant asset-freezing sanctions per UN resolution 1452 (2002). Upon request, a competent national authority may determine to release funds on the following grounds if, within the time limit provided for, there has been no objection made, or a release has been explicitly approved, by the UN Sanctions Committee.

necessary to cover basic expenses, intended for the payment of professional fees for legal services or for the payment of fees or services in relation to the maintenance of frozen funds or assets necessary for extraordinary expenses .

United Kingdom

- United Kingdom Government's Proscribed terrorist groups.
- Text of the Terrorism Act 2000 as in force today (including any amendments) within the United Kingdom, from legislation.gov.uk. .

United States

- United States State Department list of Foreign Terrorist Organizations

Terror Exclusion List (TEL)

Executive Order 13224 blocking Terrorist Property and a summary of the Terrorism Sanctions Regulations (Title 31 Part 595 of the U.S. Code of Federal Regulations), Terrorism List Governments Sanctions Regulations (Title 31 Part 596 of the U.S. Code of Federal Regulations), and Foreign Terrorist Organizations Sanctions Regulations (Title 31 Part 597 of the U.S. Code of Federal Regulations)

US Department of the Treasury, Office of Foreign Assets Control, 'What you need to know about U.S. Sanctions'

- US Department of State Terrorist Designation Lists
- US Department of State Country Reports on Terrorism 2008
- United States Department of State. "Individuals and Entities Designated by the State Department Under E.O. 13224". Retrieved 17 July 2011.
- U.S. Department of Homeland Security – Terrorist Organization Reference Guide January 2004
- List of organisations banned by the Government of India

The Ministry of Home Affairs of India has banned a number of organisations that have been proscribed as terrorist organisations under the Unlawful Activities (Prevention) Act. The banned groups are:

- Al-Badr (Jammu and Kashmir)
- All Tripura Tiger Force
- Al-Qaedaa
- Al-Umar-Mujahideen
- Babbar Khalsa International

Communist Party of India (Maoist) all its formations and front organisations.

Communist Party of India (Marxist-Leninist) People's War , All its formations and front organizations.

Deendar Anjuman

Dukhtaran-E-Millat (DEM)

Garo National Liberation Army (GNLA), all its formations and front organizations.

- Harkat-Ul-Mujahideen/Harkat-Ul-Ansar/Harkat-Ul-Jehad-E-Islami
- Hizb-Ul-Mujahideen/ Hizb-Ul-Mujahideen Pir Panjal Regiment
- Indian Mujahideen, all its formations and front organizations.
- International Sikh Youth Federation
- Islamic State/Islamic State of Iraq and Levant /Islamic State of Iraq and Syria/Daish, and all its Manifestations
- Jaish-E-Mohammed/Tahrik-E-Furqan
- Jamiat-ul-Mujahideen
- Jammu and Kashmir Islamic Front

Kamatapur Liberation Organization, all its formations and front organizations.

- Kanglei Yawol Kanna Lup (KYKL)
- Kangleipak Communist Party (KCP)
- Khalistan Commando Force
- Khalistan Zindabad Force
- Lashkar-E-Taiba/Pasban-E-Ahle Hadis
- Liberation Tigers of Tamil Eelam (LTTE)
- Manipur People's Liberation Front (MPLF)

Maoist Communist Centre (MCC), All its formations and Front Organisations

- National Democratic Front of Bodoland (NDFB) in Assam
- National Liberation Front of Tripura
- National Socialist Council of Nagaland (Khaplang), NSCN (K), all its formations and front organizations

Organisations listed in the Schedule to the U.N. Prevention and Suppression of Terrorism (Implementation of Security Council Resolutions) Order, 2007 made under section 2 of the United Nations (Security Council) Act, 1947 and amended from time to time.

- People's Liberation Army of Manipur(PLA)
- People's Revolutionary Party of Kangleipak (PREPAK)
- Students Islamic Movement of India
- Tehreek-ul-Mujahideen (TuM) active in the Kashmir valley.
- Tamil Nadu Liberation Army (TNLA)
- Tamil National Retrieval Troops (TNRT)
- United Liberation Front of Assam (ULFA)
- United National Liberation Front (UNLF)
- Islamic Research Foundation(IRF)
- Jamaat-e-Islami Kashmir(JIJK)

Stabbing

Stabbing attacks are inexpensive and easy to carry out, but very difficult for security services to prevent.

Secondary attacks

Terrorist groups may arrange for secondary devices to detonate at a slightly later time in order to kill emergency-response personnel attempting to attend to the dead and wounded. Repeated or suspected use of secondary devices can also delay emergency response out of concern that such devices may exist. Examples include a (failed) device that was meant to release cyanide-gas during the February 26, 1993 World Trade Center bombing; and a second car bomb that detonated 20 minutes after the December 1, 2001 Ben Yehuda Street Bombing by Hamas in Jerusalem.

Training

There are and have been training camps for terrorists. The range of training depends greatly on the level of support the terrorist organization receives from various organizations and states. In nearly every case the training incorporates the philosophy and agenda of the groups leadership as justification for the training as well as the potential acts of terrorism which may be committed. State sanctioned training is by far the most extensive and thorough, often employing professional soldiers and covert operatives of the supporting state.

Cover

Where terrorism occurs in the context of open warfare or insurgency, its perpetrators may shelter behind a section of the local population. Examples include the intifada on Israeli-occupied territory, and insurgency in Iraq. This population, which may be ethnically distinct from the counter-terrorist forces, is either sympathetic to their cause, indifferent, or acts under duress.

Funding

Funding can be raised in both legal and illegal ways. Some of the most common ways to raise funds are through front groups, charitable organizations, or NGOs with similar ideologies. In the absence of state funding, terrorists may rely on organized crime to fund their activities. This has included kidnapping, drug trafficking, or robbery.

Terrorist financing generated through the use of underground smuggling tunnels and the probability that a specific smuggling tunnel or terrorist criminal social network will use the smuggling tunnel to launch a kidnapping operation or terrorist attack has been addressed in the literature.

Communications

Even though older communication methods like radio are still used, the revolution in communication technology over the past 10–15 years has dramatically changed how terrorist organizations communicate. E-mails, fax transmissions, websites, cell phones, and satellite telephones have made it possible for organizations to contemplate a global strategy. However, too great a reliance on this new technology leaves organizations vulnerable to sophisticated monitoring of communication and triangulation of its source. When Osama bin Laden found out that his satellite phone conversations were being intercepted, he ceased using this method to communicate.

Fear

The primary weapon of terrorism is fear, destruction and killing are not an end in and of itself, but a tool to create fear and terror in the minds of the enemy. In an asymmetric situation an enemy who cannot be defeated militarily may be defeated psychologically, that they may come to fear attack and its consequences so much they may become willing to forgo a superior military position in order to be free of the cause of that fear.

Tactical Approach to Counter Terrorists in Cities

Addressing terrorist threats to urban spaces is a particularly challenging task in the current security climate. As one of the 11 research institutes participating in the project, RAND Europe contributed to building a decision making framework that (i) supports security forces in responding more effectively to prevent attacks or (ii) limits the consequences of those attacks, with a particular interest in urban environments.

The intensity of counterterrorism efforts has been evident in recent years as a result of traumatic events in urban areas, such as "Charlie Hebdo" and the Paris attacks. Urban areas are specifically targeted due to their high population density, the availability of multiple targets and their cultural significance. It is difficult in urban areas for security forces to differentiate unusual behaviour or to control access to urban locations. Furthermore, these forces must at all times navigate a careful balance between privacy and security.

To enhance security and mitigate the consequences of terrorism, techniques for recognising the indications of impending attacks, and for quickly assessing responsive capabilities, must be improved. The three-year FP7 project funded by the European Commission, 'Tactical Approach to Counter Terrorists in Cities' (TACTICS), was focused on approaches to enhance security and mitigate consequences of terrorism in urban cities.

Goals

Originally, the TACTICS consortium consisted of 11 partners, including RAND Europe, and was coordinated by the Dutch Organisation for Applied Scientific Research (TNO). Now a Technology Readiness Level (TRL)-5 decision support system, TACTICS aims to create a more effective counterterrorism system that incorporates mechanisms to prevent any cognitive biases and avoids false negatives or false positives when assessing threats or attacks. The TACTICS system consisted of three integrated systems.

The first system is threat management capability, which enables improved decision making based on an enhanced operational picture. TACTICS allows the input of expert knowledge to allow for quicker and more precise management of the threat. The second part is threat decomposition, improving preparedness by decomposing threats into identifiable terrorist behaviours that can be detected in urban environments. The third part is capability management, which provide improved awareness of capabilities for action in dealing with the threat and any required mitigations actions. By dividing the problem in this way, and integrating three aspects into the overall TACTICS system, TACTICS proposes a more efficient team effort through which to detect, assess and respond to threats.

Ultimately, TACTICS will improve the effectiveness of security forces in counterterrorism efforts in urban areas by aiding the prevention of attacks and/or limiting their consequences. Local forces will be able to better maintain public order and national forces will more efficiently analyse threats and risk as well as coordinate anti-terrorist security accordingly. Such contributions will be crucial in the overall fight against terrorism.

Recommendations

Based on the research, the project team proposes the following recommendations for policymakers:

Deploy appropriate counterterrorism technologies that enhance decision making, but continue to pay attention to ongoing changes in the technology landscape.

As observed in the case of the introduction of body scanners in e.g. airport security, it is necessary to continue to enhance developed technologies to overcome their potential technical limitations against new threats or the terrorists' exploitation of any limitations associated with existing technologies.

Apply a structured approach to deployment of counterterrorism technology.

This approach must include a particular emphasis on the respect for national and European legislation and on the definition and respect for appropriate safeguards. A systematic assessment of needs and requirements for counterterrorist technologies will help ensure that the technology that is procured and deployed meet the capability need as well as fit in with national and European legislation.

Carefully consider the extent to which data collection and data sharing in the context of counterterrorism is proportionate, necessary and justified.

Identify and address potential privacy issues early.

When policy-makers consider the introduction of new technologies in the context of counterterrorism, they should identify and address potential privacy issues as early as possible in the capability assessment and procurement process.

Countering terrorism requires partnerships.

These partnerships need to exist within all levels of national government, law enforcement agencies, private sector and the communities, as well as an integrated approach in collaboration with international partners and key allies. Partnership with citizens is equally important, as observed in the range of acceptance of the CT technologies in the case studies.

Carry out regular audits and evaluations on the system use.

In order to ensure that the counterterrorism technology is operationally effective, it is necessary to establish an approach to evaluating its use and effectiveness. This is often a challenge. However, another main benefit of undertaking evaluations is the potential to flag up capability needs as a result, in terms of either systems performance or operator/manager training needs.

6

Terrorist Intelligence Operations

This chapter assesses the threat posed by terrorism to the United States and examines the role that OPSEC plays in protecting U.S. interests against terrorist attack. In testimony before the House Judiciary Committee in April 1995, Admiral William 0. Studeman, the Acting Director of Central Intelligence, summarized the terrorist threat to the United States in the following manner:

International terrorism remains one of the deadliest and most persistent threats to U.S. security. The motives, perpetrators, and methods of the terrorist groups are evolving in ways that complicate analysis, collection, and counteraction and require the ability to ship resources flexibly and quickly. The rise of the new breed of terrorist who is interested in inflicting mass death and destruction does not bode well for the future security of U.S. interests. These groups can strike at any time, anywhere, spurred by seemingly unrelated events for which they judge the United States to be blameworthy. They have a widening global reach and a high degree of proficiency with more sophisticated weapons and tactics.

Terrorism is defined as the unlawful use of force or violence against persons or property for the purposes of intimidating or coercing a government, the civilian population, or any segment thereof, in furtherance of political and social objectives. There are two categories of terrorism: domestic and international. Domestic terrorism involves groups or individuals whose activities, conducted in the United States without foreign influence, are directed at elements of the United States Government or population. International terrorism involves activity committed by foreign-based groups or individuals who are either directed by countries or groups outside the United States or whose activities transcend national boundaries.

The 7/7 terrorist attacks demonstrated that there were some clear deficiencies with the organisation of the United Kingdom's counter-terrorism intelligence community. In the aftermath of the attacks, there were moves to develop a more robust 'counter-terrorism network' in the United Kingdom that would facilitate better communication and intelligence sharing. While recent developments are to be welcomed, the reforms have not addressed some of the fundamental cultural, institutional and technological issues at the heart of the problem. The creation of an effective counter-terrorism network demands that information flows more freely through the intelligence community and that institutional boundaries are broken down. Until these obstacles have been overcome, the new counter-terrorism network will continue to be hampered by the same old problems of intelligence sharing.

Terrorist group categories

Terrorist groups generally are either non-state-supported (either indigenous or transnational), state-supported, or state-directed. Non-state supported terrorist groups are autonomous and receive no significant support from a government. State-supported groups generally operate independently but receive support from one or more governments. Such support may include weapons, training, money, intelligence, or safe havens. State- directed terrorist organizations act as agents of a government. Such groups receive intelligence, logistics, and operational support from the sponsoring government, frequently through diplomatic missions. State-directed terrorism is potentially a deniable and/or relatively inexpensive method of carrying out attacks against an enemy state or its interests.

The greatest terrorist threat to the United States today comes from fundamentalist Islamic extremist groups. Some of these groups, such as the Party of God (Hizballah), the Palestinian group Islamic Resistance Movement (HAMAS), and the Algerian Armed Islamic Group fit the traditional terrorist mold. These groups have hierarchical structures and receive support from state sponsors. A new Islamic threat is on the rise as a result of the activities of ad hoc terrorist groups. These groups are even more dangerous in many ways than the traditional groups because they lack a well-established organizational identity, and they tend to decentralize and compartment their activities. They are capable of producing sophisticated conventional weapons, as well as chemical and biological agents. They are also less constrained by state sponsors or other benefactors than more traditional terrorist organizations. These new groups seek to punish the United States and other Western nations by inflicting heavy civilian casualties. The World Trade Center bombers are prime examples of this new breed of radical, transnational Islamic terrorists.

Both the traditional groups and the newer, ad hoc groups have increased their capability to attack U.S. interests. The groups are well funded, and some have developed sophisticated international support networks that provide them great freedom of movement and increase their opportunities to attack the interests of the United States on a global basis. These groups are also attracting more qualified cadres with greater technical skills. Several groups have established supporting infrastructures within the United States that provide financial, logistics, operational, and intelligence support. Although, there is no evidence that these groups are centrally coordinated, it does appear that they collaborate in terrorist actions. Evidence gathered by Federal investigators in the World Trade Center bombing case, for example, shows that leaders or representatives of five different groups - the Palestinian Islamic Jihad, HAMAS, the Sudanese National Islamic Front, the Pakistan-based al-Fuqrah, and groups funded by Persian Gulf donors - were involved in the plot. The conspirators were aided by Sudanese diplomats affiliated with the National Islamic Front, which provided them with information and credentials. Evidence seized later from the apartment of one of the conspirators revealed detailed intelligence on potential targets and plans for other attacks in the New York area.

Tactics used by Terrorist

There are six basic types of tactics that terrorist groups have used: hijackings, kidnappings, bombings, assassinations, armed assaults, and barricade-hostage incidents. A group's objectives and organizational capabilities dictate which tactics it uses. Terrorist organizations typically use hijackings, kidnapping, and barricade-hostage incidents when the group wishes to force the targeted company or government into negotiations. The terrorist group frequently is able to obtain the release of prisoners or extort money. Such incidents increase the level of risk to the terrorist organization and require a mature planning, operations, logistics, and intelligence capability to successfully conduct the operation. Bombings, assassinations, and armed assaults are less risky and generally require less organizational capabilities. These tactics tend to be used to accomplish the following goals:

Create a climate of fear in a targeted group or nation through a sustained campaign of violence;

Retaliate for previous incidents or situations affecting the terrorist organization or its causes;

Negatively affect processes that the terrorist organization sees as against its interests;

Eliminate specific individuals or groups.

Attaining the terrorist organization's goals depends on receiving adequate information for planning and executing an operation. OPSEC denies terrorist organizations the information they require for planning. The following portions of this section discuss the terrorist threat to the United States and the role of sponsoring nations and terrorist organizations in executing attacks.

Terrorist objectives

Organizations intend their terrorist activities to have an emotional impact on the target audience, causing it to act in a manner that furthers the group's objectives. Terrorist operations generally are categorized in terms of their associated goals. These goals traditionally are divided into five categories: recognition, coercion, intimidation, provocation, and insurgency support. Early in their life span, terrorist groups often carry out attacks designed to gain recognition. The objective of these attacks is national and/or international attention for the group and its stated objectives. Groups often mount such attacks, which may involve protracted hostage seizures, against highly-visible symbols of state control (e.g., national airlines). Groups intend coercion attacks to force individuals, organizations, or governments to act in a desired manner. Using this strategy, terrorists selectively target facilities with the intent of bringing increasing pressure to bear on the targeted activity. Terrorist attacks designed primarily to intimidate are a means of preventing organizations or governments from acting in a defined manner. Provocation attacks aim to force government security forces to take repressive action against the general populace. These attacks generally are against critical infrastructures, popular or high-profile individuals, or important facilities. The goal of these attacks is to demonstrate the weakness of the legitimate government, thus causing an uncoordinated backlash.

Terrorist threats to the United States

Until recently, many people believed that the United States was largely immune to terrorist attack. This belief was based on the low number of terrorist attacks that took place in the United States during the 1980s and early 1990s. The bombing of the World Trade Center on February 26, 1993, demonstrated the nation's vulnerability to terrorist attack. In retrospect, however, there was no reason to discount U.S. vulnerability to terrorist attacks. Historically, the United States has been the target of over 32 percent of all terrorist attacks worldwide, second only to Israel. Domestically, the United States averaged 100 terrorist attacks per year in the 1970s, with 112 occurring in 1977 alone. Between 1980 and 1982, 122 terrorist attacks occurred in the United States with 51 of these attacks occurring in 1982. Between 1982 and 1993, a total of 177 confirmed terrorist incidents and 46 suspected terrorist incidents took place. Additionally, law enforcement intervention prevented 81 terrorist incidents, many of which could have resulted in extensive damage to property or significant loss of life. Superior intelligence collection and the infiltration of terrorist groups with informers enabled the Federal Bureau of Investigation, in concert with the Intelligence Community, to prevent these attacks. However, if terrorist groups continue to evolve into more informal, ad hoc structures, gathering information necessary to prevent terrorist incidents may become far more difficult.

It is likely that the number of terrorist attacks taking place inside the United States will increase within the next several years. According to current projections, worldwide terrorism will increase at a rate of roughly 15 percent per year - a figure in line with historical patterns. Most terrorist attacks against American interests will still occur overseas, but more violent attacks aimed at symbolic targets and vital infrastructure are likely to occur inside the United States. Both domestic and international terrorism are likely to increase. Moreover, as terrorists gain technical skills and attempt to stay one move ahead of counterterrorist and antiterrorist forces, the weapons and operational techniques used by terrorists are likely to grow more complex and more sophisticated.

Terrorist sponsors

The Department of State currently considers seven countries to be terrorist sponsors: Libya, Syria, Iran, Cuba, Sudan, Iraq, and North Korea.

Libya

Although it has made some cosmetic changes to its terrorism apparatus, Libya retains the capability to commit terrorist acts. Despite its public renunciation of terrorism, terrorism remains an important instrument of Libyan foreign policy, which is managed at the highest levels of government. The United States has successfully sought sanctions against Libya in the United Nations aimed at forcing the extradition of the two Libyan intelligence officers implicated in the bombing of Pan American flight 103. However, Libya has still failed to comply with the demands of the U.N. Security Council for the extradition of these individuals as well as those suspected to be involved in the bombing of UTA flight 772. In December 1993, the Security Council increased sanctions against Libya to compel compliance. While it has closed some terrorist facilities, Libya still provides safe havens and financial support for the Abu Nidal Organization (ANO) and other terrorist groups. In October 1993, Qaddafi vowed to strike the United States and nations supporting U.N. sanctions against Libya. It is believed that Libya possesses chemical weapons and is actively pursuing other weapons of mass destruction.

The primary Libyan intelligence organization, the Jamahariya Security Organization (JSO), has been directly implicated in the bombing of Pan American flight 103 and UTA flight 772. The bomb used to destroy Pan American 103 was traced to a station manager for Libyan Arab Airways in Malta. The station manager, a JSO intelligence officer, checked the bag at Luqa Airport in Malta on to a KLM aircraft flying to London with instructions for transfer to a flight for John F. Kennedy International Airport in New York. Because of his position, the Libyan station manager was able to bypass airport security and forward the suitcase with the bomb without any examination. Authorities in London placed the bag on the next flight to New York, Pan American 103, assuming that it has been checked and determined to be safe in Malta. A defector from the JSO to the United States provided critical information on the role of Libyan intelligence in the bombing of the aircraft.

The JSO was also responsible for planning and executing the LaBelle Discotheque bombing in Berlin, Germany which killed U.S. Army personnel in 1986. On December 4, 1992, the Federal Republic of Germany indicted two Libyan intelligence officers for their role in the bombing. The Libyan Embassy in East Germany provided the explosives used in the bombing and collected intelligence needed to target the nightclub. The JSO has also been directly implicated in the attacks by the ANO on the Rome and Vienna Airports in 1985. Libya provided forged passports and intelligence support, and used diplomatic pouches to move weapons into the vicinity of the attacks. The JSO was also involved in the attempted assassination of a U.S. ambassador in 1977. Libyan People's Bureaus throughout the world have been used to provide monetary support, weapons, training, and intelligence to disparate terrorist groups sponsored by Libya. The Libyans have also used front companies, the offices of Libyan Arab Airlines, and the Islamic Call Society as covers for intelligence and terrorist operations. The Libyans have also used these activities to obtain embargoed technologies and information for their program to produce weapons of mass destruction.

Syria

To advance its interests in the Middle East, Syria has used terrorism as an integral part of its foreign policy. Syrian intelligence officers and diplomats have been associated with attacks on Jordanian officials and Syrian dissidents living abroad. In January 1986, the Syrian intelligence service was behind a plot to smuggle a bomb through the United Kingdom's Heathrow Airport onto an El Al aircraft. Since the end of 1986, Syrian sponsorship of terrorist activities appears to have been restricted to the Middle East. Syrian intelligence is also involved in the diversion of technologies required for the manufacture of weapons of mass destruction, and for advanced conventional munitions. It is believed that Syria possesses chemical weapons and is developing the capability to produce biological weapons. Syria continues to provide safe haven, training, financial support, and perhaps intelligence support for a number of Middle East terrorist organizations. These organizations include the Palestine Islamic Jihad (PIJ), the Popular Front for the Liberation of Palestine-General Command, Hizballah, the Japanese Red Army, and HAMAS.

Iran

Iran is the most active sponsor of terrorism in the world. Since the inception of the Islamic state in 1979, the country has used terrorism as an integral part of its foreign and military policies. Iranian leaders view terrorism as a valid tool to accomplish their political objectives. Terrorist operations are reviewed and approved at the highest levels of the Iranian government, and the President of Iran is involved in the approval process of all major terrorist operations. Iranian-sponsored terrorism has had two major goals: Punishing opponents of the Islamic regime and expanding the Islamic movement throughout the Persian Gulf region. Iran sees terrorism as a means of attacking its enemies that is less likely to result in direct retribution against the Islamic Republic. This view has been reinforced by the United States' decisive victory in the Persian Gulf War.

Despite the overall decline in state-sponsored terrorist attacks, Iranian-sponsored attacks have actually increased. The number of terrorist attacks and the centralization of oversight of terrorist operations has increased since the election of President Rafsanjani, despite the supposed moderation of his regime. Tehran and its surrogates carried out 35 terrorist attacks between 1989, when Rafsanjani was elected, and 1992. Twenty of these attacks were conducted in 1992 alone, and the trend for these attacks has been toward increased levels of lethality.

The Iranian government plays a significant role in international terrorism by providing money, training, weapons, intelligence, documentation, and cover for terrorist activities. Three government agencies play primary roles. The Ministry of Intelligence and Security (MOIS) is responsible for intelligence collection to support terrorist operations. The ministry is also responsible for liaison activities with supported terrorist groups and Islamic fundamentalist movements. MOIS has also conducted terrorist operations in support of Iranian objectives. Most of these activities have focused on attacks on Iranian dissidents. The Qods Force of the Iranian Revolutionary Guard Corps (IRGC) is responsible for extraterritorial operations, including terrorist operations. A primary focus for the Qods Force is training Islamic fundamentalist terrorist groups. Currently, the Qods Force conducts training activities in Iran and in Sudan. The Qods Force is also responsible for gathering information required for targeting and attack planning. The final operational element of the Iranian government's terrorist support infrastructure is the Ministry of Foreign Affairs (WA). The WA provides diplomatic cover for terrorist operations, diplomatic pouch service for importation of weapons and explosives, and a safe haven at Iranian diplomatic facilities for execution of terrorist operations.

Iran maintains active liaison with Hizballah, HAMAS, the PIJ, and other terrorist groups. One of these groups - the Islamic Group, an Egyptian fundamentalist terrorist group - was involved in the bombing of the World Trade Center. Subsequent investigations revealed that members of the group who participated in the bombing received bank transfers in Germany from Iran and from Iranian organizations prior to the bombing. While this does not constitute definitive proof of Iranian involvement in the bombing, these facts suggest that the Iranian government supported the activities of the ad hoc terrorist organization that carried out the bombing. The Iranians have also embarked on a long-term program to develop weapons of mass destruction.

The Intelligence Community believes that Iran is likely to continue its support for terrorist operations for the foreseeable future. Iran has never paid a significant price for any of the terrorist activities it has sponsored and has obtained tangible political benefits in the Persian Gulf region. Iran will continue to focus the majority of its attacks on Israel in hopes of derailing the Middle East peace process. The United States will also continue to be a primary target for Iranian sponsored terrorist attacks. Iran and the terrorist groups it sponsors are continuing to develop operational plans to attack the United States and its allies. Iran has an extensive intelligence collection and terrorist infrastructure throughout the world. This infrastructure is particularly well developed in the United States, Europe, and South America. Iran has also formed alliances with Islamic fundamentalists in the Philippines, Pakistan, and Afghanistan.

Sudan

In August 1993, the State Department added Sudan to its list of terrorist states. Authorities now consider Sudan to be second to Iran in its support of Muslim terrorist groups. The government of Sudan has links to radical Arab terrorist organizations, including HAMAS, ANO, and the PIJ. Sudan also provides safe haven for PLO operatives and for Egyptian fundamentalists fleeing crack- downs by the Mubarak government. The governments of Tunisia, Algeria, and Egypt have asserted that Sudan is providing weapons, funds, training, passports, and safe haven for Islamic terrorist organizations that are attempting to overthrow their governments. To date, no conclusive evidence links Sudan with any terrorist act; however, Sudanese citizens comprised five of the fifteen suspects arrested in June 1993 for plotting to bomb the United Nations Building, the Lincoln and Holland Tunnels, the New York Federal Building, and other facilities in New York City. Senior members of the National Islamic Front (NIF), which dominates the Sudanese government, have also called for attacks against the United States. The United States also suspects that Sudan provided weapons and materiel to Somali groups responsible for attacks on U.S. and U.N. forces deployed in Somalia. Iran has maintained an extremely close relationship with Sudan, and the two nations have entered into agreements for joint military and intelligence activities.

Iraq

Since the mass expulsion of its intelligence officers and diplomats from numerous countries during the Gulf War, Iraq has not fully recovered its capability to conduct terrorist operations. Nevertheless, Iraq sponsored 39 terrorist operations in 1992 - activity which was in direct violation of its cease-fire agreement with the United Nations. One notable incident was the planned assassination of former President George Bush on his visit to Kuwait in 1993. The Iraqi government was also implicated in several dozen terrorist incidents in Northern Iraq in 1993. These attacks primarily targeted U.N. food distribution activities and humanitarian relief agency operations. Indications are that the Iraqi intelligence service has resumed terrorist targeting operations throughout the world. Iraq has a well-developed chemical weapons program and possesses biological agents. U.N. disarmament operations, however, have significantly damaged Iraq's nuclear weapons program.

Cuba

In the past, Cuba was a strong supporter of terrorist activities providing training, funds, weapons, and intelligence support. The Castro regime, which has become preoccupied with its own existence, is no longer able to support armed struggle actively in Latin America or other parts of the world. Currently, the regime's focus is on economic survival, and the government is attempting to upgrade diplomatic and trade relations in Latin America. However, Cuba still provides safe haven for a number of Latin American and European terrorist organizations. It still remains likely that the Castro regime would use terrorist attacks as a means to adversely affect U.S. interests and prevent the collapse of the Cuban regime; or if U.S. military action was anticipated. Cuba has a sophisticated intelligence collection capability that could be used for targeting U.S. facilities by terrorist groups. The Cuban intelligence service, the DGI, has the ability to unilaterally carry out such attacks against the United States.

North Korea

North Korea has a worldwide capability to conduct terrorist activities against the United States or its allies. If North Korea wishes, it can mount attacks on U.S. facilities at any time. North Korea has not sponsored any terrorist activity since 1987, when it conducted a mid-flight bombing of a Korean Air Lines aircraft. The North Korean Research Department for External Intelligence (RDEI) was responsible for this attack, and an earlier attack in Rangoon, Burma that targeted an official South Korean delegation headed by South Korea's president. North Korea still provides sanctuary for terrorist groups, and military instructors at terrorist training camps in Lebanon and Sudan. The North Koreans appear to be backing away from terrorism as a means to gain economic aid and advanced technology from the United States and Japan. North Korea is believed to have chemical and biological weapons and is currently believed to be engaged in developing nuclear weapons. A significant concern has been that North Korea may be willing to sell these technologies to state supporters of terrorism or terrorist groups.

Islamic fundamentalist groups

A variety of Islamic fundamentalist and/or radical Arab groups have the ability to conduct attacks inside the United States. Such groups - HAMAS, Hizballah, PIJ, ANO, and the Islamic Group - are characterized by their increasingly strident assertions of religious justification for terrorist activities against the oppressive regimes of the developed world. In particular, groups have identified the United States as anti-Islamic. For this reason, Iran and its followers characterize the United States as the Great Satan. It is notable that from 1975 to 1987, the number of religious terrorist groups, many of which were Islamic fundamentalist, increased six-fold. In contrast, the number of Marxist-Leninist groups has remained fairly steady, while the number of ethnic terrorist groups has declined. Not only have religious terrorist groups increased in number, but they have also become increasingly more violent as a way of fulfilling their mandate from God.

Islamic Resistance Movement (HAMAS)

Formed in 1987 as an outgrowth of the Muslim Brotherhood, HAMAS is a loosely structured organization. It is the principal political rival of Yasser Arafat's Fatah organization in the occupied territories. HAMAS has engaged in terrorist operations in the Gaza Strip and West Bank and has stridently opposed any settlement with the Israeli government. During 1994, HAMAS worked to undermine the legitimacy of the Provisional Palestinian government in the Gaza Strip and conducted several major acts of terrorism against Israel. The most prominent of these incidents was a suicide attack on an Israeli bus on the main street in Tel Aviv. This incident killed 23 people. HAMAS has links to Iran and has consistently opposed U.S. policy in the Middle East. The organization has been openly involved in propaganda and fund raising operations in the United States.

Of all of the Islamic militant groups, HAMAS has developed the most sophisticated U.S. infrastructure, including charitable, political, social, and military activities. HAMAS has conducted training in the United States on military tactics and the building of explosive devices. Musa Abu Marzuk, the international political director of HAMAS, was recently arrested by immigration authorities in the United States, and his extradition to Israel for terrorist activities is currently pending. Marzuk was a resident alien in the United States until 1993 and is credited with creating much of the HAMAS infrastructure in the United States. HAMAS has threatened to conduct terrorist attacks in the United States if Marzuk is extradited to Israel.

Palestine Islamic Jihad (PIJ)

The PIJ originated in the Gaza Strip during the 1970s. Rather than a cohesive entity, the group appears to be a loose coalition of factions. The PIJ is dedicated to creating an Islamic state in Palestine and destroying Israel. In 1994, the PIJ carried out a number of attacks against Israel with the aim of destroying the peace accord with the Palestinians. In January 1995, the PIJ claimed responsibility for the bombing of an Israeli bus stop at which Israeli soldiers were awaiting transportation to their base. The attack killed 21 soldiers. The PIJ publicly has threatened to attack U.S. interests as well as Arab governments that the group believes have been tainted by Western secularism. Iran, Sudan, and Syria provide aid to some PIJ factions. The PIJ also has a sizable presence in the United States with support activities in Tampa, FL; Chicago, IL; and Brooklyn, NY.

Abu Nidal Organization (ANO)

Since 1974, the ANO has carried out over 90 terrorist attacks in 20 countries, killing or injuring more than 900 people. The ANO has an overseas support structure which includes an intelligence collection activity that is active in the United States. ANO has targeted the United States, United Kingdom, France, Israel, moderate Palestinians, the PLO, and various Arab countries. The ANO has demonstrated the capability to conduct operations worldwide.

Islamic Group (Al-Gama'a al-Islamiyya)

The Islamic Group is an Egyptian Islamic extremist group whose spiritual leader is Sheik Omar Abdel Rahman. The group's goal is to overthrow the government of Hosni Mubarak and replace it with an Islamic state. Members of this group's predecessor were involved in the assassination of Anwar Sadat and have conducted terrorist attacks inside Egypt. Having strongly condemned the United States for its participation in Middle East politics and its support of the Mubarak government, leaders of the Islamic Group have urged their followers to punish the United States. The group's financial, logistics, and training support seems to come mainly from Iran and Sudan. Sheik Rahman and a number of his followers were tried in Federal district court in New York for conspiring to conduct a series of terrorist attacks in New York City during 1993.

Party of God (Hizballah)

Hizballah, a radical Shia group, was formed in Lebanon in 1982-1983 as a result of the merger of Hussein Musawi's Islamic Amal and the Lebanese branch of the Da'wa Party. Hizballah, which is closely allied with Iran, wishes to create an Islamic republic in Lebanon. It is believed that Hizballah was responsible for the bombing of the U.S. embassy in Lebanon and the Marine barracks in Beirut, and the kidnapping and murder of Western hostages in Lebanon. Hizballah has demonstrated the ability to conduct terrorist operations outside the Middle East and has claimed responsibility for the bombing of the Israeli Embassy in Buenos Aires in March 1992. Hizballah receives substantial amounts of financial, training, weapons, explosives, political, diplomatic, and organizational aid from Iran. It is believed that Hizballah has a significant support infrastructure in the United States capable of carrying out terrorist operations. However, at this time, there is no evidence that Hizballah is contemplating any type of attack against the United States. Hizballah likely would coordinate any operation with elements of the Iranian Revolu- tionary Guard Corps who are believed to have entered the United States in the late 1980s on student visas.

Terrorism Trends

First, as generational replacement has occurred in terrorist organizations, new leaders have become less concerned with ideological constraints and adverse public opinion. As a result, they are more willing to use excessively violent or shocking tactics. Second, leaders desire to maintain media attention. As they are becoming more violent, terrorist groups also have expanded the range of targets that they consider legitimate. Brian Jenkins, formerly the director of the Rand Corporation's Program on Subnational Conflict, has postulated three reasons for this trend. Limited acts of terrorism repeated over time have failed to gain desired media attention. To receive attention, terrorists have escalated the level of violence and have used bolder, more shocking tactics designed to force the media and the public to pay attention to the terrorist group and its demands. Finally, the internal dynamics of terrorist groups require that the organization move inexorably toward its goals. Increasingly violent tactics allow group members to perceive that they are increasingly powerful and are likely to achieve their objectives.

Data gathered from 1968 to 1990 substantiates the trend that the number of terrorist groups is increasing and that groups are also more violent. In 1990, there were 70 active terrorist groups throughout the world, compared to 11 identifiable groups in 1968. Although the number of terrorist incidents identified in the 1980s increased by only one-third over those identified in the 1970s, the level of violence increased dramatically. In the 1980s, the number of deaths worldwide attributed to terrorism doubled. There was a 75 percent increase in the number of terrorist incidents resulting in fatalities, a 115 percent increase in incidents resulting in 5 or more deaths, and a 135 percent increase in incidents resulting in 10 or more deaths. Pinkerton Risk

Assessment Services, an organization that tracks terrorist incidents, recorded an unprecedented 5,404 terrorist incidents in 1992, resulting in over 10,000 deaths. These incidents represent an 11 percent increase over 1991 figures. Part of this pattern is attributable to the growth of religious terrorism. Religious terrorists differ from traditional ideological terrorists in that the former are willing to sacrifice to obtain their objective. Consequently, religious terrorists are more likely to use indiscriminate violence. They see themselves as involved in a total war in which there are no innocent parties. In determining operational matters, religious terrorists also are largely unconcerned with public opinion.

As discussed earlier, some terrorist groups are evolving into new organizational structures that are harder to detect and infiltrate. These terrorist groups are often a collection of factions with common interests. Accordingly, the groups form, change, and regroup in response to specific agendas or planned actions. The groups tend to be religious or ethnic organizations that often have major grievances with the United States. The extremist factions of Islamic fundamentalist groups that are currently emerging fit this pattern. While many are funded by Iran or supported by Sudan, the emerging groups are not controlled or directed by either state. Instead, they tend to be autonomous in their planning and decision-making functions. According to William Webster, former Director of Central Intelligence, there may be dozens of such groups in the United States waiting for the opportunity to strike. The large number of these groups as well as their lack of central direction and changing organizational structures, make them very difficult to crack.

Finally, a trend may be developing regarding a sponsoring state's use of terrorists to conduct a proxy war against the United States. Terrorist groups offer the sponsoring state a deniable method to attack primary U.S. interests. In turn, sponsoring states would provide terrorist groups with funding, access to weapons and advanced technologies, intelligence, target planning support, logistics support, and secure communications. In times of crisis or conflict, the use of terrorists as proxies is the aspect of terrorism that appears to be the most dangerous to U.S. interests because attacks could be directed at facilities critical to force mobilization or crisis management.

Counter-terrorism

Counter-terrorism (also spelled counterterrorism), also known as antiterrorism, incorporates the practice, military tactics, techniques, and strategy that government, military, law enforcement, business, and intelligence agencies use to combat or prevent terrorism. Counter-terrorism strategies include attempts to counter financing of terrorism.

If terrorism is part of a broader insurgency, counter-terrorism may employ counter-insurgency measures. The United States Armed Forces use the term foreign internal defense for programs that support other countries in attempts to suppress insurgency, lawlessness, or subversion or to reduce the conditions under which these threats to security may develop.

History of Counter-terrorism

In response to the escalating terror campaign in Britain carried out by the militant Irish Fenians in the 1880s, the Home Secretary, Sir William Harcourt, established the first counter-terrorism unit ever. The Special Irish Branch was initially formed as a section of the Criminal Investigation Department of the London Metropolitan Police in 1883, to combat Irish republican terrorism through infiltration and subversion.

Harcourt envisioned a permanent unit dedicated to the prevention of politically motivated violence through the use of modern techniques such as undercover infiltration. This pioneering branch was the first to be trained in counter-terrorism techniques.

Its name was changed to Special Branch as it had its remit gradually expanded to incorporate a general role in counterterrorism, combating foreign subversion and infiltrating organized crime. Law enforcement agencies, in Britain and elsewhere, established similar units.

Counterterrorism forces expanded with the perceived growing threat of terrorism in the late 20th century. Specifically, after the September 11 attacks, Western governments made counter-terrorism efforts a priority, including more foreign cooperation, shifting tactics involving red teams and preventive measures. Although sensational attacks in the developed world receive a great deal of media attention, most terrorism occurs in less developed countries. Government responses to terrorism in some cases generate substantial unintended consequences.

Planning

Intelligence, surveillance and reconnaissance

Most counter-terrorism strategies involve an increase in standard police and domestic intelligence. The central activities are traditional: interception of communications, and the tracing of persons. New technology has, however, expanded the range of military and law enforcement operations.

Domestic intelligence is often directed at specific groups, defined on the basis of origin or religion, which is a source of political controversy. Mass surveillance of an entire population raises objections on civil liberties grounds. Homegrown terrorists, especially lone wolves are often harder to detect because of their citizenship or legal status and ability to stay under the radar.

To select the effective action when terrorism appears to be more of an isolated event, the appropriate government organizations need to understand the source, motivation, methods of preparation, and tactics of terrorist groups. Good intelligence is at the heart of such preparation, as well as political and social understanding of any grievances that might be solved. Ideally, one gets information from inside the group, a very difficult challenge for HUMINT because operational terrorist cells are often small, with all members known to one another, perhaps even related.

Counterintelligence is a great challenge with the security of cell-based systems, since the ideal, but nearly impossible, goal is to obtain a clandestine source within the cell. Financial tracking can play a role, as can communications intercept, but both of these approaches need to be balanced against legitimate expectations of privacy.

- Legal contexts
- In response to the growing legislation.

United Kingdom

The United Kingdom has had anti-terrorism legislation in place for more than thirty years. The Prevention of Violence Act 1939 was brought in response to an Irish Republican Army (IRA) campaign of violence under the S-Plan. This act had been allowed to expire in 1953 and was repealed in 1973 to be replaced by the Prevention of Terrorism Acts a response to the Troubles in Northern Ireland. From 1974 to 1989 the temporary provisions of the act were renewed annually.

In 2000 the Acts were replaced with the more permanent Terrorism Act 2000, which contained many of their powers, and then the Prevention of Terrorism Act 2005.

The Anti-terrorism, Crime and Security Act 2001 was formally introduced into the Parliament November 19, 2001 two months after the September 11, 2001 attacks in the United States. It received royal assent and went into force on December 13, 2001. On December 16, 2004 the Law Lords ruled that Part 4 was incompatible with the European Convention on Human Rights, but under the terms of the Human Rights Act 1998 it remained in force. The Prevention of Terrorism Act 2005 was drafted to answer the Law Lords ruling and the Terrorism Act 2006 creates new offences related to terrorism, and amends existing ones. The Act was drafted in the aftermath of the 7 July 2005 London bombings, and like its predecessors some of its terms have proven to be highly controversial.

Since 1978 the UK's terrorism laws have been regularly reviewed by a security-cleared Independent Reviewer of Terrorism Legislation, whose often influential reports are submitted to Parliament and published in full.

United States

U.S. legal issues surrounding this issue include rulings on the domestic employment of deadly force by law enforcement organizations.

Search and seizure is governed by the Fourth Amendment to the United States Constitution.

The U.S. passed the USA PATRIOT Act after the September 11 attacks, as well as a range of other legislation and executive orders relating to national security.

The Department of Homeland Security was established to consolidate domestic security agencies to coordinate anti-terrorism, as well as national response to major natural disasters and accidents.

The Posse Comitatus Act limits domestic employment of the United States Army and the United States Air Force, requiring Presidential approval prior to deploying the Army and/or the Air Force. Pentagon policy also applies this limitation to the United States Marine Corps and the United States Navy, because the Posse Comitatus Act doesn't cover naval services, even though they are federal military forces. The Department of Defense can be employed domestically on Presidential order, as was done during the Los Angeles riots of 1992, Hurricane Katrina, and the Beltway Sniper incidents.

External or international use of lethal force would require a Presidential finding.

In February 2017, sources claimed that the Trump administration intends to rename and revamp the U.S. government program Countering Violent Extremism (CVE) to solely focus on Islamist extremism.

Australia

Australia has passed several anti-terrorism acts. In 2004, a bill comprising three acts Anti-terrorism Act, 2004, (No 2) and (No 3) was passed. Then Attorney-General, Philip Ruddock, introduced the Anti-terrorism bill, 2004 on March 31. He described it as "a bill to strengthen Australia's counter-terrorism laws in a number of respects – a task made more urgent following the recent tragic terrorist bombings in Spain." He said that Australia's counter-terrorism laws "require review and, where necessary, updating if we are to have a legal framework capable of safeguarding all Australians from the scourge of terrorism." The Australian Anti-Terrorism Act 2005 supplemented the powers of the earlier acts. The Australian legislation allows police to detain suspects for up to two weeks without charge and to electronically track suspects for up to a year. The Australian Anti-Terrorism Act of 2005 included a "shoot-to-kill" clause. In a country with entrenched liberal democratic traditions, the measures are controversial and have been criticized by civil libertarians and Islamic groups.

Israel

Israel monitors a list of designated terrorist organizations and has laws forbidding membership in such organizations, funding or helping them in any way.

On December 14, 2006 the Israeli Supreme Court ruled targeted killings were a permitted form of self-defense.

In 2016 the Israeli Knesset passed a comprehensive law against terrorism, forbidding any kind of terrorism and support of terrorism, and setting severe punishments for terrorists. The law also regulate legal efforts against terrorism.

Human rights

One of the primary difficulties of implementing effective counter-terrorist measures is the waning of civil liberties and individual privacy that such measures often entail, both for citizens of, and for those detained by states attempting to combat terror. At times, measures designed to tighten security have been seen as abuses of power or even violations of human rights.

Examples of these problems can include prolonged, incommunicado detention without judicial review or long periods of 'preventive detention'; risk of subjecting to torture during the transfer, return and extradition of people between or within countries; and the adoption of security measures that restrain the rights or freedoms of citizens and breach principles of non-discrimination. Examples include:

In November 2003 Malaysia passed new counter-terrorism laws that were widely criticized by local human rights groups for being vague and overbroad. Critics claim that the laws put the basic rights of free expression, association, and assembly at risk. Malaysia persisted in holding around 100 alleged militants without trial, including five Malaysian students detained for alleged terrorist activity while studying in Karachi, Pakistan.

In November 2003 a Canadian-Syrian national, Maher Arar, alleged publicly that he had been tortured in a Syrian prison after being handed over to the Syrian authorities by U.S.

In December 2003 Colombia's congress approved legislation that would give the military the power to arrest, tap telephones and carry out searches without warrants or any previous judicial order.

Images of unpopular treatment of detainees in US custody in Iraq and other locations have encouraged international scrutiny of US operations in the war on terror.

Hundreds of foreign nationals remain in prolonged indefinite detention without charge or trial in Guantánamo Bay, despite international and US constitutional standards some groups believe outlaw such practices.

Hundreds of people suspected of connections with the Taliban or al Qa'eda remain in long-term detention in Pakistan or in US-controlled centers in Afghanistan.

China has used the "war on terror" to justify its policies in the predominantly Muslim Xinjiang Uighur Autonomous Region to stifle Uighur identity.

In Morocco, Saudi Arabia, Tunisia, Yemen and other countries, scores of people have been arrested and arbitrarily detained in connection with suspected terrorist acts or links to opposition armed groups.

Until 2005 eleven men remained in high security detention in the UK under the Anti-Terrorism, Crime and Security Act 2001.

Many would argue that such violations could exacerbate rather than counter the terrorist threat. Human rights advocates argue for the crucial role of human rights protection as an intrinsic part to fight against terrorism. This suggests, as proponents of human security have long argued, that respecting human rights may indeed help us to incur security. Amnesty International included a section on confronting terrorism in the recommendations in the Madrid Agenda arising from the Madrid Summit on Democracy and Terrorism (Madrid March 8–11, 2005):

Democratic principles and values are essential tools in the fight against terrorism. Any successful strategy for dealing with terrorism requires terrorists to be isolated. Consequently, the preference must be to treat terrorism as criminal acts to be handled through existing systems of law enforcement and with full respect for human rights and the rule of law. We recommend: (1) taking effective measures to make impunity impossible either for acts of terrorism or for the abuse of human rights in counter-terrorism measures. (2) the incorporation of human rights laws in all anti-terrorism programmes and policies of national governments as well as international bodies."

While international efforts to combat terrorism have focused on the need to enhance cooperation between states, proponents of human rights (as well as human security) have suggested that more effort needs to be given to the effective inclusion of human rights protection as a crucial element in that cooperation. They argue that international human rights obligations do not stop at borders and a failure to respect human rights in one state may undermine its effectiveness in the international effort to cooperate to combat terrorism.

Preemptive neutralization

Some countries see preemptive attacks as a legitimate strategy. This includes capturing, killing, or disabling suspected terrorists before they can mount an attack. Israel, the United Kingdom, the United States, and Russia have taken this approach, while Western European states generally do not.

Another major method of preemptive neutralization is interrogation of known or suspected terrorists to obtain information about specific plots, targets, the identity of other terrorists, whether or not the interrogation subjects himself is guilty of terrorist involvement. Sometimes more extreme methods are used to increase suggestibility, such as sleep deprivation or drugs. Such methods may lead captives to offer false information in an attempt to stop the treatment, or due to the confusion brought on by it. These methods are not tolerated by European powers. In 1978 the European Court of Human Rights ruled in the Ireland v. United Kingdom case that such methods amounted to a practice of inhuman and degrading treatment, and that such practices were in breach of the European Convention on Human Rights Article 3 (art. 3).

Non-military

The human security paradigm outlines a non-military approach which aims to address the enduring underlying inequalities which fuel terrorist activity. Causal factors need to be delineated and measures implemented which allow equal access to resources and sustainability for all people. Such activities empower citizens providing 'freedom from fear' and 'freedom from want'.

This can take many forms including the provision of clean drinking water, education, vaccination programs, provision of food and shelter and protection from violence, military or otherwise. Successful human security campaigns have been characterized by the participation of a diverse group of actors including governments, NGOs, and citizens.

Foreign internal defense programs provide outside expert assistance to a threatened government. FID can involve both non-military and military aspects of counter-terrorism.

A 2017 study found that "governance and civil society aid is effective in dampening domestic terrorism, but this effect is only present if the recipient country is not experiencing a civil conflict."

Military

Terrorism has often been used to justify military intervention in countries like Pakistan where terrorists are said to be based. That was the main stated justification for the U.S. invasion of Afghanistan. It was also a stated justification for the second Russian invasion of Chechnya.

Military intervention has not always been successful in stopping or preventing future terrorism, like during the Malayan Emergency, the Mau Mau uprising, and most of the campaigns against the IRA during the Irish Civil War, the S-Plan, the Border Campaign (IRA) and the Troubles in Northern Ireland. Although military action can disrupt a terrorist group's operations temporarily, it sometimes doesn't end the threat completely.

Thus repression by the military in itself (particularly if it is not accompanied by other measures) usually leads to short term victories, but tend to be unsuccessful in the long run (e.g. the French's doctrine described in Roger Trinquier's book Modern War used in Indochina and Algeria). However, new methods (see the new Counterinsurgency Field Manual) such as those taken in Iraq have yet to be seen as beneficial or ineffectual.

Tactical units

Today, many countries have special units designated to handle terrorist threats. Besides various security agencies, there are elite tactical units, also known as special mission units, whose role is to directly engage terrorists and prevent terrorist attacks. Such units perform both in preventive actions, hostage rescue and responding to on-going attacks. Countries of all sizes can have highly trained counter-terrorist teams. Tactics, techniques and procedures for manhunting are under constant development.

Most of these measures deal with terrorist attacks that affect an area, or threaten to do so. It is far harder to deal with assassination, or even reprisals on individuals, due to the short (if any) warning time and the quick exfiltration of the assassins.

These units are specially trained in tactics and are very well equipped for CQB with emphasis on stealth and performing the mission with minimal casualties. The units include take-over force (assault teams), snipers, EOD experts, dog handlers and intelligence officers. See Counter-intelligence and counter-terrorism organizations for national command, intelligence, and incident mitigation.

The majority of counter-terrorism operations at the tactical level, are conducted by state, federal and national law enforcement agencies or intelligence agencies. In some countries, the military may be called in as a last resort. Obviously, for countries whose military are legally permitted to conduct police operations, this is a non-issue, and such counter-terrorism operations are conducted by their military.

See counter-intelligence for command, intelligence and warning, and incident mitigation aspects of counter-terror.

Designing Anti-terrorism systems

The scope for Anti-terrorism systems is very large in physical terms (long borders, vast areas, high traffic volumes in busy cities, etc.) as well as in other dimensions, such as type and degree of terrorism threat, political and diplomatic ramifications, and legal issues. In this environment, the development of a persistent Anti-terrorism protection system is a daunting task. Such a system should bring together diverse state-of-the-art technologies to enable persistent intelligence, surveillance and reconnaissance missions, and enable potential actions. Designing such a system-of-systems comprises a major technological project.

A particular design problem for this system is that it will face many uncertainties in the future. The threat of terrorism may increase, decrease or remain the same, the type of terrorism and location are difficult to predict, and there are technological uncertainties. Yet we want to design a terrorism system conceived and designed today in order to prevent acts of terrorism for a decade or more. A potential solution is to incorporate flexibility into system design for the reason that the flexibility embedded can be exercised in future as uncertainty unfolds and updated information arrives. And the design and valuation of a protection system should not be based on a single scenario, but an array of scenarios. Flexibility can be incorporated in the design of the terrorism system in the form of options that can be exercised in the future when new information is available. Using these 'real options' will create a flexible Anti-terrorism system that is able to cope with new requirements that may arise.

Law enforcement/Police

While some countries with longstanding terrorism problems, such as Israel, have law enforcement agencies primarily designed to prevent and respond to terror attacks, in other nations, counter-terrorism is a relatively more recent objective of civilian police and law enforcement agencies.

While some civil-libertarians and criminal justice scholars have called-out efforts of law enforcement agencies to combat terrorism as futile and expensive or as threats to civil liberties, other scholars have begun describing and analyzing the most important dimensions of the policing of terrorism as an important dimension of counterterrorism, especially in the post-9/11 era, and have argued how police institutions view terrorism as a matter of crime control. Such analyses bring out the civilian police role in counterterrorism next to the military model of a 'war on terror'.

Counter-Terrorism and American Law Enforcement

Pursuant to passage of the Homeland Security Act of 2002, federal, state, and local law enforcement agencies began to systemically reorganize. Two primary federal agencies (the Department of Justice (DOJ) and the Department of Homeland Security (DHS)) house most of the federal agencies that are prepared to combat domestic and international terrorist attacks. These include the Border Patrol, the Secret Service, the Coast Guard and the FBI.

Following suit from federal changes pursuant to 9/11, however, most state and local law enforcement agencies began to include a commitment to "fighting terrorism" in their mission statements. Local agencies began to establish more patterned lines of communication with federal agencies. Some scholars have doubted the ability of local police to help in the war on terror and suggest their limited manpower is still best utilized by engaging community and targeting street crimes.

While counter-terror measures (most notably heightened airport security, immigrant profiling and border patrol) have been adapted during the last decade, to enhance counter-terror in law enforcement, there have been remarkable limitations to assessing the actual utility/effectiveness of law enforcement practices that are ostensibly preventative. Thus, while sweeping changes in counter-terrorism rhetoric redefined most American post 9/11 law enforcement agencies in theory, it is hard to assess how well such hyperbole has translated into practice.

In intelligence-led policing(ILP) efforts, the most quantitatively amenable starting point for measuring the effectiveness of any policing strategy (i.e.: Neighborhood Watch, Gun Abatement, Foot Patrols, etc.) is usually to assess total financial costs against clearance rates or arrest rates. Since terrorism is such a rare event phenomena, measuring arrests or clearance rates would be a non-generalizable and ineffective way to test enforcement policy effectiveness. Another methodological problem in assessing counter-terrorism efforts in law enforcement hinges on finding operational measures for key concepts in the study of homeland security. Both terrorism and homeland security are relatively new concepts for criminologists, and academicians have yet to agree on the matter of how to properly define these ideas in a way that is accessible.

International Counter-Terrorism Agencies

Albania: RENEA

Algeria: GIS, DSI [fr], GOSP.

Argentina: GEOF (Special Group of Federal Operations, Federal Arg Police) Falcon Commando (Comando Halcon, State Buenos Aires Police)

Australia: State and Australian Federal Police, Police Tactical Groups, Tactical Assault Group (TAG East & TAG West), and Australian Security and Intelligence Organization (ASIO)

- Austria: EKO Cobra; Austrian Military Police; Jagdkommando
- Bangladesh: 1st Para-commando Battalion, Navy Special Warfare Diving and Salvage (BN SWADS)
- Brazil: State/local Police SWAT teams: BOPE, COE, GATE, COT
- Belgium: Directorate of special units (DSU) Federal Police Special Units
- Bosnia and Herzegovina: SIPA
- Bulgaria: Specializiran Otriad za Borba s Terorizma
- Canada: Emergency Task Force, Joint Task Force 2
- Chile: GOPE (Police Special Operations Group, Chilean Carabineros) ERTA (Tactic Reaction Team, PDI Chilean Civil Police)
- China: Snow Leopard Commando Unit+, Beijing SWAT.
- Colombia: AFEUR+, GAULA, COPES
- Croatia: Lučko Anti-Terrorist Unit, RH Alfa
- Czech Republic: URNA National Police Rapid Response Unit or Útvar rychlého nasazení

Denmark: Politiets Aktionsstyrke

- Dominican Republic: Anti-terrorism Special Command – Comando Especial Contra Terrorismo
- Egypt: Unit 777, Hostage Rescue Force HRF
- Finland: Karhu-ryhmä, Utti Jaeger Regiment, Guard Jaeger Regiment
- France: BRI-BAC (Paris Police Prefecture), RAID (National Police) and GIGN (National Gendarmerie)
- Georgia: Designated - Counter Terrorism Center State Security Service, Federal: MIA - Special Emergency and Crisis Center
- Germany: Federal Police: GSG 9 and BFE– / State Police: SEK and MEK
- Greece: Anti-Terror Division, Greek Police and Special Anti-Terrorist Unit.
- Hungary: Counter Terrorism Centre, Alert Police, Hungarian Homeland Defence Forces
- Hong Kong : Special Duties Unit, Airport Security Unit, Counter Terrorism Response Unit

Iceland: Víkingasveitin

India: Rashtriya Rifles, NSG, NIA, Anti Terrorist Squad, Force One, Thunderbolt, state/local Police SWAT teams

Indonesia: Detachment 88 (Police), Satuan 81/Gultor (Army)+, Detachment Bravo 90+ (Air Force), Jala Mengkara Detachment+ (Navy)

Iran: NAJA (Iranian Police), NOPO (Counter-terrorism Special Force), Police Amniat (Security Police)

Iraq: Iraqi Hillah Swat, Kurdish anti terror, Iraqi Counter Terrorism Force

Ireland: Garda Special Detective Unit, Garda Emergency Response Unit,

Garda National Surveillance Unit, Defence Forces Directorate of Military Intelligence+, Defence Forces Army Ranger Wing+

Israel: YAMAM – elite Israeli Police anti-terror unit (counter-terror, foiling terrorism, hostages rescue etc.), "Mistaaravim" – IDF and Border Guard undercover units for foiling terrorism, Shin Bet – counter-terrorism intelligence and security agency

Italy: NOCS, GIS, A.P.I. Aliquota Primo Intervento, ATPI

Japan: Special Assault Teams and Anti-firearms squads (Prefectural police departments), Special Security Team (Japan Coast Guard), Central Readiness Force (JGDSF)

- Kosovo: NJSI-SIU Special Intervenation Unit
- Latvia: OMEGA police unit
- Lithuania: ARAS (Force) Lithuanian Police force of antiterrorism operations

Malaysia: Royal Malaysia Police Special Task Force (Operations / Counter Terrorism), Royal Malaysia Police Pasukan Gerakan Khas, UNGERIN, Rapid Actions Troops, STAR APMM

- Mexico: Mexican Army Special Reaction Force, Federal Police GOPES
- Morocco: Groupement de Sécurité Gendarmerie Royale

Netherlands: DSI (Dutch: Dienst Speciale Interventies, Special Interventions Service) and police special arrest teams Royal Marechaussee (Dutch: Brigade Speciale Beveiligingsopdrachten, Special Security Task Brigade) Dutch marines BBE

New Zealand: NZ Police Special Tactics Group, New Zealand Special Air Service

- Nigeria: National Intelligence Agency MOPOL
- Norway: Emergency Response Unit, FSK+

Pakistan: Special Service Group, Pakistan Army Rangers, Elite Police Commandos, Counter Terrorism Department

Philippines: Philippine Army-Light Reaction Regiment, PNP-Special Action Force, Philippine Navy-Naval Special Warfare Group, Philippine Air Force – 710th Special Operations Wing, Philippine Coast Guard-Special Operations Group and police SWAT teams

- Poland: BOA, SPAP, ABW V Directoriate of III Departament
- Portugal: GOE and COE

Romania: Brigada Antiteroristă, (counter-terrorist brigade)

Russia: Spetsgruppa A, Vympel, OMON, Spetsnaz GRU, Vityaz, Rus, SOBR

- Serbia: SAJ, PTJ, Cobras MP, MP-CT Battalion
- Slovenia: Special Police Unit, SEP Slovenian national police forces

South Korea: 707th Special Mission Unit, Republic of Korea Navy Special Warfare Flotilla

Sri Lanka: 3rd Sri Lanka Army Special Forces Regiment, 3rd Sri Lanka Army Commando Regiment, Special Task Force

Spain: GEO, UEI and GEI, CITCO

Sweden: National Task Force (Nationella Insatsstyrkan) and Särskilda operationsgruppen (Special Forces)

Taiwan: Thunder Squad

- Turkey: Özel tim-Özel Harekat Timi (Special Team) and Maroon Berets
- Tunisia: BAT and USGN
- United Kingdom: Counter Terrorism Command, Special Air Service

United States: FBI Counter-terrorism Special Agents, FBI Hostage Rescue Team, FBI Special Weapons and Tactics Teams, (FBI SWAT) Federal Air Marshal Service, Delta Force, (US Army), Naval Special Warfare Development Group, CIA Special Activities Division, (SAD) Diplomatic Security Service, Immigration and Customs Enforcement, BORTAC, state/local Police SWAT teams

Uruguay: GEO (Uruguayan Police) and Escorpión Commando Group (Uruguayan Army)

Military

Given the nature of operational counter-terrorism tasks national military organizations do not generally have dedicated units whose sole responsibility is the prosecution of these tasks. Instead the counter-terrorism function is an element of the role, allowing flexibility in their employment, with operations being undertaken in the domestic or international context.

In some cases the legal framework within which they operate prohibits military units conducting operations in the domestic arena; United States Department of Defense policy, based on the Posse Comitatus Act, forbids domestic counter-terrorism operations by the U.S. military. Units allocated some operational counter-terrorism task are frequently Special Forces or similar assets.

Intelligence agency

An intelligence agency is a government agency responsible for the collection, analysis, and exploitation of information in support of law enforcement, national security, military, and foreign policy objectives.

Means of information gathering are both overt and covert and may include espionage, communication interception, cryptanalysis, cooperation with other institutions, and evaluation of public sources. The assembly and propagation of this information is known as intelligence analysis or intelligence assessment.

Intelligence agencies can provide the following services for their national governments.

Give early warning of impending crises;

Serve national and international crisis management by helping to discern the intentions of current or potential opponents;

Inform national defense planning and military operations (military intelligence);

Protect sensitive information secrets, both of their own sources and activities, and those of other state agencies;

May act covertly to influence the outcome of events in favor of national interests, or influence international security; and

Defense against the efforts of other national intelligence agencies (counter-intelligence).

There is a distinction between "security intelligence" and "foreign intelligence". Security intelligence pertains to domestic threats (e.g., terrorism, espionage). Foreign intelligence involves information collection relating to the political, or economic activities of foreign states.

Some agencies have been involved in assassination, arms trafficking, coups d'état, and the placement of misinformation (propaganda) as well as other covert operations, in order to support their own or their governments' interests.

Mass surveillance

Mass surveillance is the intricate surveillance of an entire or a substantial fraction of a population in order to monitor that group of citizens. The surveillance is often carried out by local and federal governments or governmental organisations, such as organizations like the NSA and the FBI, but it may also be carried out by corporations (either on behalf of governments or at their own initiative). Depending on each nation's laws and judicial systems, the legality of and the permission required to engage in mass surveillance varies. It is the single most indicative distinguishing trait of totalitarian regimes. It is also often distinguished from targeted surveillance.

Mass surveillance has often been cited as necessary to fight terrorism, prevent crime and social unrest, protect national security, and control the population. Conversely, mass surveillance has equally often been criticized for violating privacy rights, limiting civil and political rights and freedoms, and being illegal under some legal or constitutional systems. Another criticism is that increasing mass surveillance could lead to the development of a surveillance state or an electronic police state where civil liberties are infringed or political dissent is undermined by COINTELPRO-like programs. Such a state could be referred to as a totalitarian state.

In 2013, the practice of mass surveillance by world governments was called into question after Edward Snowden's 2013 global surveillance disclosure. Reporting based on documents Snowden leaked to various media outlets triggered a debate about civil liberties and the right to privacy in the Digital Age. Mass surveillance is considered a global issue.

By country

Privacy International's 2007 survey, covering 47 countries, indicated that there had been an increase in surveillance and a decline in the performance of privacy safeguards, compared to the previous year. Balancing these factors, eight countries were rated as being 'endemic surveillance societies'. Of these eight, China, Malaysia and Russia scored lowest, followed jointly by Singapore and the United Kingdom, then jointly by Taiwan, Thailand and the United States. The best ranking was given to Greece, which was judged to have 'adequate safeguards against abuse'.

Many countries throughout the world have already been adding thousands of surveillance cameras to their urban, suburban and even rural areas. For example, in September 2007 the American Civil Liberties Union (ACLU) stated that we are "in danger of tipping into a genuine surveillance society completely alien to American values" with "the potential for a dark future where our every move, our every transaction, our every communication is recorded, compiled, and stored away, ready to be examined and used against us by the authorities whenever they want."

On 12 March 2013, Reporters Without Borders published a Special report on Internet Surveillance. The report included a list of "State Enemies of the Internet", countries whose governments are involved in active, intrusive surveillance of news providers, resulting in grave violations of freedom of information and human rights. Five countries were placed on the initial list: Bahrain, China, Iran, Syria, and Vietnam.

Australia

Bahrain

Bahrain is one of the five countries on Reporters Without Borders' March 2013 list of "State Enemies of the Internet", countries whose governments are involved in active, intrusive surveillance of news providers, resulting in grave violations of freedom of information and human rights. The level of Internet filtering and surveillance in Bahrain is one of the highest in the world. The royal family is represented in all areas of Internet management and has sophisticated tools at its disposal for spying on its subjects. The online activities of dissidents and news providers are closely monitored and the surveillance is increasing.

Canada

China

China is one of the five countries on Reporters Without Borders' March 2013 list of "State Enemies of the Internet", countries whose governments are involved in active, intrusive surveillance of news providers, resulting in grave violations of freedom of information and human rights. All Internet access in China is owned or controlled by the state or the Communist Party. Many foreign journalists in China have said that they take for granted that their telephones are tapped and their email is monitored.

The tools put in place to filter and monitor the Internet are collectively known as the Great Firewall of China. Besides the usual routing regulations that allow access to an IP address or a particular domain name to be blocked, the Great Firewall makes large-scale use of Deep Packet Inspection (DPI) technology to monitor and block access based on keyword detection. The Great Firewall has the ability to dynamically block encrypted connections. One of the country's main ISPs, China Unicom, automatically cuts a connection as soon as it is used to transmit encrypted content.

The monitoring system developed by China is not confined to the Great Firewall, monitoring is also built into social networks, chat services and VoIP. Private companies are directly responsible to the Chinese authorities for surveillance of their networks to ensure banned messages are not circulated. The QQ application, owned by the firm Tencent, allows the authorities to monitor in detail exchanges between Internet users by seeking certain keywords and expressions. The author of each message can be identified by his or her user number. The QQ application is effectively a giant Trojan horse. And since March 2012, new legislation requires all new users of micro-blogging sites to register using their own name and telephone number.

Skype, one of the world's most popular Internet telephone platforms, is closely monitored. Skype services in China are available through a local partner, the TOM media group. The Chinese-language version of Skype, known as TOM-Skype, is slightly different from the downloadable versions in other countries. A report by OpenNet Initiative Asia says everyday conversations are captured on servers. Interception and storage of a conversation may be triggered by a sender's or recipient's name or by keywords that occur in the conversation.

On 30 January, the New York Times reported that it had been the target of attacks by the Chinese government. The first breach took place on 13 September 2012 when the newspaper was preparing to publish an article about the fortune amassed by the family of outgoing Prime Minister Wen Jiabao. The newspaper said the purpose of attacks was to identify the sources that supplied the newspaper with information about corruption among the prime minister's entourage. The Wall Street Journal and CNN also said they had been the targets of cyber attacks from China. In February, Twitter disclosed that the accounts of some 250,000 subscribers had been the victims of attacks from China similar to those carried out on the New York Times. Mandiant, the company engaged by the NYT to secure its network, identified the source of the attacks as a group of hackers it called Advanced Persistent Threat 1, a unit of the People's Liberation Army operating from a 12-story building in the suburbs of Shanghai that had hundreds, possibly thousands, of staff and the direct support of the Chinese government.

The newest form of mass surveillance in China is the Social Credit System, where citizens and businesses are given or deducted good behavior points depending on their choices.

East Germany

Before the Digital Revolution, one of the world's biggest mass surveillance operations was carried out by the Stasi, the secret police of the former East

Germany. By the time the state collapsed in 1989, the Stasi had built up an estimated civilian network of 300,000 informants (approximately one in fifty of the population), who monitored even minute hints of political dissent among other citizens. Many West Germans visiting friends and family in East Germany were also subject to Stasi spying, as well as many high-ranking West German politicians and persons in the public eye.

Most East German citizens were well aware that their government was spying on them, which led to a culture of mistrust: touchy political issues were only discussed in the comfort of their own four walls and only with the closest of friends and family members, while widely maintaining a façade of unquestioning followership in public.

European Union

The right to privacy is a highly developed area of law in Europe. The Data Protection Directive regulates the processing of personal data within the European Union. For comparison, the US has no data protection law that is comparable to this; instead, the US regulates data protection on a sectoral basis.

Since early 2012, the European Union has been working on a General Data Protection Regulation to replace the Data Protection Directive and harmonise data protection and privacy law. On 20 October 2013, a committee at the European Parliament backed the measure, which, if it is enacted, could require American companies to seek clearance from European officials before complying with United States warrants seeking private data. The vote is part of efforts in Europe to shield citizens from online surveillance in the wake of revelations about a far-reaching spying program by the U.S. National Security Agency. European Union justice and rights commissioner Viviane Reding said "The question has arisen whether the large-scale collection and processing of personal information under US surveillance programmes is necessary and proportionate to meet the interests of national security." The EU is also asking the US for changes to US legislation to match the legal redress offered in Europe; American citizens in Europe can go to the courts if they feel their rights are infringed but Europeans without right of residence in America cannot. When the EU / US arrangement to implement International Safe Harbor Privacy Principles were struck down by the European Court of Justice, a new framework for transatlantic data flows, called the "EU-US Privacy Shield", was adopted in July 2016.

In April 2014, the European Court of Justice declared invalid the EU Data Retention Directive. The Court said it violates two basic rights - respect for private life and protection of personal data. The legislative body of the European Union passed the Data Retention Directive on 15 December 2005. It requires that telecommunication operators retain metadata for telephone, Internet, and other telecommunication services for periods of not less than six months and not more than two years from the date of the communication as determined by each EU member state and, upon request, to make the data available to various governmental bodies. Access to this information is not limited to investigation of serious crimes, nor is a warrant required for access.

Undertaken under the Seventh Framework Programme for research and technological development (FP7 - Science in Society) some multidisciplinary and mission oriented mass surveillance activities (for example INDECT and HIDE) were funded by the European Commission in association with industrial partners.

The INDECT Project ("Intelligent information system supporting observation, searching and detection for security of citizens in urban environment") develops an intelligent urban environment observation system to register and exchange operational data for the automatic detection, recognition and intelligent processing of all information of abnormal behaviour or violence.

The main expected results of the INDECT project are:

Trial of intelligent analysis of video and audio data for threat detection in urban environments,

Creation of tools and technology for privacy and data protection during storage and transmission of information using quantum cryptography and new methods of digital watermarking,

Performing computer-aided detection of threats and targeted crimes in Internet resources with privacy-protecting solutions,

Construction of a search engine for rapid semantic search based on watermarking of content related to child pornography and human organ trafficking,

Implementation of a distributed computer system that is capable of effective intelligent processing.

HIDE ("Homeland Security, Biometric Identification & Personal Detection Ethics") was a research project funded by the European Commission within the scope of the Seventh RTD Framework Programme (FP7). The consortium, coordinated by Emilio Mordini, explored the ethical and privacy implications of biometrics and personal detection technologies, focusing on the continuum between personal detection, authentication, identification and mass surveillance.

Germany

In 2002 German citizens were tipped off about wiretapping when a software error led to a phone number allocated to the German Secret Service being listed on mobile telephone bills.

India

The Indian parliament passed the Information Technology Act of 2008 with no debate, giving the government fiat power to tap all communications without a court order or a warrant. Section 69 of the act states "Section 69 empowers the Central Government/State Government/ its authorized agency to intercept, monitor or decrypt any information generated, transmitted, received or stored in any computer resource if it is necessary or expedient so to do in the interest of the sovereignty or integrity of India, defence of India, security of the State, friendly relations with foreign States or public order or for preventing incitement to the commission of any cognizable offence or for investigation of any offence."

India is setting up a national intelligence grid called NATGRID, which would be fully set up by May 2011 where each individual's data ranging from land records, Internet logs, air and rail PNR, phone records, gun records, driving license, property records, insurance, and income tax records would be available in real time and with no oversight. With a UID from the Unique Identification Authority of India being given to every Indian from February 2011, the government would be able track people in real time. A national population registry of all citizens will be established by the 2011 census, during which fingerprints and iris scans would be taken along with GPS records of each household.

As per the initial plan, access to the combined data will be given to 11 agencies, including the Research and Analysis Wing, the Intelligence Bureau, the Enforcement Directorate, the National Investigation Agency, the Central Bureau of Investigation, the Directorate of Revenue Intelligence and the Narcotics Control Bureau.

Several states within India have already installed CCTV surveillance systems with face matching capabilities using biometrics in Aadhaar. Andhra Pradesh and Telangana are using information linked with Aadhaar across different agencies to create a 360-degree profile of a person, calling it the Integration Information Hub. Other states are now planning to follow this model.

Iran

Iran is one of the five countries on Reporters Without Borders' March 2013 list of "State Enemies of the Internet", countries whose governments are involved in naturally active efforts to news providers . The government runs or controls almost all of the country's institutions for regulating, managing or legislating on telecommunications. The Supreme Council for Cyberspace, which was headed by President Ahmadinejad, was established in March 2012 and now determines digital policy. The construction of a parallel "Iranian Internet", with a high connection speed but fully monitored and censored, is almost complete.

The tools used by the Iranian authorities to monitor and control the Internet include data interception tools capable of Deep Packet Inspection. Interception products from leading Chinese companies such as ZTE and Huawei are in use. The products provided by Huawei to Mobin Net, the leading national provider of mobile broadband, can be used to analyze email content, track browsing history and block access to sites. The products that ZTA sold to the Telecommunication Company of Iran (TCI) offer similar services plus the possibility of monitoring the mobile network. European companies are the source of other spying and data analysis tools. Products designed by Ericsson and Nokia Siemens Networks (later Trovicor) are in use. These companies sold SMS interception and user location products to Mobile Communication Company of Iran and Irancell, Iran's two biggest mobile phone companies, in 2009 and they were used to identify Iranian citizens during the post-election uprising in 2009. The use of Israeli surveillance devices has also been detected in Iran. The network traffic management and surveillance device NetEnforcer was provided by Israel to Denmark and then resold to Iran. Similarly, US equipment has found its way to Iran via the Chinese company ZTE.

Malaysia

In July 2018, the Malaysian police announced the creation of the Malaysian Internet Crime Against Children Investigation Unit (Micac) that is equipped with real-time mass internet surveillance software developed in the United States and is tasked with the monitoring of all Malaysian internet users, with a focus on pornography and child pornography. The system creates a "data library" of users which includes details such as IP addresses, websites, locations, duration and frequency of use and files uploaded and downloaded.

Mexico

After struggling with drug trafficking and criminal groups for decades Mexico has been strengthening their military mass surveillance. Approximately half of the population in Mexico does not support democracy as a form of government, and believe an authoritarian system is better if social matters are solved through it. The relevance of these political beliefs may make it easier for mass surveillance to take spread within the country. "This does not necessarily mean the end of democratic institutions as a whole—such as free elections or the permanence of critical mass media—but it means strengthening the mechanisms for exercising power that exclude dialogue, transparency and social agreement." Developing intelligence agencies has been on Mexico's radar for a while for means of security.

Netherlands

According to a 2004 report, the government of the Netherlands carries out more clandestine wire-taps and intercepts than any country, per capita, in the world. The Dutch military intelligence service MIVD operates a satellite ground station to intercept foreign satellite links and also a facility to eavesdrop on foreign high-frequency radio traffic.

North Korea

Having attained the nickname 'surveillance state', North Korea's government has complete control over all forms of telecommunications and Internet. It is routine to be sent to a prison camp for communicating with the outside world. The government enforces restrictions around the types of appliances North Koreans may own in their home, in case radio or TV sets pick up signals from nearby South Korea, China and Russia. There is no attempt to mask the way this government actively spies on their citizens. In North Korea, an increasing number of citizens do have smartphones. However, these devices are heavily controlled and are being used to censor and observe everything North Koreans do on their phones. Reuters reported in 2015 that Koryolink, North Korea's official mobile phone network, has around 3 million subscribers in a country of 24 million. Obviously, in order to have digital data to draw from, the citizens must have access to phones and other things online.

Russia

The SORM (and SORM-2) laws enable complete monitoring of any communication, electronic or traditional, by eight state agencies, without warrant. These laws seem to be in conflict with Article 23 of the Constitution of Russia which states:

Everyone shall have the right to the inviolability of private life, personal and family secrets, the protection of honour and good name.

Everyone shall have the right to privacy of correspondence, of telephone conversations, postal, telegraph and other messages. Limitations of this right shall be allowed only by court decision.

In 2015, the European Court for Human Rights ruled that the legislation violated Article 8 of the European Convention on Human Rights (Zakharov v. Russia).

Yarovaya Law required storage and unconditional access to private communication data for law enforcement.

Singapore

Singapore is known as a city of sensors. Singapore's surveillance structure spreads widely from Closed-circuit television in public areas even around the neighbourhood, internet monitoring/ traffic monitoring and to the use of surveillance metadata for government initiatives. In Singapore, SIM card registration is mandatory even for prepaid card. Singapore's government have the rights to access communication data. Singapore's largest telecompany, Singtel, has close relations to the government and Singapore's laws are broadly phrased to allow the government to obtain sensitive data such as text-messages, email, call logs and web surfing history from its people without the need for court permission.

The installation of mass surveillance cameras in Singapore is an effort to act as a deterrence not only for terror attacks but also for public security such as loan sharks, illegal parking and more. As part of Singapore's Smart Nation initiative to build a network of sensors to collect and connect data from city life (including the citizen's movement), the Singapore government rolled out 1000 sensors ranging from computer chips to surveillance cameras, to track almost everything in Singapore from air quality to public safety in 2014.

In 2016, in a bid to increase security, the Singapore Police Force installed 62,000 police cameras in 10,000 Housing and Development Board (HDB) blocks covering the lifts and multi-storey car parks. With rising security concerns, the number of CCTV cameras in public areas such as monitoring of the public transport system and commercial/ government buildings in Singapore is set to increase.

In 2018, the Singapore government would be rolling out new and more advanced surveillance systems. Starting with Singapore's maritime borders, new panoramic electro-optic sensors will be put in place on the north and south coasts, monitoring a 360-degree view of the area. A tethered unmanned aerial vehicle (UAV) will also be operational, which can be used during search and rescue operations including hostage situations and public order incidents.

Spain

According to a 2017 report by Privacy International, Spain may be part of a group of 21 European countries that is withholding information, also known as data retention. In 2014, many defense lawyers tried to overturn multiple cases that used mass storage as their evidence to convict, according to the European Agency for Fundamental Rights.

Sweden

Prior to 2009, the National Defence Radio Establishment (FRA) was limited to wireless signals intelligence (SIGINT), although it was left largely unregulated. In December 2009, new legislation went into effect, allowing the FRA to monitor cable bound signals passing the Swedish border. Communications service providers are legally required, under confidentiality, to transfer cable communications crossing Swedish borders to specific "interaction points", where data may be accessed after a court order.

The FRA has been contested since the change in its legislation, mainly because of the public perception the change would enable mass surveillance. The FRA categorically deny this allegation, as they are not allowed to initialize any surveillance on their own, and has no direct access to communication lines. All SIGINT has to be authorized by a special court and meet a set of narrow requirements, something Minister for Defence Sten Tolgfors have been quoted as saying, "should render the debate on mass surveillance invalid." Due to the architecture of Internet backbones in the Nordic area, a large portion of Norwegian and Finnish traffic will also be affected by the Swedish wiretapping.

Syria

Syria is one of the five countries on Reporters Without Borders' March 2013 list of "State Enemies of the Internet", countries whose governments are involved in active, intrusive surveillance of news providers, resulting in grave violations of freedom of information and human rights. Syria has stepped up its web censorship and cyber-monitoring as the country's civil war has intensified. At least 13 Blue Coat proxy servers are in use, Skype calls are intercepted, and social engineering techniques, phishing, and malware attacks are all in use.

Turkey

The failed coup attempt June 15, 2016 led to an authoritarian shift that uses mass surveillance to suppress opposite views. Digital surveillance is part of everyday life due to the box the government puts the Turkish citizens in. It is increasingly difficult to release any academic knowledge beyond what the Turkish government wants to be released. They have a digital and physical strong hold over any knowledge that goes against their regime. Today, the surveillance of academicians goes along with the state's oppression in Turkey. It is hard to say what will happen in the next few years in Turkey as they become increasingly more authoritarian. The centralization of state power along with digitalization expands the scope of the state surveillance. The digitalization and the centralization of state power are closely related to the regime of power that becomes prominent in this conjuncture. National security and terrorism are Turkey's main explanations to the world on this topic, although there is clearly more happening there. According to the report of Human Rights Joint Platform published on February 23, 2017, during the nine months period of the state of emergency, the number of dismissed academicians reached 4,811, increasing to 7,619 with the addition of academicians who were working in the universities closed after the failed coup attempt. The extended surveillance in Turkey helped them to control the population at a massive scale.

United Kingdom

State surveillance in the United Kingdom has formed part of the public consciousness since the 19th century. The postal espionage crisis of 1844 sparked the first panic over the privacy of citizens. However, in the 20th century, electronic surveillance capabilities grew out of wartime signal intelligence and pioneering code breaking. In 1946, the Government Communications Headquarters (GCHQ) was formed. The United Kingdom and the United States signed the bilateral UKUSA Agreement in 1948. It was later broadened to include Canada, Australia and New Zealand, as well as cooperation with several "third-party" nations. This became the cornerstone of Western intelligence gathering and the "Special Relationship" between the UK and the USA.

After the growth of the Internet and development of the World Wide Web, a series of media reports in 2013 revealed more recent programs and techniques involving GCHQ, such as Tempora.

The Investigatory Powers Tribunal, a judicial oversight body for the intelligence agencies, ruled in December 2014 that the legislative framework in the United Kingdom does not breach the European Convention on Human Rights. However, the Tribunal stated in February 2015 that one particular aspect, the data-sharing arrangement that allowed UK Intelligence services to request data from the US surveillance programs Prism and Upstream, had been in contravention of human rights law prior to this until two paragraphs of additional information, providing details about the procedures and safeguards, were disclosed to the public in December 2014.

In its December 2014 ruling, the Investigatory Powers Tribunal found that the legislative framework in the United Kingdom does not permit mass surveillance and that while GCHQ collects and analyses data in bulk, it does not practice mass surveillance. A report on Privacy and Security published by the Intelligence and Security Committee of Parliament also came to this view, although it found past shortcomings in oversight and said the legal framework should be simplified to improve transparency. This view is supported by independent reports from the Interception of Communications Commissioner. However, notable civil liberties groups continue to express strong views to the contrary and plan to appeal the ruling to the European Court of Human Rights, while others have criticised these viewpoints in turn.

The Regulation of Investigatory Powers Act 2000 (RIP or RIPA) is a significant piece of legislation that granted and regulated the powers of public bodies to carry out surveillance and investigation. In 2002 the UK government announced plans to extend the Regulation of Investigatory Powers Act so that at least 28 government departments would be given powers to access metadata about citizens' web, e-mail, telephone and fax records, without a warrant and without a subject's knowledge.

The Protection of Freedoms Act 2012 includes several provisions related to controlling and restricting the collection, storage, retention, and use of information in government databases.

Supported by all three major political parties, the UK Parliament passed the Data Retention and Investigatory Powers Act in July 2014 to ensure police and security services retain existing powers to access phone and Internet records.

This was superseded by the Investigatory Powers Act 2016, a comprehensive statute which made public a number of previously secret powers (equipment interference, bulk retention of metadata, intelligence agency use of bulk personal datasets), and enables the Government to require internet service providers and mobile phone companies to maintain records of (but not the content of) customers' Internet connections for 12 months. In addition, it created new safeguards, including a requirement for judges to approve the warrants authorised by a Secretary of State before they come into force. The Act was informed by two reports by David Anderson QC, the UK's Independent Reviewer of Terrorism Legislation: A Question of Trust (2015) and the report of his Bulk Powers Review (2016), which contains a detailed appraisal (with 60 case studies) of the operational case for the powers often characterised as mass surveillance. It may yet require amendment as a consequence of legal cases brought before the Court of Justice of the European Union and the European Court of Human Rights.

The UK is a member of the European Union, participates in its programs, and is subject to EU policies and directives on surveillance.

The vast majority of video surveillance cameras in the UK are not operated by government bodies, but by private individuals or companies, especially to monitor the interiors of shops and businesses. According to 2011 Freedom of Information Act requests, the total number of local government operated CCTV cameras was around 52,000 over the entirety of the UK. The prevalence of video surveillance in the UK is often overstated due to unreliable estimates being requoted; for example one report in 2002 extrapolated from a very small sample to estimate the number of cameras in the UK at 4.2 million (of which 500,000 in London). More reliable estimates put the number of private and local government operated cameras in the United Kingdom at around 1.85 million in 2011.

United States

Historically, mass surveillance was used as part of wartime censorship to control communications that could damage the war effort and aid the enemy. For example, during the world wars, every international telegram from or to the United States sent through companies such as Western Union was reviewed by the US military. After the wars were over, surveillance continued in programs such as the Black Chamber following World War I and project Shamrock following World War II. COINTELPRO projects conducted by the U.S. Federal Bureau of Investigation (FBI) between 1956 and 1971 targeted various "subversive" organizations, including peaceful anti-war and racial equality activists such as Albert Einstein and Martin Luther King Jr.

Billions of dollars per year are spent, by agencies such as the National Security Agency (NSA) and the Federal Bureau of Investigation (FBI), to develop, purchase, implement, and operate systems such as Carnivore, ECHELON, and NarusInsight to intercept and analyze the immense amount of data that traverses the Internet and telephone system every day.

Since the September 11, 2001, terrorist attacks, a vast domestic intelligence apparatus has been built to collect information using the NSA, FBI, local police, state homeland security offices and military criminal investigators. The intelligence apparatus collects, analyzes and stores information about millions of (if not all) American citizens, many of whom have not been accused of any wrongdoing.

The FBI developed the computer programs "Magic Lantern" and CIPAV, which they can remotely install on a computer system, in order to monitor a person's computer activity.

The NSA has been gathering information on financial records, Internet surfing habits, and monitoring e-mails. They have also performed extensive analysis of social networks such as Myspace.

The PRISM special source operation system legally immunized private companies that cooperate voluntarily with U.S. intelligence collection. According to The Register, the FISA Amendments Act of 2008 "specifically authorizes intelligence agencies to monitor the phone, email, and other communications of U.S. citizens for up to a week without obtaining a warrant" when one of the parties is outside the U.S. PRISM was first publicly revealed on 6 June 2013, after classified documents about the program were leaked to The Washington Post and The Guardian by American Edward Snowden.

The Communications Assistance for Law Enforcement Act (CALEA) requires that all U.S. telecommunications and Internet service providers modify their networks to allow easy wiretapping of telephone, VoIP, and broadband Internet traffic.

In early 2006, USA Today reported that several major telephone companies were providing the telephone call records of U.S. citizens to the National Security Agency (NSA), which is storing them in a large database known as the NSA call database. This report came on the heels of allegations that the U.S. government had been conducting electronic surveillance of domestic telephone calls without warrants. In 2013, the existence of the Hemisphere Project, through which AT&T provides telephone call data to federal agencies, became publicly known.

Traffic cameras, which were meant to help enforce traffic laws at intersections, may be used by law enforcement agencies for purposes unrelated to traffic violations. Some cameras allow for the identification of individuals inside a vehicle and license plate data to be collected and time stamped for cross reference with other data used by police. The Department of Homeland Security is funding networks of surveillance cameras in cities and towns as part of its efforts to combat terrorism.

The New York City Police Department infiltrated and compiled dossiers on protest groups before the 2004 Republican National Convention, leading to over 1,800 arrests.

Modern surveillance in the United States was thought of more of a wartime effort before Snowden disclosed in depth information about the National Security Agency in June 2013. The constant development and improvements of the Internet and technology has made it easier for mass surveillance to take hold. Such revelations allow critical commentators to raise questions and scrutinize the implementation, use, and abuse of networking technologies, devices, and software systems that partake in a "global surveillant assemblage" (Bogard 2006; Collier and Ong 2004; Haggerty and Ericson 2000; Murakami Wood 2013). The NSA collected millions of Verizon user's telephone records in between 2013-2014. The NSA also collected data through Google and Facebook with a program called 'Prism'. Journalists through Snowden published nearly 7,000 top-secret documents since then, yet the information disclosed seems to be less than 1% of the entire information. Having access to every individual's private records seems to directly contradict the fourth amendment.

Vietnam

Vietnam is one of the five countries on Reporters Without Borders' March 2013 list of "State Enemies of the Internet", countries whose governments are involved in active, intrusive surveillance of news providers, resulting in grave violations of freedom of information and human rights. Most of the country's 16 service providers are directly or indirectly controlled by the Vietnamese Communist Party. The industry leader, Vietnam Posts and Telecommunications Group, which controls 74 per cent of the market, is state-owned. So is Viettel, an enterprise of the Vietnamese armed forces. FPT Telecom is a private firm, but is accountable to the Party and depends on the market leaders for bandwidth.

Service providers are the major instruments of control and surveillance. Bloggers monitored by the government frequently undergo man-in-the-middle attacks. These are designed to intercept data meant to be sent to secure (https) sites, allowing passwords and other communication to be intercepted. According to a July 2012 Freedom House report, 91 percent of survey respondents connected to the Internet on their mobile devices and the government monitors conversations and tracks the calls of "activists" or "reactionaries."

Commercial mass surveillance

As a result of the digital revolution, many aspects of life are now captured and stored in digital form. Concern has been expressed that governments may use this information to conduct mass surveillance on their populations. Commercial mass surveillance often makes use of copyright laws and "user agreements" to obtain (typically uninformed) 'consent' to surveillance from consumers who use their software or other related materials. This allows gathering of information which would be technically illegal if performed by government agencies. This data is then often shared with government agencies - thereby - in practice - defeating the purpose of such privacy protections.

One of the most common forms of mass surveillance is carried out by commercial organizations. Many people are willing to join supermarket and grocery loyalty card programs, trading their personal information and surveillance of their shopping habits in exchange for a discount on their groceries, although base prices might be increased to encourage participation in the program.

Through programs like Google's AdSense, OpenSocial and their increasing pool of so-called "web gadgets", "social gadgets" and other Google-hosted services many web sites on the Internet are effectively feeding user information about sites visited by the users, and now also their social connections, to Google. Facebook also keep this information, although its acquisition is limited to page views within Facebook. This data is valuable for authorities, advertisers and others interested in profiling users, trends and web site marketing performance. Google, Facebook and others are increasingly becoming more guarded about this data as their reach increases and the data becomes more all inclusive, making it more valuable.

New features like geolocation give an even increased admission of monitoring capabilities to large service providers like Google, where they also are enabled to track one's physical movements while users are using mobile devices, especially those which are syncing without any user interaction. Google's Gmail service is increasingly employing features to work as a stand-alone application which also might activate while a web browser is not even active for synchronizing; a feature mentioned on the Google I/O 2009 developer conference while showing the upcoming HTML5 features which Google and others are actively defining and promoting.

In 2008 at the World Economic Forum in Davos, Google CEO Eric Schmidt, said: "The arrival of a truly mobile Web, offering a new generation of location-based advertising, is set to unleash a 'huge revolution'". At the Mobile World Congress in Barcelona on 16 February 2010, Google presented their vision of a new business model for mobile operators and trying to convince mobile operators to embrace location-based services and advertising. With Google as the advertising provider, it would mean that every mobile operator using their location-based advertising service would be revealing the location of their mobile customers to Google.

Organizations like the Electronic Frontier Foundation are constantly informing users on the importance of privacy, and considerations about technologies like geolocation.

Computer company Microsoft patented in 2011 a product distribution system with a camera or capture device that monitors the viewers that consume the product, allowing the provider to take "remedial action" if the actual viewers do not match the distribution license.

Reporters Without Borders' March 2013 Special report on Internet Surveillance contained a list of "Corporate Enemies of the Internet", companies that sell products that are liable to be used by governments to violate human rights and freedom of information. The five companies on the initial list were: Amesys (France), Blue Coat Systems (U.S.), Gamma Group (UK and Germany), Hacking Team (Italy), and Trovicor (Germany), but the list was not exhaustive and is likely to be expanded in the future.

Surveillance state

A surveillance state is a country where the government engages in pervasive surveillance of large numbers of its citizens and visitors. Such widespread surveillance is usually justified as being necessary for national security, such as to prevent crime or acts of terrorism, but may also be used to stifle criticism of and opposition to the government.

Examples of early surveillance states include the former Soviet Union and the former East Germany, which had a large network of informers and an advanced technology base in computing and spy-camera technology. But these states did not have today's technologies for mass surveillance, such as the use of databases and pattern recognition software to cross-correlate information obtained by wire tapping, including speech recognition and telecommunications traffic analysis, monitoring of financial transactions, automatic number plate recognition, the tracking of the position of mobile telephones, and facial recognition systems and the like which recognize people by their appearance, gait, DNA profiling, etc.

Smart cities

The development of smart cities has seen the increased adoption of surveillance technologies by governments, although the primary purpose of surveillance in such cities is to use information and communication technologies to improve the urban environment. The implementation of such technology by a number of cities has resulted in increased efficiencies in urban infrastructure as well as improved community participation. Sensors and systems monitor a smart city's infrastructure, operations and activities and aim to help it run more efficiently. For example, the city could use less electricity; its traffic run more smoothly with fewer delays; its citizens use the city with more safety; hazards can be dealt with faster; citizen infractions of rules can be prevented, and the city's infrastructure; power distribution and roads with traffic lights for example, dynamically adjusted to respond to differing circumstances.

The development of smart city technology has also led to an increase in potential unwarranted intrusions into privacy and restrictions upon autonomy. The widespread incorporation of information and communication technologies within the daily life of urban residents results in increases in the surveillance capacity of states - to the extent that individuals may be unaware of what information is being accessed, when the access occurs and for what purpose. It is possible that such conditions could give rise to the development of an electronic police state. Shanghai, Amsterdam, San Jose, Dubai, Barcelona, Madrid, Stockholm, and New York are all cities that use various techniques from smart city technology.

Electronic police state

An electronic police state is a state in which the government aggressively uses electronic technologies to record, collect, store, organize, analyze, search, and distribute information about its citizens. Electronic police states also engage in mass government surveillance of landline and cellular telephone traffic, mail, email, web surfing, Internet searches, radio, and other forms of electronic communication as well as widespread use of video surveillance. The information is usually collected in secret.

The crucial elements are not politically based, so long as the government can afford the technology and the populace will permit it to be used, an electronic police state can form. The continual use of electronic mass surveillance can result in constant low-level fear within the population, which can lead to self-censorship and exerts a powerful coercive force upon the populace.

Seventeen factors for judging the development of an electronic police state were suggested in The Electronic Police State: 2008 National Rankings:

Daily documents: Requirement for the use and tracking of state-issued identity documents and registration.

Border and travel control: Inspections at borders, searching computers and cell phones, demanding decryption of data, and tracking travel within as well as to and from a country.

Financial tracking: A state's ability to record and search financial transactions: checks, credit cards, wires, etc.

Gag orders: Restrictions on and criminal penalties for the disclosure of the existence of state surveillance programs.

Anti-crypto laws: Outlawing or restricting cryptography and/or privacy enhancing technologies.

Lack of constitutional protections: A lack of constitutional privacy protections or the routine overriding of such protections.

- Data storage: The ability of the state to store the data gathered.
- Data search: The ability to organize and search the data gathered.

Data retention requirements: Laws that require Internet and other service providers to save detailed records of their customers' Internet usage for a minimum period of time.

Telephone data retention requirements: Laws that require telephone companies to record and save records of their customers' telephone usage.

Cell phone data retention requirements: Laws that require cellular telephone companies to record and save records of their customers' usage and location.

Medical records: Government access to the records of medical service providers.

Enforcement: The state's ability to use force to seize anyone they want, whenever they want.

Lack of habeas corpus: Lack of a right for a person under arrest to be brought before a judge or into court in a timely fashion or the overriding of such rights.

Lack of a police-intel barrier: The lack of a barrier between police organizations and intelligence organizations, or the overriding of such barriers.

Covert hacking: State operatives collecting, removing, or adding digital evidence to/from private computers without permission or the knowledge of the computers' owners.

Loose or no warrants: Arrests or searches made without warrants or without careful examination and review of police statements and justifications by a truly independent judge or other third-party.

The list includes factors that apply to other forms of police states, such as the use of identity documents and police enforcement, but go considerably beyond them and emphasize the use of technology to gather and process the information collected.

7

Suicide Bombers: A Global Problem

A suicide attack is any violent attack in which the attacker accepts their own death as a direct result of the method used to harm, damage or destroy the target. Suicide attacks have occurred throughout history, often as part of a military campaign such as the Japanese kamikaze pilots of World War II, and more recently as part of terrorist campaigns, such as the September 11 attacks. While there were few, if any, successful suicide attacks anywhere in the world from the end of World War II until 1980, between 1981 and September 2015, a total of 4,814 suicide attacks occurred in over 40 countries, killing over 45,000 people. During this time the global rate of such attacks grew from an average of three a year in the 1980s, to about one a month in the 1990s, to almost one a week from 2001 to 2003, to approximately one a day from 2003 to 2015.

Suicide attacks tend to be more deadly and destructive than other terror attacks because they give their perpetrators the ability to conceal weapons, make last-minute adjustments, and because they dispense with the need for remote or delayed detonation, escape plans or rescue teams. They constituted only 4% of all terrorist attacks around the world over one period (between 1981 and 2006), but caused 32% of all terrorism-related deaths (14,599). Ninety percent of those attacks occurred in Afghanistan, Iraq, Israel, the Palestinian territories, Pakistan, and Sri Lanka. Overall, as of mid-2015 about three-quarters of all suicide attacks occurred in just three countries: Afghanistan, Pakistan, and Iraq. Suicide attacks have been described as a weapon of psychological warfare to instill fear in the target population, a strategy to eliminate or at least drastically diminish areas where the public feels safe, and the "fabric of trust that holds societies together", as well as demonstrate the lengths to which perpetrators will go to achieve their goals.

The motivation of suicide attackers varies. Kamikaze acted under military orders and were motivated by obedience and nationalism. Before 2003, most attacks targeted forces occupying the attackers' homeland, according to analyst Robert Pape. Anthropologist Scott Atran states that since 2004 the overwhelming majority of bombers have been motivated by the ideology of Islamist martyrdom.

Definitions

Terrorism

Suicide attacks include both suicide terrorism—terrorism often defined as any action "intended to cause death or serious bodily harm to civilians or non-combatants" for the purpose of intimidation—and suicide attacks not targeting non-combatants. An alternative definition is provided by Jason Burke, a journalist who has lived among Islamic militants, and suggests that most define terrorism as 'the use or threat of serious violence' to advance some kind of 'cause', stressing that terrorism is a tactic. Academic Fred Halliday, has written that assigning the descriptor of 'terrorist' or 'terrorism' to the actions of a group is a tactic used by states to deny 'legitimacy' and 'rights to protest and rebel'.

Suicide terrorism

The definition of "suicide" is another issue. Suicide terrorism itself has been defined by one source (Ami Pedahzur) as "violent actions perpetrated by people who are aware that the odds they will return alive are close to zero". Other sources exclude from their work "suicidal" or high risk attacks, such as the Lod Airport massacre or "reckless charge in battle", focusing only on true "suicide attacks", where the odds of survival are not "close to zero" but required to be zero, because "the perpetrator's ensured death is a precondition for the success of his mission".

Also excluded from the definition are:

"proxy bombings", which may have political goals and may be designed to look like suicide bombing, but where the "proxy" is forced to carry a bomb under threat (such as having his/her Il, not political, social or religious, motives.

It may not always be clear to investigators which type of killing is which. Suicide attack campaigns sometimes also using proxy bombers (as alleged in Iraq). or manipulating the vulnerable to be bombers, At least one researcher (Adam Lankford) argues that the motivation to kill and be killed connects some suicide attackers more closely to "suicidal rampage" murderers than is commonly thought.

Usage

The usage of the term "suicide attack" goes back a long way but "suicide bombing" dates back to at least 1940 when a New York Times article mentions the term in relation to German tactics. Less than two years later that newspaper referred to a Japanese kamikaze attempt on an American carrier as a "suicide bombing". In 1945 The Times of London, referred to a kamikaze plane as a "suicide-bomb", and two years later an article there referred to a new British pilot-less, radio-controlled rocket missile as originally designed "as a counter-measure to the Japanese 'suicide-bomber'".

Alternative terms

Sometimes, to assign either a more positive or negative connotation to the act, suicide bombing is referred to by different terms.

Istishhad

Islamist supporters often call a suicide attack Istishhad (often translated as "martyrdom operation"), and the suicide attacker shahid (pl. shuhada, literally 'witness' and usually translated as 'martyr'). The idea being that the attacker died in order to testify his faith in God, for example while waging jihad bis saif (jihad by the sword). The term "suicide" is never used because Islam has strong strictures against taking one's own life. The terms Istishhad / "martyrdom operation" have been embraced by the Palestinian Authority, and by Hamas, Al-Aqsa Martyrs' Brigades, Fatah and other Palestinian factions.

Homicide bombing

Some efforts have been made to replace the term "suicide bombing" with "homicide bombing", on the grounds that since the primary purpose of such a bombing is to kill other people, homicide is a more apt adjective than "suicide".

The first to use the term for a wide audience was White House Press Secretary Ari Fleischer in April 2002. The only major media outlets to use it were Fox News Channel and the New York Post (both of which are owned by News Corporation and have since mostly abandoned the term).

Emeritus Professor Robert Goldney, of the University of Adelaide, has argued in favor of the term "homicide bomber", arguing that studies show that there is little in common between people who blow themselves up, intending to kill as many people as possible in the process, and actual suicide victims. Fox News producer Dennis Murray argued that a suicidal act should be reserved for a person who does something to kill themselves only. CNN Producer Christa Robinson argued that the term "homicide bomber" reflects only that you have killed other people, but not that you have also killed yourself.

Genocide bombing

"Genocide bombing" was coined in 2002 by Irwin Cotler, a member of the Canadian parliament, in an effort to focus attention on the alleged intention of genocide by militant Palestinians in their calls to "wipe Israel off the map".

Sacrifice bombing

In the German-speaking area the term "sacrifice bombing" (Ger. Opferanschlag) was proposed in 2012 by German scholar Arata Takeda. The term is intended to shift the focus away from the suicide of the perpetrators and towards their use as weapons by their commanders.

Post-1980 attacks

History

The concept of self-sacrifice as a means to killing others dates back to antiquity with Samson's suicidal mass killing of the Philistine leaders, but the idea of suicide bombing "as a tool of stateless terrorists" was only "dreamed up a hundred years ago by the European anarchists", according to author Noah Feldman. It was not until 1983 when Shiite militants blew up the U.S. Marine barracks in Lebanon, that it became "tool of modern terrorist warfare". Modern suicide bombing has been defined as "involving explosives deliberately carried to the target either on the person or in a civilian vehicle and delivered by surprise". (Noah Feldman and many others exclude terror attacks such as the Lod Airport massacre where "the perpetrator's ensured death" was not "a precondition for the success of his mission".) The intended targets are often civilian, not just military or political.

The U.S. Embassy in Dar es Salaam, Tanzania, in the aftermath of August 7, 1998, Al-Qaeda suicide bombing

Suicide bombing was used by factions of the Lebanese Civil War and especially by the Tamil Tigers (LTTE) of Sri Lanka.

The Islamic Dawa Party's car bombing of the Iraqi embassy in Beirut in December 1981 and Hezbollah's bombing of the U.S. embassy in April 1983 and attack on United States Marine and French barracks in October 1983 brought suicide bombings international attention. Other parties to the civil war were quick to adopt the tactic, and by 1999 factions such as Hezbollah, the Amal Movement, the Ba'ath Party, and the Syrian Social Nationalist Party had carried out around 50 suicide bombings between them. (The latter of these groups sent the first recorded female suicide bomber in 1985.)

During the Sri Lankan Civil War, the Tamil Tigers (LTTE) adopted suicide bombing as a tactic, using bomb belts and female bombers. The LTTE carried out their first suicide attack in July 1987, and their Black Tiger unit committed 83 suicide attacks from 1987 to 2009, killing 981 people, including former Indian Prime Minister Rajiv Gandhi, and the president of Sri Lanka, Ranasinghe Premadasa.

Another non-religious group involved in suicide attacks was the Kurdistan Workers' Party which began their insurgency against the Turkish state in 1984. According to the Chicago Project on Security and Terrorism's Suicide Attack Database, as of 2015, ten suicide attacks by the PKK from 1996 to 2012 killed 32 people and injured 116. (Suicide attacks are only part of the PKK's militant arsenal as they have killed or wounded hundreds of government workers and destroyed or damaged hundreds of school, post offices and mosques.)

Al-Qaeda carried out its first suicide attack in the mid-1990s, and they first appeared in Israel and the Palestinian Territories in 1989.

In early 2000, one analyst (Yoram Schweitzer) saw a pause in bombing campaigns and argued that "most of the groups that were involved in suicide terrorism either stopped using it or eventually reduced it significantly."

The number of attacks using suicide tactics grew from an average of fewer than five per year during the 1980s to 81 suicide attacks in 2001 to 460 in 2005. By 2005, the tactic had spread to dozens of countries.

Suicide bombing became a popular tactic among Palestinian militant organizations such as Hamas, Islamic Jihad, the Al-Aqsa Martyrs Brigade, and occasionally by the PFLP. The first suicide bombing in Israel was by HAMAS in 1994. Attacks peaked from 2001–2003 with over 40 bombings and over 200 killed in 2002. Bombers affiliated with these groups often use so-called "suicide belts", explosive devices (often including shrapnel) designed to be strapped to the body under clothing. In order to maximize the loss of life, the bombers seek out enclosed spaces, such as cafés or city buses crowded with people at rush hour. Less common are military targets (for example, soldiers waiting for transport at roadside).

These bombings have tended to have more popular support than in other Muslim countries, and more music videos and announcements that promise eternal reward for suicide bombers can be found on Palestinian television (according to Palestinian Media Watch). Israeli sources observed that Hamas, Islamic Jihad and Fatah operate "Paradise Camps", training children as young as 11 to become suicide bombers.

The September 11, 2001 attacks, orchestrated by al-Qaeda, has been called "the worst attack on American soil since the Japanese attack on Pearl Harbor which thrust the United States into World War II". They involved the hijacking of four large passenger jet airliners because their long transcontinental flight plans meant they carried more fuel, allowing a bigger explosion on impact (unlike earlier airline hijackings, the primary focus was the planes, not the passengers). Two planes were deliberately flown into the Twin Towers of the World Trade Center in New York City, destroying both 110 story skyscrapers within less than two hours, and a third was flown into the Pentagon in Arlington County, Virginia, causing severe damage to the west side of the building. These attacks resulted in the deaths of 221 people (including the 15 hijackers) on board the three planes as well as 2,731 more in and around the targeted buildings. A fourth plane crashed into a field near Shanksville, Pennsylvania, after a revolt by the plane's passengers, killing all 44 people (including the four hijackers) on board. In total, the attacks killed 2,996 people and injured more than 6,000 others. The U.S. stock market closed for four trading days after the attacks (the first time it had an unscheduled closing since the Great Depression). Nine days after the attack, U.S. President George W. Bush called for a "War on Terror" and shortly thereafter launched the War in Afghanistan to find and capture Osama bin Laden, the head of the al-Qaeda organization that mounted the 9/11 attacks.

After the U.S.-led invasion of Iraq in 2003, Iraqi and foreign insurgents carried out waves of suicide bombings. More attacks have been carried out in Iraq (1938 as of mid-2015) than in any other country In addition to United States military targets, they attacked many civilian targets such as Shiite mosques, international offices of the UN and the Red Cross. Iraqi men waiting to apply for jobs with the new army and police force were targets. In the lead up to the Iraqi parliamentary election, on January 30, 2005, suicide attacks upon civilian and police personnel involved with the elections increased. There were also reports of the insurgents co-opting disabled people as involuntary suicide bombers.

Other major locations of suicide attack are Afghanistan (1059 attacks as of mid-2015) and Pakistan (490 attacks). In the first eight months of 2008, Pakistan overtook Iraq and Afghanistan in suicide bombings, with 28 bombings killing 471 people. Suicide bombings have become a tactic in Chechnya, first being used in the conflict in 2000 in Alkhan Kala, and spreading to Russia, notably with the Moscow theater hostage crisis in 2002 to the Beslan school hostage crisis in 2004.

In Europe four Islamist suicide bombers exploded home-made peroxide explosives on three London underground trains and a bus on 7 July 2005, during the morning rush hour. These "7/7" bombings killed 52 civilians and injured 700. Since 2006, al-Shabaab and its predecessor, the Islamic Courts, have carried out major suicide attacks in Somalia, the worse year so far being 2014 with 16 attacks and over 120 killed.

Weapons and methods

- On foot: explosive belt, satchel charge: many, including the assassination of Rajiv Gandhi
- With a plane as target and explosives hidden inside attackers shoe: Richard Reid on American Airlines Flight 63
- With explosives hidden inside the body: 2009 attack on a Saudi prince, Muhammad bin Nayef
- By car bomb: 1983 Beirut barracks bombing, Sri Lankan Central Bank bombing, numerous incidents in Iraq since 2003
- By a boat with explosives: USS Cole bombing attacks in Aden, Yemen by Al-Qaeda; SLNS Sagarawardena sinking in Sri Lanka by Tamil Tigers.
- By a submarine with explosives (human-steered torpedo): Kaiten, used by Japan in World War II
- By a bicycle with explosives: Assassination of Sri Lankan President Ranasinghe Premadasa by the Liberation Tigers of Tamil Eelam (LTTE)
- By a hijacked commercial jet airliner with fuel: September 11 attacks, attempted on Air France Flight 8969 and by Samuel Byck
- By private plane: 2010 Austin plane crash
- By diverting a bus to an abyss: Tel Aviv Jerusalem bus 405 attack
- By a car by using a fast driving car to drive intentionally into a crowd of people or breaching a security barrier: 2009 attack on the Dutch royal family

Strategy and advantages

According to author Jeffrey William Lewis, to succeed, campaigns of suicide bombing need: willing individuals organizations to train and use them a society willing to accept such acts in the name of a greater good

The organizations work to guarantee individual suicide bombers that they "will be remembered as martyrs dying for their communities". By imbuing suicide bombing/attacks with "reverence and heroism", it becomes more attractive to recruits. According to Yoram Schweitzer, modern suicide terrorism is "aimed at causing devastating physical damage, through which it inflicts profound fear and anxiety". Its goal is not to produce a negative psychological effect only on the victims of the actual attack, but on the entire target population. Attackers themselves have often framed suicide attacks as acts of courageous self-sacrifice in made necessary by the superior military or security strength of the enemy. The technique has also been called "the atomic weapon of the weak". According to Sheikh Ahmed Yassin, the former leader of Hamas, "Once we have warplanes and missiles, then we can think of changing our means of legitimate self-defense. But right now, we can only tackle the fire with our bare hands and sacrifice ourselves." While arguably this explains the motivation of many early suicide bombings in the 1980s and 90s, it cannot explain many later attacks, such as on funeral processions of the minority Shia in Pakistan.

A major reason for the popularity of suicide attacks despite the sacrifice involved for its perpetrators is its tactical advantages over other types of terrorism, such as the ability to conceal weapons, make last-minute adjustments, increased ability to infiltrate heavily guarded targets, lack of need for remote or delayed detonation, escape plans or rescue teams. Robert Pape observes: "Suicide attacks are an especially convincing way to signal the likelihood of more pain to come, because if you are willing to kill yourself you are also willing to endure brutal retaliation. "... The element of suicide itself helps increase the credibility of future attacks because it suggests that attackers cannot be deterred."

Bruce Hoffman describes the characteristics of suicide bombing, as "universal": "Suicide bombings are inexpensive and effective. They are less complicated and compromising than other kinds of terrorist operations. They guarantee media coverage. The suicide terrorist is the ultimate smart bomb. Perhaps most important, coldly efficient bombings tear at the fabric of trust that holds societies together."

Attacker profiles and motivations

Studies of who becomes a suicide attacker and what motivates them have often come to different conclusions. According to Riaz Hassan, "apart from one demographic attribute—that the majority of suicide bombers tend to be young males—the evidence has failed to find a stable set of demographic, psychological, socioeconomic and religious variables that can be causally linked to suicide bombers' personality or socioeconomic origins." Scott Atran agrees: "In targeting potential recruits for suicide terrorism, it must be understood that terrorist attacks will not be prevented by trying to profile terrorists. They are not sufficiently different from everyone else. Insights into homegrown jihadi attacks will have to come from understanding group dynamics, not individual psychology. Small-group dynamics can trump individual personality to produce horrific behavior in otherwise ordinary people." Reasons vary greatly, and are different in the case of each individual. Fanaticism (nationalist or religious, or both), results from brain-washing, negative experiences regarding "the enemy", the lack of a perspective in life. Suicides want to hurt or kill their targets because they hold them responsible for all bad things that has happened to them or in the world or simply just because they want to escape misery and poverty.

Based on biographies of more than seven hundred foreign fighters uncovered at an Iraqi insurgent camp, researchers believe that the motivation for suicide missions (at least in Iraq) was not "the global jihadi ideology", but "an explosive mix of desperation, pride, anger, sense of powerlessness, local tradition of resistance and religious fervor".

Criminal Justice professor Adam Lankford argues that suicide terrorists are not psychologically normal or stable, and are motivated to suicide/killing to mask their desire to die beneath a "veneer of heroic action", because of the religious consequences of killing themselves outright. He has identified more than 130 individual suicide terrorists, including 9/11 ringleader Mohamed Atta, with classic suicidal risk factors, such as depression, post-traumatic stress disorder, other mental health problems, drug addictions, serious physical injuries or disabilities, or having suffered the unexpected death of a loved one or from other personal crises.

A study of the remains of 110 suicide bombers in Afghanistan for the first part of 2007 by Afghan pathologist Dr. Yusef Yadgari, found 80% were suffering from physical aliments such as missing limbs (before the blasts), cancer, or leprosy. Also in contrast to earlier findings of suicide bombers, the Afghan bombers were "not celebrated like their counterparts in other Arab nations. Afghan bombers are not featured on posters or in videos as martyrs."

Anthropologist Scott Atran's research has found that the attacks are not organized from the top down, but occurs from the bottom up. That is, it is usually a matter of following one's friends, and ending up in environments that foster groupthink. Atran is also critical of the claim that terrorists simply crave destruction; they are often motivated by beliefs they hold sacred, as well as their own moral reasoning.

Robert Pape, director of the Chicago Project on Suicide Terrorism, found the majority of suicide bombers came from the educated middle classes. (Humam Balawi, who perpetrated the Camp Chapman attack in Afghanistan in 2010, was a medical doctor.) A 2004 paper by Harvard University Professor of Public Policy Alberto Abadie "cast[s] doubt on the widely held belief that terrorism stems from poverty, finding instead that terrorist violence (not just suicide terrorism) is "related to a nation's level of political freedom", with countries "in some intermediate range of political freedom" more prone to terrorism than countries with "high levels" of political freedom or countries with "highly authoritarian regimes". "When governments are weak, political instability is elevated, so conditions are favorable for the appearance of terrorism".

A study by German scholar Arata Takeda analyzes analogous behavior represented in literary texts from the antiquity through the 20th century (Sophocles' s Ajax, Milton's Samson Agonistes, Friedrich Schiller's The Robbers, Albert Camus's The Just Assassins) and comes to the conclusion "that suicide bombings are not the expressions of specific cultural peculiarities or exclusively religious fanaticisms. Instead, they represent a strategic option of the desperately weak who strategically disguise themselves under the mask of apparent strength, terror, and invincibility."

Pape found other factors associated with suicide attacks included the government of the targeted country being democratic and the public opinion of the country playing a role in determining policy. a difference in religion between the attackers and occupiers; grassroots support for the attacks; attackers disproportionately from the educated middle classes; high levels of brutality and cruelty by the occupiers, and competition among militant groups fighting the occupiers.

Other researchers contend that Pape's analysis is flawed, particularly his contention that democracies are the main targets of such attacks. Atran argues that suicide bombing has moved on from the days of Pape's study, that non-Islamic groups have carried out very few bombings since 2003, while bombing by Muslim or Islamist groups associated with a "global ideology" of "martyrdom" has skyrocketed. In one year, in one Muslim country alone – 2004 in Iraq – there were 400 suicide attacks and 2,000 casualties. Other researchers (such as Yotam Feldner) argue that perceived religious rewards in the hereafter are instrumental in encouraging Muslims to commit suicide attacks, or ask why prominent secular anti-occupation terrorist groups—such as the Provisional IRA, ETA or anti-colonialist insurgents in Vietnam, Algeria, etc.—have not used suicide, why he does not mention that the very first suicide attack in Lebanon (in 1981) targeted the embassy of Iraq, a country which was not occupying Lebanon.

Mia Bloom agrees with Pape that competition among insurgents groups is a significant motivator, arguing the growth in suicide as a tactic is a product of "outbidding", i.e. the need by competing insurgent groups to demonstrate their commitment to the cause to broader public—making the ultimate sacrifice for the insurgency being a "bid" impossible to top. (This explains its use by Palestinian groups, but not that by the Tamil Tigers.) Still other researchers have identified sociopolitical factors as more central in the motivation of suicide attackers than religion.

According to Atran and former CIA case officer Marc Sageman, support for suicide actions is triggered by moral outrage at perceived attacks against Islam and sacred values, but this is converted to action as a result of small-world factors (such as being part of a football club with other jihadis). Millions express sympathy with global jihad (according to a 2006 Gallup study involving more than 50,000 interviews in dozens of countries, seven percent or at least 90 million of the world's 1.3 billion Muslims consider the 9/11 attacks "completely justified").

Also arguing that the increase in suicide terrorism since 2001 is really driven by Salafi/Jihadist ideology and Al-Qaeda is Assaf Moghadam.

Updating his work in a 2010 book Cutting the Fuse, Pape reported that a fine-grained analysis of the time and location of attacks strongly support his conclusion that "foreign military occupation accounts for 98.5%—and the deployment of American combat forces for 92%—of all the 1,833 suicide terrorist attacks around the world" between 2004 and 2009 Moreover, "the success attributed to the surge in 2007 and 2008 was actually less the result of an increase in coalition forces and more to a change of strategy in Baghdad and the empowerment of the Sunnis in Anbar." (emphasis in the original)

The same logic can be seen in Afghanistan. In 2004 and early 2005, NATO occupied the north and west, controlled by the Northern Alliance, whom NATO had previously helped fight the Taliban. An enormous spike in suicide terrorism only occurred later in 2005 as NATO moved into the south and east, which had previously been controlled by the Taliban and locals were more likely to see NATO as a foreign occupation threatening local culture and customs. Critics argue the logic cannot be seen in Pakistan, which has no occupation and the second highest number of suicide bombing fatalities as of mid-2015.

Islam

What connection the high percentage of suicide attacks executed by Islamist groups since 1980 has to do with the religion of Islam is disputed. Specifically, scholars, researchers, and others, disagree over whether Islam forbids suicide in the process of attacking enemies or the killing of civilians. According to a report compiled by the Chicago Project on Suicide Terrorism, 224 of 300 suicide terror attacks from 1980 to 2003 involved Islamist groups or took place in Muslim-majority lands. Another tabulation found more than a fourfold increase in suicide bombings in the two years following Papes study and that the overwhelming majority of these bombers were motivated by the ideology of Islamist martyrdom. (For example, as of early 2008, 1121 Muslim suicide bombers have blown themselves up in Iraq.)

Recent history

Islamic suicide bombing is a fairly recent event. It was totally absent from the 1979–1989 Afghan jihad against the Soviet Union, (an asymmetrical war where the mujahideen fought Soviet warplanes, helicopters and tanks primarily with light weapons). According to author Sadakat Kadri, "the very idea that Muslims might blow themselves up for God was unheard of before 1983, and it was not until the early 1990s that anyone anywhere had tried to justify killing innocent Muslims who were not on a battlefield." After 1983 the process was limited among Muslims to Hezbollah and other Lebanese Shi'a factions for more than a decade.

Since then, the "vocabulary of martyrdom and sacrifice", videotaped pre-confession of faith by attackers have become part of "Islamic cultural consciousness", "instantly recognizable" to Muslims (according to Noah Feldman), while the tactic has spread through the Muslim world "with astonishing speed and on a surprising course".

First the targets were American soldiers, then mostly Israelis, including women and children. From Lebanon and Israel, the technique of suicide bombing moved to Iraq, where the targets have included mosques and shrines, and the intended victims have mostly been Shiite Iraqis. ... [In] Afghanistan, ... both the perpetrators and the targets are orthodox Sunni Muslims. Not long ago, a bombing in Lashkar Gah, the capital of Helmand Province, killed Muslims, including women, who were applying to go on pilgrimage to Mecca. Overall, the trend is definitively in the direction of Muslim-on-Muslim violence. By a conservative accounting, more than three times as many Iraqis have been killed by suicide bombings in just three year (2003–6) as have Israelis in ten (from 1996–2006). Suicide bombing has become the archetype of Muslim violence – not just to Westerners but also to Muslims themselves

Recent research on the rationale of suicide bombing has identified both religious and sociopolitical motivations. Those who cite religious factors as an important influence note that religion provides the framework because the bombers believe they are acting in the name of Islam and will be rewarded as martyrs. Since martyrdom is seen as a step towards paradise, those who commit suicide while discarding their community from a common enemy believe that they will reach an ultimate salvation after they die.

Support for "martyrdom operations"

Islamist militant organisations (including al-Qaeda, Hamas and Islamic Jihad) argue that despite what some Muslims claim is Islam's strict prohibition of suicide and murder, suicide attacks fulfill the obligation of jihad against the "oppressor", "martyrs" will be rewarded with paradise, and have the support of (some) Muslim clerics. Clerics have supported suicide attacks largely in connection with the Palestinian issue. Prominent Sunni cleric Yusuf al-Qaradawi previously had supported such attacks by Palestinians in perceived defense of their homeland as heroic and an act of resistance. Shiite Lebanese cleric Muhammad Husayn Fadlallah, the spiritual authority recognized by Hezbollah, holds similar views. According to the conservative Iranian Shi'ah cleric Ayatollah Mohammad Taghi Mesbah Yazdi, "When protecting Islam and the Muslim community depends on martyrdom operations, it not only is allowed, but even is an obligation as many of the Shi'ah great scholars and Maraje', including Ayatullah Safi Golpayegani and Ayatullah Fazel Lankarani, have clearly announced in their fatwas."

The Quranic verse used by Zarein Ahmedzay (an Afghanistan-born New York City cab driver who traveled to Waziristan for terrorist training and discussed possible suicide bombing target locations in crowded parts of Manhattan) in support of his actions was 9:111 (Surah At-Tawba):

Verily, Allah has purchased of the believers their lives and their wealth for the price of Paradise, to fight in the way of Allah, to kill and be killed. It is a promise binding on the truth in the Torah, the Gospel and the Qur'an.

Supporters of the Taliban insist their attacks are "martyrdom operations" and not suicide. The June 2013 issue of the Taliban magazine Azan extolled the virtues of suicide attacks, claiming that "suicide bombing" is a "false term" for jihad martyrdom attacks. "So martyrdom operation ≠ Suicide bombing".

The articles maintains that Abu Huraira (a companion of the Muhammad) and Umar ibn Khattab (the third caliph of Islam), approved acts in which the Muslims knew would lead to certain death, and that the Islamic prophet Muhammad also approved of such acts (according to authors Maulana Muawiya Hussaini and Ikrimah Anwar cited numerous Hadith of Muhammad on the authority of Islamic jurist Muslim ibn al-Hajjaj). "The Sahaba [companions of the Islamic prophet Muhammad] who carried out the attacks almost certainly knew that they were going to be killed during their operations but they still carried them out and such acts were extolled and praised in the sharia."

Opposition and responses from Muslim scholars

Others (such as Middle East historian Bernard Lewis) disagree, noting

... a clear difference was made between throwing oneself to certain death at the hands of an overwhelmingly strong enemy, and dying by one's own hand. The first, if conducted in a properly authorized [jihad], was a passport to heaven; the second to damnation. The blurring of their previously vital distinction was the work of some twentieth-century theologians who outlined the new theory which the suicide bombers put into practice."

The difference between engaging in an act where the perpetrator plans to fight to the death but where the attack does not require their death, is important to at least one Islamist terror group—Lashkar-e-Taiba (LeT). While the group extols "martyrdom" and has killed many civilians, LeT believes suicide attacks where the attackers dies by their own hand (such as by pressing a detonation button), are haram (forbidden). Its "trademark" is that of perpetrators fighting "to the death" but escaping "if practical". "This distinction has been the subject of extensive discourse among radical Islamist leaders."

A number of Western and Muslim scholars of Islam have posited that suicide attacks are a clear violation of classical Islamic law and characterized such attacks against civilians as murderous and sinful.

According to Bernard Lewis, "the emergence of the now widespread terrorism practice of suicide bombing is a development of the 20th century. It has no antecedents in Islamic history, and no justification in terms of Islamic theology, law, or tradition." Islamic legal rules of armed warfare or military jihad are covered in detail in the classical texts of Islamic jurisprudence, which forbidding the killing of women, children or non-combatants, and the destroying of cultivated or residential areas. For more than a millennium, these tenets were accepted by Sunnis and Shiites; however, since the 1980s militant Islamists have challenged the traditional Islamic rules of warfare to justify suicide attacks.

A number of respected Muslim scholars have provided scholastic refutations of suicide bombings, condemning them as terrorism prohibited in Islam and leading their perpetrators to hell. In his 400+-page Fatwa on Terrorism condemning suicide attacks, Muslim Islamic scholar Muhammad Tahir-ul-Qadri directly disputed the rationale of Islamists, arguing among other things that the indiscriminately killing of both Muslims and non-Muslims is unlawful, and brings the Muslim ummah into disrepute, no matter how lofty the killers intentions. Tahir-ul-Qadri states terrorism "has no place in Islamic teaching, and no justification can be provided to it...good intention cannot justify a wrong and forbidden act".

pecific groups

Studies have attempted to learn the history and motivation of suicide attackers.

Al Qaeda

Analysis of the 9/11 Al Qaeda attackers found almost all had joined the group with someone else. About 70% joined with friends, 20% with kin. Interviews with friends of the 9/11 pilots reveal they weren't "recruited" into Qaeda. They were Middle Eastern Arabs isolated even among the Moroccan and Turkish Muslims who predominate in Germany. Seeking friendship, they began hanging out after services at the Masjad al-Quds and other nearby mosques in Hamburg, in local restaurants and in the dormitory of the Technical University in the suburb of Harburg. Three (Mohamed Atta, Ramzi bin al-Shibh, Marwan al-Shehhi) wound up living together as they self-radicalized. They wanted to go to Chechnya, then Kosovo.

Hamas

Hamas's most sustained suicide bombing campaign in 2003–04 involved several members of Hebron's Masjad (mosque) al-Jihad soccer team. Most lived in the Wad Abu Katila neighborhood and belonged to the al-Qawasmeh hamula (clan); several were classmates in the neighborhood's local branch of the Palestinian Polytechnic College. Their ages ranged from 18 to 22. At least eight team members were dispatched to suicide shooting and bombing operations by the Hamas military leader in Hebron, Abdullah al-Qawasmeh (killed by Israeli forces in June 2003 and succeeded by his relatives Basel al-Qawasmeh, killed in September 2003, and Imad al-Qawasmeh, captured on October 13, 2004). In retaliation for the assassinations of Hamas leaders Sheikh Ahmed Yassin (March 22, 2004) and Abdel Aziz al-Rantissi (April 17, 2004), Imad al-Qawasmeh dispatched Ahmed al-Qawasmeh and Nasim al-Ja'abri for a suicide attack on two buses in Beer Sheva (August 31, 2004). In December 2004, Hamas declared a halt to suicide attacks.

On January 15, 2008, the son of Mahmoud al-Zahar, the leader of Hamas in the Gaza Strip, was killed (another son was killed in a 2003 assassination attempt on Zahar). Three days later, Israel Defense Minister Ehud Barak ordered Israel Defense Forces to seal all border crossings with Gaza, cutting off the flow of supplies to the territory in an attempt to stop rocket barrages on Israeli border towns. Nevertheless, violence from both sides only increased. On February 4, 2008, two friends (Mohammed Herbawi, Shadi Zghayer), who were members of the Masjad al-Jihad soccer team, staged a suicide bombing at commercial center in Dimona, Israel. Herbawi had previously been arrested as a 17-year-old on 15 March 2003 shortly after a suicide bombing on Haifa bus (by Mamoud al-Qawasmeh on March 5, 2003) and coordinated suicide shooting attacks on Israeli settlements by others on the team (March 7, 2003, Muhsein, Hazem al-Qawasmeh, Fadi Fahuri, Sufian Hariz) and before another set of suicide bombings by team members in Hebron and Jerusalem on May 17–18, 2003 (Fuad al-Qawasmeh, Basem Takruri, Mujahed al-Ja'abri). Although Hamas claimed responsibility for the Dimona attack, the politburo leadership in Damascus and Beirut was clearly initially unaware of who initiated and carried out the attack. It appears that Ahmad al-Ja'abri, military commander of Hamas's Izz ad-Din al-Qassam Brigades in Gaza requested the suicide attack through Ayoub Qawasmeh, Hamas's military liaison in Hebron, who knew where to look for eager young men who had self-radicalized together and had already mentally prepared themselves for martyrdom.

LTTE

The Liberation Tigers of Tamil Eelam were thought to have mastered the use of suicide terrorism and had a separate unit, "The Black Tigers", consisting "exclusively of cadres who have volunteered to conduct suicide operations".

Islamic State in Iraq and the Levant

The Islamic State in Iraq and the Levant utilizes suicide attacks against government targets before they attack. The attackers can use a wide range of methods, from suicide vests and belts to bomb trucks and cars and APCs filled to the brim with explosives. Usually, the suicide bomber involved in a "martyrdom operation" will record his last words in a martyrdom video before they start their attack and will be released after the suicide attack was done.

A study published by The Guardian in 2017 analyzed 923 attacks done between December 2015 and November 2016 and compared the military tactic to those used by kamikaze operations. Charlie Winter, author of the study, indicated that ISIL had "industrialized the concept of matyrdom". Most (84%) of suicide attacks were directed towards military targets usually with armed vehicles. About 80% of the attackers were of Iraqi or Syrian origin.

Response and results

Response

Suicide bombings are often followed by heightened security measures and reprisals by their targets. Because a successful suicide bomber cannot be targeted, the response is often a targeting of those believed to have sent the bomber. Because future attacks cannot be deterred by the threat of retaliation if the attackers were already willing to kill themselves, pressure is great to employ intensive surveillance of virtually any potential perpetrator, "to look for them almost everywhere, even if no evidence existed that `they` were `there` at all".

In the West Bank the IDF has at times demolished homes that belong to families whose children (or landlords whose tenants) had volunteered for such missions (whether successfully or not). Other military measures that were taken during the suicide attack campaign included: A widescale re-occupation of the West Bank and blockading of Palestinian towns; "targeted assassinations" of militants, (an approach used since the 1970s); raids against militants suspected of plotting attacks, mass arrests, curfews, and stringent travel restrictions; and physical separation from Palestinians via the 650-km (400-mile) "security barrier" in and around the West Bank. cide bombing campaign in 2003–04 involThe Second Intifada and its suicide attacks are often dated as ending around the time of an unofficial ceasefire by some of the most powerful Palestinian militant groups in 2005. A new "knife intifada" started in September 2015, but although many Palestinians were killed in the process of stabbing or attempting to stab Israelis, their deaths were not "a precondition for the success" of their mission and so are not considered suicide attacks by many observers.)

In the United States, the element of suicide in the major attack on it (the 9/11 attacks) persuaded many that previously unthinkable, "out of the box" strategic policies in a "war on terrorism" — from "preventive war" against countries not immediately attacking the US, to almost unlimited surveillance of virtually any person in the United States by the government without normal congressional and judicial oversight—was necessary. These responses "produced their own costs and risks—in lives, national debt, and America's standing in the world".

The "heightened security measures" also affected the target populations. During the bombing campaign Israelis were questioned by armed guards and given a quick pat down before being let into cafes. In the US, the post-9/11 era meant "previously inconceivable security measures—in airports and other transportation hubs, hotels and office buildings, sports stadiums and concert halls".

Suicide bombing as a strategic weapon

Militant groups employ suicide bombing not only for the practical reasons described above but also for broader strategic goals. The Canadian political scientist Mia Bloom noted that suicide bombings are frequently part of a competition between groups for legitimacy, as when the Islamic group amās used the willingness of some of its members to kill themselves in attacks against Israel to claim moral superiority over the ruling political party, Fatah, within the Palestinian Authority. Pape, on the other hand, pointed out that suicide bombing can be an effective method to pressure democracies to quit foreign interventions, as happened in the withdrawal of Western forces from Lebanon after 1983 and in India's decision not to reintroduce military forces into Sri Lanka after Gandhi's assassination in 1991.

Whatever their long-range goals, it is clear that the leaders of some groups, as part of their campaigns to exploit political, social, and economic conditions, utilize suicide bombing in a rational and calculated manner. Yet the success of the tactic does not always translate into success within a strategy of political violence, for suicide bombing is a double-edged sword. If used too frequently and too indiscriminately, it can become less shocking over time and can even alienate the populations that militants need to sustain their long-term struggle. For instance, according to a Pew Global Attitudes study, the very people in Muslim countries who looked favourably upon suicide bombing in 2002, including residents of Lebanon, Indonesia, and Pakistan, clearly expressed their rejection of suicide bombing as a tactic some five years later.

Confronting suicide bombing

Despite the difficulty, states confronting suicide attacks must take measures to prevent them. Such measures can be active or offensive, ranging from aggressive law enforcement (including the profiling of select population and age groups) to violent counterterrorist missions against cells, organizations, and leaders. Other measures can be passive or defensive; these might range from highway checkpoints and screening of airline passengers to legal measures against travel or even to the building of walls and fences in order to control movement. Regardless of what measures are used, they must be balanced against the gravity of the threat, lest they erode the values of the community or society under siege and thus cause more damage than the worst suicide attack. For example, although Israel's security fence, construction of which began in 2002, effectively reduced suicide bombings within Israel, the system of walls and barriers in the West Bank significantly reduced international support and sympathy for Israel in its continuing struggle against Palestinian radicals. Within the United States the ability of the National Security Agency to conduct "warrantless wiretapping," or electronic monitoring of domestic communication, led legislators and civil liberty groups to declare that such powers endanger due process and the personal freedoms guaranteed by law.

Results

One of the first bombing campaigns utilizing primarily suicide attacks had considerable success. In the early 1980s Hezbollah used these bombing attacks targeting first foreign peacekeepers and then Israel. The result in both cases was withdrawal from Lebanon by the targets.

Other groups have had mixed results. The Liberation Tigers of Tamil Eelam (LTTE) pioneered the use of suicide bombings against civilian and political targets and in 2000 were called (by Yoram Schweitzer) "unequivocally the most effective and brutal terrorist organization ever to utilize suicide terrorism". Their struggle for an independent state in the North and East of the island lasted for 26 years and led to the deaths of two heads of state or government, several ministers, and up to 100,000 combatants and civilians (by a UN estimate). Politically its attacks succeeded in halting the deployment of the Indian peace keeping troops to Sri-Lanka and the subsequent postponement of the peace-talks in Sri-Lanka. Nonetheless it ended in May 2009 not with an independent "Eelam", but with the overrunning of LTTE strongholds and the killing of its leadership by the Sri Lankan military and security forces.

It is more difficult to determine whether Palestinian suicide bombings have proved to be a successful tactic. Hamas "came to prominence" after the first intifada as "the main Palestinian opponent of the Oslo Accords" ("the US-sponsored peace process that oversaw the gradual and partial removal of Israel's occupation in return for Palestinian guarantees to protect Israeli security") according to the BBC. The accords were sidetracked after the election in 1996 of right wing Israeli leader Benjamin Netanyahu. Hamas's suicide bombings of Israeli targets (from 1994–1997 there were 14 suicide attacks killing 159—not all of which were attributed to Hamas) "were widely" credited for the popularity among Israelis of the hardline Netanyahuof, who—like HAMAS—was a staunch opponent of the Oslo accords, but an even stauncher enemy of HAMAS).

The efficacy of suicide bombing however, does not appear to have demonstrated by the al-Aqsa Intifada. During this Intifada, the number of suicide attacks increased markedly, but petered out around 2005 following harsh Israeli security measures (mentioned above) such as "targeted assassinations" of Palestinians reportedly involved in terrorism, and the building of a "separation barrier" that severely hampered Palestinian travel, but with no withdrawal by the Israelis from any occupied territory.

The drop in suicide bombings in Israel has been explained by the many security measures taken by the Israeli government, especially the building of the "separation barrier", and a general consensus among Palestinians that the bombings were a "losing strategy". The suicide (and non-suicide) attacks on civilians had "a major impact" on the attitudes of the Israeli public/voters, creating not demoralization, but even greater support for the right-wing Likud party, bringing to office another hardliner, former general, prime minister Ariel Sharon. In 2001, 89% of Israeli Jews supported the Sharon government's policy of "targeted assassinations" of Palestinian militants involved in terrorism against Israel, the number rising to 92% in 2003. Opinion polls of the Jewish Israelis found 78–84% support for the "separation barrier" in 2004.

The rise of suicide bombing

Accessible and stable high explosives such as trinitrotoluene (TNT) have been available for more than a century, but suicide bombing is a more recent phenomenon. Modern suicide bombers can trace their roots to radical 19th-century anarchists, or "dynamiters," who espoused a doctrine of action and a "propaganda of the deed." Few dynamiters, however, sought to destroy themselves with the same weapons that they directed against monarchs and other leaders. Contemporary suicide bombing began in 1981 in Lebanon. However, it achieved worldwide notoriety in 1983, first with an attack against the U.S. embassy in Beirut that killed 63 people and then with simultaneous car bombings of U.S. and French military barracks, also in Beirut, that killed 299 more. These attacks, mounted by the Shi□ite Islamic group Hezbollah, were credited with forcing the withdrawal of Western military forces from Lebanon.

Since 1983, suicide bombing has become a favourite terrorist tactic of insurgent groups from Sri Lanka to Chechnya to Afghanistan. One indication of this growing preference is the number of attacks, which rose from 1 in 1981 to more than 500 in 2007. The use of suicide bombing has grown for three primary reasons. First, suicide bombing is almost impossible for security forces to prevent. Bombers such as the three second-generation Pakistani Britons and one young immigrant from Jamaica who killed 52 people in the London bombings of 2005 are almost unstoppable once they are committed to die and kill others. Second, suicide bombing generates publicity. Media attention is like oxygen to terrorists, and suicide bombings receive enormous news coverage owing to the willingness of the bombers to die for a cause and the shocking damage inflicted indiscriminately against targets and bystanders alike—as happened in the assassination in 1991 of Indian Prime Minister Rajiv Gandhi and 16 others by a woman associated with the Liberation Tigers of Tamil Eelam. Third, a successful suicide bombing requires little expertise and few resources beyond a bomb and someone willing to carry it. Therefore, for groups determined to spread terror, suicide bombing is much more cost-effective than other tactics such as hostage taking, which requires considerably greater investment in resources, planning, and training. Instruction manuals, videos, and other training materials, some of them available online, have allowed groups like the London bombers to construct bombs with little guidance.

Religion and the question of motivation

The growth in suicide bombing has also been linked with the rise of militant religious-inspired terrorist violence. However, religion is not the sole motivation for suicide bombing. American political scientist Robert Pape argued that, prior to 2003, the group that used suicide bombing the most was the Tamil Tigers, a largely secular ethnic separatist group from Sri Lanka. Nevertheless, suicide bombings since 2003 have been mounted almost exclusively by groups espousing religious causes. One compelling explanation for the role of religion involves justification and persuasion. As a means to justify indiscriminate killing and to overcome the natural aversion against taking one's own life, militant groups (and the religious leaders and interpreters who speak for them) use faith to elevate their causes to religious crusades. In this way the act of suicide bombing becomes not a social or religious aberration but rather a sacred duty and obligation. At various times and for various reasons, communities have been manipulated into sanctifying those "martyred" in suicide bombings and have become a source of new recruits. The reasons can include resentment against a perceived occupier or some other historical and social injustice as well as economic and social incentives for the families of martyrs.

Religion may justify suicide bombing on one level, but on another level the act springs from the motivation of the individual bomber. Studies have shown that many suicide bombers, particularly in developed societies, are not deranged or wild-eyed fanatics with nothing to live for; indeed, a significant number of bombers have come from income and education levels well above their countries' norms. Another broad trend, noticeable in the numerous suicide bombings in Iraq and Afghanistan, has been the recruitment of individuals who are physically or mentally ill, impoverished, suggestible, or alienated in some way from their society. Individual purposes or motivations can range broadly, from revenge for the death of a family member (for instance, the female suicide bombers, or "Black Widows," in Chechnya) to outrage against an occupying power (for instance, in Iraq or the Palestinian territories) or against some incident (e.g., the abuse of prisoners at the Abu Ghraib prison in Iraq) to coercion or even the payment of money to one's family (as has occurred in Afghanistan and elsewhere). Neither altruism nor anomie figures much in such individual calculations.

Female suicide bomber

Female suicide bombers are women who carry out a suicide attack, wherein the bomber kills herself while simultaneously killing targeted people. Suicide bombers are normally viewed as male political radicals, but since the 1960s female suicide attacks have been on the rise. Through 1985-2006, 15% of all suicide attacks were conducted by female suicide bombers. There are many organizations, such as Boko Haram (which is the first group to use females in a majority of their suicide bombings and surpassed the Tamil Tigers in using more female suicide-bombers than any other terrorist group in history), ISIS, and the Al Aqsa Martyrs Brigade, that recently started using women as tools in their attacks, since they are normally viewed as less of a threat than their male counterparts. This includes women having the element of surprise, a hesitancy to search females, increased publicity for female suicide bombing attacks, and the female stereotype as non-violent.

Background

Women have an extensive and complex history in political violence. While the typical terrorist of the 1960s tended to be an educated male from an upper-middle-class background, many left-wing terrorist groups in the 1960s and 1970s had prominent women active within these groups. Ulrike Meinhof, a German left-wing terrorist and journalist, co-founded the Red Army Faction and participated in a range of bombings and bank robberies. The Popular Front for the Liberation of Palestine (PFLP)'s Leila Khaled is considered to be the first women to hijack an airplane, drawing international attention. Fusako Shigenobu founded and led the Japanese Red Army, a communist militant group that conducted hijackings and massacres. A number of Italian women were active in Italian terrorist organizations between 1970-1984. Females played fundamental roles in Puerto Rican nationalist movements such as the Puerto Rican Armed Forces of National Liberation (FLAN) and Los Macheteros, two groups designated as terrorist organizations. Women served visible roles in American groups, such as the Symbionese Liberation Army. Women also served as mobilizing agents for Weather Underground, recruiting people into the organization. Women have been more active in left-wing groups as these groups' ideologies tend to be more conducive to women's participation in combatant and other non-traditional roles.

Female bombers have emerged as an area of particular study, with the circumstances of female involvement garnering a great deal of research. The number of female suicide bombers has been steadily increasing. Existing models of terrorism emphasize that these acts begin with a group promoting, supporting, or praising acts such as martyrdom. Their decisions to engage in suicide bombings contradicts theories that dictate that women prefer peaceful conflict resolution mechanisms as compared to men.

Organizations have differing stances on female suicide bombers. For example, in 2002, the spiritual leader of Hamas "categorically renounced the use of women as suicide bombers." In fact, in early 2002, he reported that "Hamas was far from enthusiastic about the inclusion of women in warfare, for reasons of modesty." This stance shifted in 2004, when the first female suicide bomber was used. Officials exclaimed that the act was a "significant evolution in our fight. The male fighters face many obstacles...Women are like the reserve army□when there is a necessity, we use them." The LTTE attracted thousands of women and their militarization shaped women's identity from the "traditional ideal of the auspicious, fecund wife to the androgynous Armed Virgin." Rajini Thiranagama exclaimed, "One cannot but be inspired when one sees the women of the LTTE in the night with their AKs slung over the shoulder ... One cannot but admire the dedication and toughness of their training … One could see the nationalist fervor and the romantic vision of women in arms defending the nation."

Characteristics of female suicide bombers

There is much variation among female suicide bombers. A number of studies have attempted to compare suicide attackers across different suicide groups. It was found that groups that used women the least were Islamist fundamentalist groups. When dealing with age, female suicide bombers followed the same age trend as males, they usually fall within the early to mid 20s. They also tend to have more secular ties than presumed. Some are married while others are widows. Socioeconomic status also varies among female attackers.

Women's involvement is mediated differently than men's; they are more likely to be involved through personal contacts or family members, while men's process of involvement is more likely to stem from movement affiliation and disenchantment with nonviolent forms of political activism. Differences in men and women's need for revenge (and subsequent use of suicide attacks) has been studied, with inconsistent findings reported. Some argue men are more vengeful than women, while others find no such claims.

Examples

Sana'a Mehaidli, a 17-year-old member of the Syrian Socialist Party (SSNP/PPS), a pro-Syrian Lebanese organization, is believed to have been the first female suicide bomber. On April 9, 1985, she blew up herself and a truck of explosives next to an Israeli convoy in Lebanon during the Israeli occupation of south Lebanon. She worked at a video store where she recorded her will, saying "I am very comfortable with carrying out this operation. I choose to do this because I am fulfilling my duty towards my land and my people...Now I am loving my country, sacrificing my life and respecting the people of the south."

Thenmozhi Rajaratnam, also known as Dhanu, is thought to have been a member of the Liberation Tigers of Tamil Eelam (Tamil Tigers), and involved in the Assassination of Rajiv Gandhi, the ex-Prime minister of India, and sixteen other bystanders in 1991. She allegedly had been raped by Indian Peace Keeping Force soldiers and her four brothers were killed. Sri Lanka's political group, Liberation Tigers of Tamil Ealam (LTTE) includes the Black Tigers, and the Black Tigers are known for suicide bombing attacks, and also for the fact that mostly women execute them.

Wafa Idris Arafat was the first female suicide bomber in the Israeli–Palestinian conflict; in 2002 she detonated a 22-pound bomb in the center of Jerusalem outside a shoe store on Jaffa Road that killed her, Pinhas Tokatli (81), and injured more than 100 others. The attack took place on 27 January 2002 but the identity of the bomber wasn't confirmed until 30 January 2002. Wafa carried the bomb in a backpack, rather than strapped to her body. Since, prior to this attack, women had only helped plant bombs, the use of a backpack and the lack of the usual note or video led to confusion regarding her suicide motives and speculation that she did not intend to detonate the bomb, but that the explosion was accidental. However, after investigation of the explosion, Israel declared Wafa a suicide bomber around 9 February 2002. Prior to this Wafa called for an "Army of Roses." Wafa became an icon and served under Al Aqsa Martyrs Brigade. Wafa was born in a refugee camp, and her father died in when she was a child. During the First Intifada, she served on the refugee camp's women's committee, helping prisoners' families and distributing food. When she delivered a stillborn and was told she would never be able to carry a baby to full-term, her husband divorced her.

Muriel Degauque was a Belgian convert to Islam who performed a suicide car bomb attack on November 9, 2005 against a U.S. military convoy in Iraq. She originally worked at a bakery and after marrying a Muslim man, she moved to Iraq and became radicalized.

In Dagestan, Russia in 2010 a 17-year-old widow of a Caucasus militant wearing a suicide bomb vest approached a Ministry of the Interior office in the village of Gubden . She was apparently stopped at a security post outside the office where she detonated her explosives, killing one police officer and injuring four others. The attack was claimed by the Caucasus Emirate militant Jihadist group, Dokku Umarov.

Blasts from two female suicide bombers at a crowded fish market in Nigeria's northeastern city of Maiduguri killed at least 20 people on June 22, 2015.

On December 23, 2016, the first female suicide bomber in Bangladesh detonated her explosive during a police raid.

In 2018, Puji Kuswati became Indonesia's first female suicide bomber when she and her daughters, Fadila Sari, and Pamela Rizkita, (twelve and nine years old respectively, and thus not counted as choosing to be bombers) bombed the GKI Diponegoro church·.

Causes and reasons

There are a number of reasons as to why female suicide bombers are used by groups. Terrorists use bombers as they are cheaper than purchasing arms. They are considered a low risk weapon and require low technology. They do not require much training, do not leave much of a trace behind, have the element of surprise, have easier access to targeted populations as well as soft targets, and tend to frighten the general population. As female combatants are seen as less likely to engage in lethal actions and can thus avoid suspicion, they are regarded as ideal combatants. Dress and gender stereotypes are often utilized by women to bypass security defenses. For example, women who appear pregnant appropriate related expectations and stereotypes to their benefit, discouraging invasive body searchers. Women may also "westernize" their appearance in an attempt at covering their actions and avoiding detection. Women are also deployed as suicide bombers as they tend to "elicit greater public sympathy and publicity for an organization." By some research, female bombers receive eight times more press coverage than their male counterparts.

Insurgent groups also face pressure when it comes to recruiting members, causing the group to expand their bases to sustain the group's position. It has been argued that the introduction of women and girls into combat "generally came about in response to logistical demands: the mounting number of casualties, the intensified crackdowns by government, and the ability to escape detection more easily than men." An example of this was in January 2002 when the spiritual leader of Hamas renounced the use of female bombers. Later on in the same year, Hamas wasn't enthusiastic about adding women into their ranks.Then in January 2004, Hamas used their first female suicide bomber. Hamas defense to this was evolution of their fight. Citing easier access to reach targets, Hamas stated that women are the reserve army. When there is a need they will use them. On average, it is calculated that terrorist groups that use suicide bombing as a tactic wait around 13.5 years before employing women. However, women are reported to have higher kill rates than men, on average killing four times as many people as men do.

Terrorist and insurgent groups may also appropriate media coverage to benefit from the portrayal of female suicide bombers. Women's media portrayal may help various organizations recruit and motivate men, and coverage of women in the media allows groups to differentiate themselves from one another. It also may help deliver group-based messages. For example, media coverage may highlight that the group, by using women, had been driven to extreme measures. Media attention on female suicide bombers tends to examine emotional explanations for women's involvement, as opposed to ideological justifications.

Another reason for the use of female suicide bombers may be based in culture. In the Middle East, use of female bombers by groups can be used as an image to emasculate males in the region. Using the idea that the situation is dire that the women have to fight.

Individual motivations

There are different causes and reasons as to why female suicide bombers perform these deadly actions. For one, many cite personal feelings of sacrifice in conducting such missions. The missions become more successful to the public when they are framed as forms of sacrifice. Society would be "hard pressed to accept, a female who offers her life in this context is seen as engaging in the most profound form of selflessness." Other research suggests that women resort to terrorism to "redeem their fallen reputations, such as being barren, divorced, defiled, unchaste, and so on." Struggling for the pursuit of freedom through the LTTE can be seen as a way in which women can redeem themselves. Tamil rape victims tend to be prohibited from marriage and childbearing. Conceptualizing female bombers as mothers allows suicide bombings to serve as offerings for women who cannot become mothers.

In literature on female suicide bombers, exploitation of women is a distinctive factor that separates them from male suicide bombers. Research has examined cases of women's exploitation by their own families, often for monetary compensation.

Women can also be motivated by political/and or historical contexts to take action against their enemy. For example, in the context of the Israeli–Palestinian conflict, it has been noted that Palestinian female suicide bombers are often motivated by anti-Zionism and the Israeli occupation of their homeland to take action. According to Palestinian legal scholar Noura Erakat, the "Israeli military occupation [is] a significant, if not the most significant, factor contributing to the subjugation of Palestinian women's rights." They are often motivated by the politics of their environment to take action in this situation. Western feminist critic Amal Amireh notes examples of how the women exercise their political agency in the conflict, including the fact that the bomber often declares in public her political group and nationalism, as well as the fact that they commit the act in public as a spectacle to be observed. There is also a case to made toward religion/political indoctrination. Some recruiters, like the LTTE, would concentrate on recruiting orphans due to their young age and they are much easier to indoctrinate and condition.

Individual motivations to become suicide bombers vary. Motives include "to avenge a personal loss, to redeem the family name, to escape a life of sheltered monotony and achieve fame, or to equalize the patriarchal societies in which they live." The death of a relative triggers the decision to commit a suicide attack. Some women join to seek revenge. For example, studies have shown that some women join the Liberation Tigers of Tamil Eelam seeking revenge against crimes the government has committed against the group, from disappearances to torture. Government oppression has only emboldened the LTTE, and women have increasingly become more publicly involved.

In Chechnya, female bombers originally became involved for more personal reasons, avenging the deaths of Chechen male relatives killed by Russian forces. They are referred to as "Black Widows" because many were the wives, mothers, sisters, or female relatives of men killed in battle. The activities of the Black Widows are regarded to support the theory that suicide bombings may alter societal gender norms. With militant involvement usually seen as being performed by men, engaging in violent actions counters notions of women's traditional roles, such as raising children. Clara Beyler, a counter-terrorism analyst writes that "There is a difference between men and women suicide attackers: women consider combat as a way to escape the predestined life that is expected of them. When women become human bombs, their intent is to make a statement not only in the name of a country, a religion, a leader, but also in the name of their gender." Some argue that violence serves to empower women. In this sense, some argue that understanding women's motivations should be understood through cultural contexts.

Effects

Organizations of female suicide bombers

Al Aqsa Martyrs Brigade is a known terrorist organization that trained many female suicide bombers since their uprising as political weapons. In January 2002, the group claimed responsibility for the first female suicide bombing attack inside of Israel, in efforts to push Israel settlers out of west bank and to form an entirely Palestinian state. The group is known to be most active in the Gaza strip, but also attacks inside of Israel and the West Bank.

Palestinian bombers

On the same day Darine Abu Aisha committed a suicide bombing, Sheikh Ahmed Yassin, the religious leader of Islamist militant group Hamas, issued a fatwa, or religious rule, that gave permission to women to participate in suicide attacks as well as listing the rewards in "Paradise" that these female martyrs would receive upon their deaths. He also promised Hamas will send many female suicide bombers in order to strike Israelis.

Reactions to this in the Islamic world were mixed. While many hailed the female suicide bomber and urged full involvement of all in Jihad, some criticized the cruelty of tearing mothers from their children and sending them to explode themselves.

Notable female Palestinian suicide bombers include

- Wafa Idris - first suicide bomber (bombing date: January 27, 2002)
- Darine Abu Aisha- second suicide bomber (bombing date: February 27, 2002)
- Ayat al-Akhras - third suicide bomber (bombing date: March 29, 2002)
- Andalib Suleiman - fourth suicide bomber (bombing date: April 12, 2002)
- Hanadi Jaradat - sixth suicide bomber (bombing date: October 4, 2003)
- Reem Al-Reyashi- eighth suicide bomber (bombing date: January 15, 2004). Al-Reyashi, a 22-year-old mother of two, detonated an explosive pack at the Erez crossing point on the frontier of the Gaza Strip.

Chechnya

The Shahidka, commonly called the "Black widows" are a group of Islamist Chechen separatist suicide bombers. Khava Barayeva blew herself up at a Russian Army outpost in June 7, 2000. In 2001, Aiza Gazuyeva killed Russian general Gaidar Gadzhiyev in a suicide bombing, the first female suicide bomber of the Chechen insurgency. The group carried out the Moscow theater hostage crisis and some were involved in the Beslan school siege. A bombing that killed 10 people at Rizhskaya metro station in Moscow was thought to be carried out by a woman who was identified as a Beslan school captor. The 2004 Russian aircraft bombings are believed to be carried out by female bombers. Two of the perpetrators of the 2010 Moscow Metro bombings were women; Dzhanet Abdullayeva, who was married to a militant,and Maryam Sharipova. The October 2013 Volgograd bus bombing was carried out by a woman.

8

Future of Terrorism

Terrorism, both domestic and international, shows every sign of increasing. In looking at the future of terrorism, this chapter acknowledges the evaluative nature of the concept of terrorism, and attempts to distinguish it from other forms of violence. Three major forms of terrorism are examined, and in each case an attempt is made to specify the general context and forms of terror employed, the conditions conducive to terror and those factors tending to inhibit or reduce terror. Possible new types of weapons and tactics likely to be employed by terrorists in the future are investigated, and the danger of nuclear terrorism is evaluated.

The future of terrorism and terrorism of the future are two different issues. It can be safely said that the future of terrorism is, in a manner of speaking, 'secure' in that society and states that may be able to manage terrorism with the correct instruments and policies but it cannot be totally eliminated from society no matter what laws and counter-terror measures that are taken. Some terrorist groups fade away quickly, almost as suddenly as they appeared on the scene, while others run through a mixture of fluctuating fortunes depending on the kind of support they are able to derive from their benefactors and empirical geopolitical conditions that exist and which might vary. For long, it was considered that Islamic terrorism was something that happened only in Africa and Asia untill 11 September, 2001. The narrative began to change but not fast enough. Today, terror is to be found in San Bernardino in California, Orlando in Florida USA, Brussels and Paris; the idea is spreading from West Asia but the act often carried out by the locals. The narrative still has not changed adequately enough.

Besides the need to eliminate radical Islamic terrorism through military domination, it is necessary that the voice of the moderate must be strengthened for the battle is internal, within Islam as well. But so long as pre-eminent global leaders like President Obama and US Presidential hopefuls like Hillary

Clinton fudge and refuse to describe recent attacks in Orlando as Islamic terror and bend the narrative away from this, the moderate feels weakened. This is precisely what moderate Muslims settled in the West and even in some Muslim countries have been urging. If the power that proclaims to lead the world in getting rid of terrorism is unable to unequivocally condemn such acts of Islamic terror, then this only strengthens radical Islamist violence.

Pakistan's Jihad fixation

This is not surprising in a country where even the fiery speeches of Mullah Aziz of Red Mosque and videos of Jamia Hafza are not described as a threat to the State by government representatives in the court. Pakistani rulers, especially its military mindset against India and Afghanistan, have remained unchanged. Even with some acceptance of civilian control, there is unlikely to be any course correction by the military. Jihad as a tool of Pakistan's foreign and national security policies is now a permanent fixture. Pakistan claims to be a victim of terrorism while the world at large sees it as a major backer of jihadism. American officials have described Pakistan as the 'ally from hell' and its officials as 'duplicitous'. Curiously, Afghanistan is portrayed as a potential collaborator of India while the fact is that during the 1965 and 1971 wars between Pakistan and India, Afghanistan sided with the former Professor C Christine Fair in her book 'Fighting to the End: The Pakistan Army's Way of War' effectively counters the claim that Pakistan is a security-seeking State facing hostile neighbours and if the international powers, especially the US, could guarantee or facilitate its well-being by leaning on India and to an extent on Afghanistan, Pakistan could be weaned away from jihad. The truth is that under the façade of Islam, jihad and patriotism is a mega business entity, which has actually become an economic class in its own right. Pakistani scholar Dr Ayesha Siddiqa describes the military as an economic class that is out to keep its chokehold on the nation's resources through whatever means necessary. (Dr Mohammed Taqi, Whither Dr Jekyll and Mr Hyde) The main threat to the Pakistan Army is that if peace might happen between India and Pakistan then it would lose its stranglehold on the country. That is why there is the perennial need to keep the jihadis going, creating new ogres, activating defunct outfits, renaming others and keeping both countries in mutual antagonism. Jihad or its variations will continue. We should remain prepared for the long haul.

Rise of the Caliphate

According to a Gallup poll in 2007 in Indonesia, Pakistan, Egypt and Morocco, 71 per cent of those interviewed agreed that there should be a strict application of the Shariah law in every Islamic country and about 65 per cent agreed that all Islamic countries should be unified into one single State or a Caliphate. This is similar to the orthodox Islamic goal which says that there should be a single ruler for the entire Muslim world. Moreover, 75 per cent wanted all western values be kept out of Islamic countries. The question would be who will be that single ruler. Right now, there are several claimants. Ayman al-Zawahiri also referred to Caliphates as a goal of Al Qaeda. Lashkar-e-Toiba has dreamt of three Caliphates in India and that is not something the ISIS has adopted as a slogan. The business of Caliphates is serious business in the Muslim world. Hizb ut-Tehrir had organised a series of conferences on this issue some years ago, from the UK to Indonesia. But the movement for a Caliphate is not monolithic and apart from Shia reservations, the Saudis have their own agenda with their Wahabbi Islam. There are regional conflicts like the oldest, Sunni versus Shia, at play as well. John Cooley in his book 'Unholy Wars' had predicted, "The world will continue to experience this blowback from the Afghanistan war of 1979-89 well into the new century". And it shows no sign of ending.

Western interests

Western, primarily the US, commercial and strategic interests in the entire region seek to control the production and distribution of the world's energy reserves, to be paid for in the US dollars. This interest is exhibited through the massive private US investments in Saudi Arabia and the Gulf, the oil and gas interests of Western companies in drilling, refining and transporting. ExxonMobil, Chevron, Royal Dutch, BP and Total are some of the oil giants in the playing fields of West Asia. It is this interest and the commitment of the Saudi Kings to the US that it would sell its oil in Dollars and the massive US investments in the kingdom that prevents the US from taking any action against Saudi rulers in financing terrorism and spreading Wahabbi Islam across the globe. This remains a major impediment in controlling, financing, weaponisation and the spread of terror.

It has become fashionable since then as a force equaliser in some cases (against India) or force multiplier against others (in the Arab world). There is blow-back in most sponsoring countries. There is a third epicentre evolving and this is expected to be in Libya from where ISIS hordes will fan out into the rest of Africa: Algeria, Niger, Nigeria, Somalia and also spill into Europe. There is no knowing how, when and where this will end. One of the main reasons has been an inability to define terror and over-emphasis on political correctness of the narrative. For us in India, we have the problem that confirmed terrorist organisations like Lashkar-e-Toiba in Pakistan plans Ghazwa-eHind and dream of establishing three Caliphates in India. This fits admirably with the dreams of the military mindset that seeks equality with India through confrontation. Pakistani terror outfits dreamt of Caliphates in India decades before Abu Bakr al-Baghdadi announced his Caliphate in Iraq in 2014.

Tolerance is at dangerously low ebb in all our societies. We see signs of this in Europe and America as well. An inability of the world powers to agree on a common definition of terror and terrorism has been a major hindrance in international cooperation in tackling terror. Political correctness has been carried to absurd limits and we are not able to describe what is happening in West Asia as acts of intolerance, brutality and violence perpetrated by some Muslims in the name of Islam. The unwillingness of political leaders and society to truthfully and accurately describe such atrocities as the handiwork of Muslim extremists only hurts the interests of the moderates. It is this section of society that seeks international support to be able to stand up to this brutality in the name of Islam as these extremists chase their Armageddon. While many would reject the vision of the Islamic State, the fact was that this entity and Al Qaeda and various Islamic groups like Lashkar-e-Toiba have drawn on the scholarship of Ibn Taymiyyah in the 14th century to Sayyid Qutb in the 20th century, whom many Muslims considered as 'religious leaders'. One of the major results of this politically correct narrative has been that counter-terror has become politicised.

Terrorism of the future

Terrorists and terrorism will evolve with time and as always prove themselves far more nimble than the State to adapt to new tactics and technology in the furtherance of their goals. They will evolve as the society evolves and as the State reacts to them. The ability to handle them will also depend on how the society reacts and how efficient and nimble the State is. Technology will continue to develop and improve, not along a linear path but exponentially. Learning to dream, think and act exponentially is going to be the new battle ground between the terrorists and the counter terrorists. Tipping points will be reached far more suddenly and sharply. Given the age old symbiotic relationship between crime of various kinds and terrorism, the two together will use these technologies far more quickly and efficiently. Financial transactions will move even faster than now, borders would not have to be crossed and worse, for the counter terrorists, he will not know the source or origin of the attack. And we are only talking of internet aided, computer based terrorists acting in a group with or without miniaturised robots.

A lone terrorist acting similarly is a counter terrorist's or counter-intelligence agent's worst nightmare. And we are not even talking of artificial intelligence-based devices here. Far more is also the problem that while the terrorist and the criminal finds these methods price friendly, a counter to this runs into billions of dollars and massive manpower with limited chances of success. It was this fear that led Bertrand Russell to remark that, "Technological progress is like an axe in the hands of pathological criminal." This fear is becoming a reality of the 21st century.

The use of the social media has been maximised by jihadist organisations as they use 21st century technology to knock their people back to the 7th century. Al Qaeda has its own glossy magazine to inspire while ISIS has Dabiq. The content of the English version is designed for Western audiences and is therefore different from the one in Arabic. Quite often counter terrorist experts refer to the Internet as a "terrorist university", "where terrorists can learn new technologies to make them even more effective in their attack methodologies." (Marc Goodman, Future Crime – A Journey to the Dark Side of Technology and How to Survive It).

All this has made the task of the counter-terrorists and the Intelligence agencies extremely complicated and at times, seemingly hopeless. In

Facebook, for instance, with its more than 1.5 billion members, uploading 350 million photographs with the 'Like' button being used six billion times every day. Google, the other giant which the world swears by today, processes so much data every day that if converted into books, this would reach half way to the moon from earth. This happens EVERY DAY. Is there an Intelligence agency in the world that can access all this data, sift it and then convert the rest into information which is then processed as knowledge and along with other inputs finally get them converted into actionable intelligence that is usable, against terrorists? After the 11 September, 2001 attacks the US security apparatus led by George Bush had gone into a massive revamp and reorientation overdrive of its security and intelligence systems. Not even the US, with all its financial resources and technology at its disposal, after having privatised intelligence collection and total electronic surveillance of all manner of transmissions, has been unable to prevent all terror attacks. That is how it is going to be in the future except that techniques, targets, sponsors may vary and may not be identifiable, making retaliation difficult, even impossible.

Increasing Capabilities of Terrorists

Terrorists are improving their sophistication and abilities in virtually all aspects of their operations and support. The aggressive use of modern technology for information management, communication and intelligence has increased the efficiency of these activities. Weapons technology has become more increasingly available, and the purchasing power of terrorist organizations is on the rise. The ready availability of both technology and trained personnel to operate it for any client with sufficient cash allows the well-funded terrorist to equal or exceed the sophistication of governmental counter-measures.

Likewise, due to the increase in information outlets, and competition with increasing numbers of other messages, terrorism now requires a greatly increased amount of violence or novelty to attract the attention it requires. The tendency of major media to compete for ratings and the subsequent revenue realized from increases in their audience size and share produces pressures on terrorists to increase the impact and violence of their actions to take advantage of this sensationalism.

Today, most experts believe that certain parts of the Middle East, Pakistan and Afghanistan are turning out to be the main power centers for terrorism. Decades of lawlessness and corruption have seen Islamic terrorist groups fill the power vaccum in this region and continue to turn out an alarming number of religiously motivated terrorists.

The Evolution of Terrorism

Terrorism is continually changing

While at the surface it remains "the calculated use of unlawful violence or threat of unlawful violence to inculcate fear" it is rapidly becoming the predominant strategic tool of our adversaries. As terrorism evolves into the principal irregular warfare strategy of the 21st century, it is adapting to changes in the world socio-political environment. Some of these changes facilitate the abilities of terrorists to operate, procure funding, and develop new capabilities. Other changes are gradually moving terrorism into a different relationship with the world at large.

In order to put these changes into context, it will be necessary to look at the historical evolution of terrorism, with each succeeding evolution building upon techniques pioneered by others. This evolution is driven by ongoing developments in the nature of conflict and international relations. It is also necessary to consider some of the possible causes of future conflicts, in order to understand the actors and their motivations. Finally, we examine how terrorism will be integrated into this evolution of conflict, and what that will mean for U.S. military forces.

When describing the evolution of terrorism and the use of terror through history, it is essential to remember that forms of society and government in the past were significantly different than they are today. Modern nation-states did not exist in their present form until 1648 (Treaty of Westphalia), and the state's monopoly on warfare, or inter-state violence, is even more recent. The lack of central governments made it impossible to use terror as a method of affecting a political change, as there was no single dominant political authority. Also, the absence of central authority meant that the game of warfare was open to many more players. Instead of national armies, a variety of non-sovereign nobility, mercenaries, leaders of religious factions, or mercantile companies participated in warfare. Their involvement in warfare was considered to be perfectly legitimate. This is in contrast to the modern era, where nations go to war, but private participation is actually illegal.

Early Theories of Terrorism

Early practitioners of terrorism, such as the Zealots and the Assassins did not leave any particular philosophy or doctrine on their use of terrorism. With the exception of spectacular failures such as Guy Fawkes' religiously inspired attempt to assassinate King James I and both Houses of Parliament in England, terrorism did not separate itself or progress beyond the normal practices of warfare at that time. As political systems became more sophisticated, and political authority was viewed as less of a divine gift and more as a social construct, new ideas about political conflict developed.

The period of warfare and political conflict that embroiled Europe after the French Revolution provided inspiration for political theorists during the early 1800s. Several important theories of social revolution developed during this time (see text box on the next page for summaries of the key revolutionary thinkers). The link between revolutionary violence and terror was developed early on. Revolutionary theories rejected the possibility of reforming the system and demanded its destruction. This extremism laid the groundwork for the use of unconstrained violence for political ends.

Two ideologies that embraced violent social change were Marxism, which evolved into communism, and anarchism. Both were utopian; they held that putting their theories into practice could produce ideal societies. Both advocated the complete destruction of the existing system. Both acknowledged that violence outside the accepted bounds of warfare and rebellion would be necessary. Communism focused on economic class warfare, and assumed seizure of state power by the working class (proletariat) until the state was no longer needed, and eventually disposed of. Anarchism advocated more or less immediate rejection of all forms of governance. The anarchist's belief was that after the state is completely destroyed, nothing will be required to replace it, and people could live and interact without governmental coercion. In the short term, communism's acceptance of the need for organization and an interim coercive state made it the more successful of the two ideologies. Anarchism survived into the modern era and retains attraction for violent extremists to this day.

20th Century Evolution of Terrorism

In the early years of the 20th Century nationalism and revolutionary political ideologies were the principal developmental forces acting upon terrorism. When the Treaty of Versailles redrew the map of Europe after World War I by breaking up the Austro-Hungarian Empire and creating new nations, it acknowledged the principle of self-determination for nationalities and ethnic groups. This encouraged minorities and ethnicities not receiving recognition to campaign for independence or autonomy. However, in many cases self-determination was limited to European nations and ethnic groups and denied others, especially the colonial possessions of the major European powers, creating bitterness and setting the stage for the long conflicts of the anti-colonial period.

In particular, Arab nationalists felt that they had been betrayed. Believing they were promised post-war independence, they were doubly disappointed; first when the French and British were given authority over their lands; and then especially when the British allowed Zionist immigration into Palestine in keeping with a promise contained in the Balfour Declaration.

Since the end of World War II, terrorism has accelerated its development into a major component of contemporary conflict. Primarily in use immediately after the war as a subordinate element of anti-colonial insurgencies, it expanded beyond that role. In the service of various ideologies and aspirations, terrorism sometimes supplanted other forms of conflict completely. It also became a far-reaching weapon capable of effects no less global than the intercontinental bomber or missile. It has also proven to be a significant tool of diplomacy and international power for states inclined to use it.

The seemingly quick results and shocking immediacy of terrorism made some consider it as a short cut to victory. Small revolutionary groups not willing to invest the time and resources to organize political activity would rely on the "propaganda of the deed" to energize mass action. This suggested that a tiny core of activists could topple any government through the use of terror alone. The result of this belief by revolutionaries in developed countries was the isolation of the terrorists from the population they claimed to represent, and the adoption of the Leninist concept of the "vanguard of revolution" by tiny groups of disaffected revolutionaries. In less developed countries small groups of foreign revolutionaries such as Che Guevara arrived from outside the country, expecting to immediately energize revolutionary action by their presence.

Future Trends in Terrorism

As a conflict method that has survived and evolved through several millennia to flourish in the modern information age, terrorism continues to adapt to meet the challenges of emerging forms of conflict, and exploit developments in technology and society. Terrorism has demonstrated increasing abilities to adapt to counter-terrorism measures and political failure. Terrorists are developing new capabilities of attack and improving the efficiency of existing methods. Additionally, terrorist groups have shown significant progress in escaping from a subordinate role in nation-state conflicts, and becoming prominent as international influences in their own right. They are becoming more integrated with other sub-state entities, such as criminal organizations and legitimately chartered corporations, and are gradually assuming a measure of control and identity with national governments.

Adaptive Capabilities of Terror Groups

Terrorists have shown the ability to adapt to the techniques and methods of counter-terror agencies and intelligence organizations over the long term. The decentralization of the network form of organization is an example of this. Adopted to reduce the disruption caused by the loss of key links in a chain of command, a network organization also complicates the tasks of security forces, and reduces predictability of operations.

Terrorists have also been quick to use new technologies, and adapt existing ones to their uses. The debate over privacy of computer data was largely spurred by the specter of terrorists planning and communicating with encrypted data beyond law enforcement's ability to intercept or decode this data. To exchange information, terrorists have exploited disposable cellular phones, over the counter long-distance calling cards, Internet cafes, and other means of anonymous communications. Embedding information in digital pictures and graphics is another innovation employed to enable the clandestine global communication that modern terrorists require.

Terrorists have also demonstrated significant resiliency after disruption by counter-terrorist action. Some groups have redefined themselves after being defeated or being forced into dormancy. The Shining Path of Peru (Sendero Luminosa) lost its leadership cadre and founding leader to counter-terrorism efforts by the Peruvian government in 1993. The immediate result was severe degradation in the operational capabilities of the group. However, the Shining

Path has returned to rural operations and organization in order to reconstitute itself. Although not the threat that it was, the group remains in being, and could exploit further unrest or governmental weakness in Peru to continue its renewal.

In Italy, the Red Brigades (Brigate Rossi) gradually lapsed into inactivity due to governmental action and a changing political situation. However, a decade after the supposed demise of the Red Brigades, a new group called the Anti-Capitalist Nuclei emerged exhibiting a continuity of symbols, styles of communiqus, and potentially some personnel from the original Red Brigade organization. This ability to perpetuate ideology and symbology during a significant period of dormancy, and re-emerge under favorable conditions demonstrates the durability of terrorism as a threat to modern societies.

Increasing Capabilities of Terrorists

Terrorists are improving their sophistication and abilities in virtually all aspects of their operations and support. The aggressive use of modern technology for information management, communication and intelligence has increased the efficiency of these activities. Weapons technology has become more increasingly available, and the purchasing power of terrorist organizations is on the rise. The ready availability of both technology and trained personnel to operate it for any client with sufficient cash allows the well-funded terrorist to equal or exceed the sophistication of governmental counter-measures.

Likewise, due to the increase in information outlets, and competition with increasing numbers of other messages, terrorism now requires a greatly increased amount of violence or novelty to attract the attention it requires. The tendency of major media to compete for ratings and the subsequent revenue realized from increases in their audience size and share produces pressures on terrorists to increase the impact and violence of their actions to take advantage of this sensationalism.

Today, most experts believe that certain parts of the Middle East, Pakistan and Afghanistan are turning out to be the main power centers for terrorism. Decades of lawlessness and corruption have seen Islamic terrorist groups fill the power vaccum in this region and continue to turn out an alarming number of religiously motivated terrorists.

The future of terrorism in India

Things have remained volatile between India and its neighbors, Pakistan and China, since independence was granted to India and Pakistan by the British in 1947. Considering that the partitioning of the subcontinent has triggered Indo-Pakistan rivalry due to border disputes, these countries have emerged as bitter enemies. Four wars have been fought between them during the last seventy years of their cagey and difficult relationship. Besides its bête noire Pakistan, India has fought a brief but devastating war with China in 1962, with bitter memories still passing on to next generations. Apart from dealing with two nuclear armed nemeses, India has another problem: terrorism. A variety of violent non-state actors (insurgents, terrorists) operates in India. Perhaps no other country is as diverse as the Indian society, having a plethora of ethnic, communal, religious and sectarian groups including some who have indeed resorted to violence because of a wide range of issues.

While studying India's decades-long fight against terrorism, it is evident that the Indian counter-terrorism efforts have yielded positive results up till recently. Law enforcement and paramilitary forces in India have combatted a range of terrorist groups in 13 India states, and have significantly reduced the number of attacks. Counter-terrorism operations, anti-terrorism legislations, peace agreements and grant of rights to local people have gradually reduced terrorism by manifold in Seven Sister States in Northeast India, and Punjab. Despite these efforts, Islamist terrorism in Indian Kashmir and Maoist insurgency in Indian Red Corridor remain perennial problems in Northern and Central India.

The raison d'être of this article is to analyze the recent rise in incidents of terrorism in India and what would be its possible future course. According to a report, the number of fatalities in terrorist incidents has risen by 17% (289 in 2015 to 337 in 2016). It is expected that the number of terrorist attacks will grow, keeping in view of the surfacing of Hindu nationalist wave also known as Hindutva.

The recent surge of Hindu nationalism, after the 2014 electoral victory of ultra-Hindu nationalist Bhartiya Janata Party (BJP), is indeed alarming. The BJP draws its origins from Sangh Pariwar, an agglomerate of ultra-orthodox Hindu nationalist organizations like Vishva Hindu Parishad (VHP), Rashtriya Swayamsevak Sangh (RSS) and others. The current BJP reign has ushered in a wave of violent and vigilant activities against minority groups (Muslims, Christians, Dalits).

In total, 28 people (24 Muslims, and 4 scheduled caste Dalits) were killed and 124 were injured in 63 attacks, lynchings and other violent activities triggered by radical and violent Hindu groups against people suspected of eating or supplying beef. The intensity of communal violence could be gauged from one incident in Mewa (state of Haryana), where two Muslim women were gang-raped and their relatives murdered on suspicion of eating beef in August 2016.

Considering the demographics of India, a highly diverse society divided on religious, communal, caste, sectarian, and ethnic lines, the majoritarianism policy of BJP would likely to be a blowback for the Indian State. As prominent terrorism scholar Jessica Stern has pointed out, the major root causes of terrorism are humiliations, alienation and revenge. Hence, it could be projected that the growing alienation coupled with humiliation of minority groups may bring waves of communal violence and particularly pave the way for Muslim youth, living under deeply divided society, to join jihadist groups.

It would be naïve to consider that Islamist terrorist groups only operate in Indian Kashmir. A number of Islamist terrorist groups operate in mainland

India, such as Indian Mujahedeen and Student Islamic Movement of India (SIMI). Hitherto the Islamic State of Iraq and Sham (ISIS) has been able to lure in only a handful of Indians, but the current situation may increase ISIS recruitment among the 172 million Muslim community of India. The communal riots of 1992 and 2002 should have been eye-openers for Indian policy makers in order to comprehend and analyze the alienation and revengefulness of Muslim youth. The BJP-led National Democratic Alliance government needs to examine their current reluctance in reining over their irregulars and creating havoc in the Indian society. Whether Islamist or Hindu nationalist, vigilantism is precursor to terrorist activities, and the resulting humiliation of minority communities works as catalyst for them to embrace violent groups. The birth of Irish Republican Army (IRA) in Northern Ireland in the early 1970s was because of the upsurge in violent vigilantism of Ulster Unionists against Catholic community of Northern Ireland. It took British government 20 years to finally resolve the matter in 1998 with Good Friday Agreement.

Impact on Terrorism in the Future

Information warfare tactics allow a terrorist group to operate without the support of a large terrorist organization or a wealthy state sponsor. In addition, terrorists will utilize the emerging cryptography and global telecommunications system to climb out of the "dragonworld" of covert communications as described by J. Bowyer Bell and enhance their ability to communicate in a secure fashion with members scattered across the globe. These tactics may have several effects on future terrorist organizations.

Demassification

First, terrorist groups may become more "demassified." In The Third Wave, Alvin Toffler describes how society is shifting away from large, centralized organizations to smaller, more distributed elements. The ability to steal $10 million electronically overnight, and the ability to exercise command and control utilizing "off the shelf" commercial technology may sound the death knell for state sponsored terrorism. Groups that formerly took direction and were controlled or supported by state actors, will now move into cyberspace, supporting themselves through criminal activities and removing the need for basing by becoming distributed organizations around the world. This lack of state control and funding will remove one of the key elements in present counter-terrorism planning-the punishment or coercion of the sponsoring state. The freedom from state imposed restraints will also allow terrorists to target all states in the future, not only those directed by the sponsor.

New State Sponsors

The lower level of support required to execute a cyberterrorist strategy may have the opposite effect, actually increasing state sponsorship. Poor states that did not have the means to support an international terrorist organization are now becoming connected to the world via the Internet and new telecommunications systems. Argentina, Iran, Peru, Egypt and the

Philippines had the highest percentage growth in Internet connections from July to October of 1994. Each experienced growth ranging from 419% to 134%. All regions of the world do not match these numbers. Africa has 35 of the world's least developed states tin terms of telecommunications, an essential ingredient for connectivity with the rest of the world. Over the last 10 years, Africa has had the lowest growth in teledensity, the number of main telephone lines per 100 inhabitants. It was estimated to be .91 in 1991. States such as Sweden, with an index of 68, Switzerland, Canada, Denmark, Finland, and the United States, all with indexes in the 50s, lead the world in teledensity. The increasing numbers of connections from states that have sponsored terrorism in the past, such as Iran, as well as those that have not, is a new threat. These states may view cyberterrorism as an ideal tool with which to strike the information dependent first world. Cyberterrorism may also appeal to states as it has the added benefit of plausible deniability. There will be no large money, material, or communications "trail" to lead back to the sponsor state.

Targeted Message

While the world (and terrorist groups) are demassifying, industry and business are pursuing more "targeted" production and advertising. This strategy attempts to focus the manufacturing and selling of products to a select audience. Technology is emerging to allow advertising to just those customers who are most likely to purchase a product. Terrorists in the information age may also mirror this trend, with new techniques and weapons that allow them to affect a target audience without resorting to violence against the general population. This technology also allows a terrorist message or action to affect many more people than was possible before. Thus, the "target" for terrorism can be as large or as small as the terrorist sees fit. The growing, worldwide, interconnectedness of individuals and organizations may change the role played by the media in past terrorist events. While terrorists have staged many events in the last 25 years to garner maximum worldwide media attention ('72 Olympics, World Trade Center bombing, Airplane hijackings), the exponential growth of the Internet and the introduction of Direct Broadcast Satellites with more than 500 channels and an 18" receive dish may allow terrorists to formulate, create, and distribute their own "news" to millions around the globe. The role of computers and fax machines in the Tiananmen square uprising is well documented. The Zapatista rebel organization in Mexico used the Internet and World Wide Wed extensively to promote their cause and get their "message" to sympathetic audiences around the world.

Rise of Disruption not Destruction

The final change that information warfare tactics may bring to terrorism is a shift in terrorism itself. In the future, terrorist organizations may move toward tactics that attempt to achieve the terrorist goals without physical violence. This corresponds to the current thinking about the future of warfare. John Arquilla and David Ronfeldt have stated:

Warfare is no longer primarily a function of who puts the most capital, labor, and technology on the battlefield, but of who has the best information about the battlefield. What distinguishes the victors is their grasp of information, not only from the mundane standpoint of knowing how to find the enemy while keeping it in the dark, but also in doctrinal and organizational terms.

In the information age, shifting the definition of terrorism to include violence in cyberspace may be necessary, where electrons, not people are attacked, in the same manner as physical violence is presently included.

Despite these changes, many "classical" terrorist organizations motivated by "conventional" objectives will remain viable. Terrorist groups, regardless of their level of sophistication, will adhere to the logic of symbolic violence and the creation of terror. While it is likely that conventional terrorist groups will evolve into hybrid groups employing both violence and information warfare cyberviolence, we may see the creation of new and unique terrorist organizations unlike those of the past, where close personal ties and ideology were necessary to maintain security. The terrorist organization of the future may not have any "homeland" other than cyberspace. While it is difficult to track selected individuals in just one country or region, tracking a small number of individuals who could be anywhere on the globe, who can communicate in a secure and instantaneous fashion with each other, is likely to pose an order of magnitude increase in the problem.

New Tools for Attacker and Defender

The "information age" provides many tools to assist in countering conventional terrorism. It also presents a host of new problems associated with countering techno and cyberterrorism. The standard offense/defense and prevention/preemption/disruption dynamics of counter and anti-terrorism in the physical world do not have direct counterparts in cyberspace. In the virtual world, a small number of individuals, with the right information, are as powerful as large state actors. The "balance of power" in cyberspace can shift in a matter of seconds, with the insertion or deletion of several lines of code to a program, or the installation of a new security protocol. The lessons from past conventional counter and anti-terrorism tactics are only of limited value in understanding the effectiveness of offense and defense in cyberspace.

Offense and Defense in Cyberspace

The initiative in cyberspace does not necessarily rest with those pursuing an offensive strategy. In keeping with conventional terrorism, it is the terrorist group that normally attempts to seize the initiative by launching an offensive attack on a symbolic target. This attack is usually meant to undermine the belief that the government can protect its citizens. The government is then forced to reexamine and often change the way it attempts to maintain security. In cyberspace, no government has promised to guarantee "safety and security" as they have in the physical world. In the anarchic world of cyberspace, each individual serves as their own sovereign state. The government has addressed the security of individuals only in limited form, with passage of several laws concerning computer security. The commercial sector has attempted to defend the individual with the introduction of virus detection and encryption programs. Neither business nor government has advocated an offensive posture against computer hackers and potential cyberterrorists. The focus has, out of necessity, been directed toward defense. The use of offensive tactics would work well if the enemy could be unambiguously identified. A skilled cyberterrorist can make the identification of those responsible, a cornerstone of conventional U.S. counterterrorism policy, exponentially more difficult in cyberspace. Even if an attacker in cyberspace can be identified, the range of responses open to the defender is somewhat limited. In the case of an unsophisticated hacker or criminal, access to the network can be denied.

Future Research

While the government may be called upon to assist in the defense of cyberspace, the doctrinal and organizational foundations have not yet been established to allow for this involvement. Further study of this problem is necessary to ensure that any government involvement is proportional and effective. While cyberspace can place individuals and states on equal footing, the state clearly retains an advantage in the physical world. This advantage may provide a useful tool in the prosecution of cyberterrorism. While the doctrine of asymmetric response was utilized during the Cold War to deter a nuclear exchange, a cyberspace equivalent of this doctrine may prove useful in the information age. If a state commits to defending cyberspace, the first course of action is likely to be the securing of systems to prevent unauthorized access. By raising the threshold of skill and technology required to penetrate a system, amateurs and unskilled cyberterrorists may be deterred from pursuing an offensive in cyberspace. By securing systems from "low level" attacks, the various government agencies involved in counter and anti-terrorism will be free to pursue the "high level" threats that are sure to exist in cyberspace. It remains to be seen if an offensive response, such as a military strike against a computer center or selected organizations, will be tolerated by the citizens of the United States. Will people be willing to launch an air strike against computer terrorists in the same fashion as they were launched against terrorists training bases in Libya? The implications of an offensive, asymmetric response to the terrorist problem must be explored, as a response that exists exclusively in cyberspace may not be sufficient to deter, or even slow down a cyberterrorist. At the dawn of the information age, the borders of the United States are no longer secure. We must recognize the potential threat and adjust our thinking to formulate an effective individual and state response.

The New Face of Terrorism

The threat posed by Middle Eastern terrorists has been shrinking for some time. Even during the war against the Islamic State, Russian speakers from former Soviet countries were already committing many of the major attacks in the West. Those included relatively simple lone-wolf events, such as the 2017 truck strikes on pedestrians in New York and Stockholm—both conducted by Uzbeks—but also more complicated operations, such as the 2016 suicide bombing of Istanbul's airport—which was allegedly organized by a Russian national—and the 2017 attack on a nightclub in the same city, led by an Uzbek.

There are several reasons for the relative increase in anti-Western terrorism coming out of the post-Soviet world. For starters, in recent years Middle Eastern jihadis have been too preoccupied with local conflicts in Iraq, Syria, and Yemen to head elsewhere. The pull of the Islamic State, meanwhile, has faded after its almost total defeat in Iraq and Syria.

At the same time, the wars in the Middle East have transformed militants from Russian-speaking areas, who previously focused on fighting repressive governments at home, into global terrorists. By 2017, at least 8,500 fighters from former Soviet republics had flocked to Syria and Iraq to join the Islamic State. That experience gave many of these jihadis their first taste battling U.S. and NATO troops, and it left them looking for vengeance, convinced that future operations should be aimed at the West.

Ahmed Chataev, for example, who allegedly organized the attack on Istanbul's airport, apparently first cooked up plans to strike Western targets while fighting in Iraq and Syria. A phone conversation leaked last year between Chataev and another Russian-speaking terrorist, Islam Atabiev, revealed that the two were planning to collect intelligence on several U.S. consulates and restaurants popular with Americans in Turkey and Georgia.

In the coming years, the terrorist threat from Russia and beyond will only increase. With the fall of the Islamic State, Russian-speaking terrorists were mostly able to flee Iraq and Syria with more ease than Middle Eastern foreign fighters and are now back in hiding in the former Soviet sphere or in Europe. Having escaped the reach of the U.S. military, they may find it easier to bring their plots to fruition. Local sympathies will help. Government neglect and outright repression have made religious Muslims in Kazakhstan, Tajikistan, and Uzbekistan attractive targets for radicals looking for new recruits. Several popular sheikhs from the Middle East, including the Saudi cleric Abdulaziz al-Tarefe, now have significant Russian- and Arabic-language followings on social media.

As the locus of terrorism changes, the United States and its allies will have to update their strategies for fighting it. Over the last two decades, Washington built up a huge bureaucracy around Middle Eastern terrorism. Untold millions of dollars were poured into finding and training Arabic-speaking researchers and analysts. According to data from a critical language scholarship program run by the U.S. government, out of 550 university students who will be admitted in 2019, 105 will be studying Arabic and only 60 Russian. And according to professors with whom I've spoken—from top policy schools such as the Harvard Kennedy School, Johns Hopkins School of Advanced International Studies, and Texas A&M's Bush School of Government and Public Service—the overwhelming majority of college students who plan to work in counterterrorism still minor in Middle Eastern studies or Arabic.

There's also a dearth of experts who've specialized in Central Asia and can teach a new generation of analysts.

Reorienting the West's focus will also involve political challenges, since the United States will have to find a way to cooperate with Russia and its neighbors. Over the last several years, for example, U.S. companies have gotten good at deleting jihadi propaganda from U.S.-based social media platforms, but the same propaganda is still widely available on Russian-language apps such as VK and OK, which are popular across post-Soviet states. Telegram, which was founded by a Russian national, has likewise become a major communications tool for terrorists of all backgrounds, and cell phones captured from the Islamic State revealed that they were operating on Ukrainian SIM cards. Monitoring these systems and others will require deep cooperation and intelligence sharing with Russia. But such cooperation does not seem likely in the immediate future. There may simply be too much animosity between Washington and Moscow to allow for effective collaboration.

There's also the problem of the quality of intelligence. Many of those who end up on domestic terrorist watchlists and even Interpol lists throughout the region are actually members of the domestic opposition. Meanwhile, lots of known terrorists are never singled out: Russia is well-known for providing passports to radicals from the Caucasus on the grounds that letting would-be jihadis leave the country is easier than dealing with them at home.

The West should have recognized this shift long ago. It didn't, but that doesn't mean that it should sit on its hands now. The United States and its allies need to recognize that future attacks are more likely to come from the East than the Middle East and that there is no other option than to cooperate with Russia and its neighbors to stop them.

Bibliography

- Antipenko, V.F. (2011). International criminology: The experience of the study of terrorism. Odessa: Phoenix.
- Axelrod, Alan; Phillips, Charles, eds. (2004). Encyclopedia of Wars (Vol.3). Facts on File. pp. 1484-1485 Index entry for "Religious wars" category. ISBN 0816028516.
- Barskiy, L.A. (2007). Roots and faces of terror: Historical and journalistic detective. Moscow: LCI.
- Booth, William (May 21, 2017). "Israel wants Trump to stop Palestinian payments to prisoners and families of 'martyrs'". Washinington Post. Retrieved June 5, 2017.
- Cavanaugh, William T. (2009). The Myth of Religious Violence : Secular Ideology and the Roots of Modern Conflict. Oxford: Oxford University Press. ISBN 978-0-19-538504-5.
- Cohen-Almagor, R. (2005). Media coverage of acts of terrorism: Troubling episodes and suggested guidelines. Canadian journal of communication, 30(3), 383-409.
- CUNNINGHAM, KARLA J. (2003-05-01). "Cross-Regional Trends in Female Terrorism". Studies in Conflict & Terrorism. 26 (3): 171–195. doi:10.1080/10576100390211419. ISSN 1057-610X.
- Dowling, R.E. (1982). The rhetorical genre of terrorism. identification and policy implications. ERIC, 26.
- Dowling, R.E. (1989). Terrorism and the media: A rhetorical genre. Journal of Communication, 36(1), 12-24.
- Dremin, V.N. (2000). The socio-psychological mechanism for the reproduction of terrorism. Current Problems of State and Law,8, 78-83.
- Dunne, T. (2011). The terrorism industry. International Affairs, 87(4), 965-973.

- Dunne, T. (2016). Terrorism and the News Media. Retrieved from https://www.researchgate.net/publication/299158905_Terrorism_and_the_News_Media.
- Edwards, John. "Review: Was the Spanish Inquisition Truthful?" The Jewish Quarterly Review 87 (1997): 351-66.
- Ellens, J. Harold, ed. Destructive Power of Religion: Violence in Judaism, Christianity, and Islam Vol 4. Westport: Praegers, 2004.
- Ellens, J. Harold, ed. The Destructive Power of Religion: Violence in Judaism, Christianity, and Islam Vol. 3. Westport: Praegers, 2004.
- Eviatar, Daphne (June 13, 2013). "Is 'Terrorism' a War Crime Triable by Military Commission? Who Knows?". Huffington Post. Retrieved April 29, 2017.
- Farr, Thomas. "Islam's Way to Freedom." First Things 187 (2008): 24-28.
- Fine, Jonathan (2010). "Political and Philological Origins of the Term 'Terrorism' from the Ancient Near East to Our Times". Middle Eastern Studies. 46 (2): 271–288. doi:10.1080/00263201003619927. JSTOR 20720662.
- Fitch, Asa; Dana Ballout (2 March 2016). "Gulf Cooperation Council Labels Hezbollah a Terrorist Group". The Wall Street Journal. Retrieved 1 December 2016.
- Fortna, Virginia Page (May 20, 2015). "Do Terrorists Win? Rebels' Use of Terrorism and Civil War Outcomes". International Organization. 69 (3): 519–556. doi:10.1017/S0020818315000089. hdl:1811/52898.
- Fortna, Virginia Page (May 20, 2015). "Do Terrorists Win? Rebels' Use of Terrorism and Civil War Outcomes". International Organization. 69 (3): 519–556. doi:10.1017/S0020818315000089. hdl:1811/52898.
- Frey, .S. (2004). Dealing with terrorism:Stick or Carrot? Northampton: Elgar Publishers.
- Halibozek, Edward P.; Jones, Andy; Kovacich, Gerald L. (2008). The corporate security professional's handbook on terrorism (illustrated ed.). Elsevier (Butterworth-Heinemann). pp. 4–5. ISBN 978-0-7506-8257-2. Retrieved December 17, 2016.
- Halibozek, Edward P.; Jones, Andy; Kovacich, Gerald L. (2008). The corporate security professional's handbook on terrorism (illustrated ed.). Elsevier (Butterworth-Heinemann). pp. 4–5. ISBN 978-0-7506-8257-2. Retrieved December 17, 2016.
- Harrison, Peter (2015). The Territories of Science and Religion. University of Chicago Press. ISBN 022618448X.
- Heryanto, Ariel (April 7, 2006). State Terrorism and Political Identity in Indonesia: Fatally Belonging. Routledge. p. 161. ISBN 978-1-134-19569-5.